Giant

Terrace Books, a trade imprint of the University of Wisconsin Press, takes its name from the Memorial Union Terrace, located at the University of Wisconsin–Madison. Since its inception in 1907, the Wisconsin Union has provided a venue for students, faculty, staff, and alumni to debate art, music, politics, and the issues of the day. It is a place where theater, music, drama, literature, dance, outdoor activities, and major speakers are made available to the campus and the community. To learn more about the Union, visit www.union.wisc.edu

Giant

George Stevens, a Life on Film

Marilyn Ann Moss

TERRACE BOOKS
A trade imprint of the University of Wisconsin Press

The University of Wisconsin Press
1930 Monroe Street, 3rd Floor
Madison, Wisconsin 53711-2059
uwpress.wisc.edu

3 Henrietta Street, Covent Garden
London WC2E 8LU, United Kingdom
eurospanbookstore.com

Printed in the United States of America

Library of Congress Cataloging-in-Publication Data

Moss, Marilyn Ann.
Giant: George Stevens, a life on film / Marilyn Ann Moss.
p.   cm.
Includes bibliographical references and index.
ISBN 0-299-20430-8 (hardcover: alk. paper)
1. Stevens, George Cooper, 1904—
2. Motion picture producers and directors—United States—Biography
I. Title.
PN1998.3.S738M67   2004
791.4302´33´092—dc22
2004007797

ISBN 978-0-299-20434-1 (pbk.: alk. paper)
ISBN 978-0-299-20433-4 (e-book)

For James Wilson
Resplendent

and
for my daughter, Lizzi
In Mr. Dingle's words, "Damn the torpedoes . . . full speed ahead!"

George Stevens's method was called "the Indian look." After five days' shooting he would usually be three weeks behind schedule, whereupon the desperate producer would come crying on the set, "George, the picture is out of control, it will cost millions, the boys in New York are very upset . . . " Stevens would just sit there and listen without any expression on his big, impassive face, never say a word, and when the producer ran out of breath, he would say, "Thank you very much," get up and go back to work. His pictures made millions.

— Fred Zinnemann, *An Autobiography: A Life in the Movies*

Contents

Acknowledgments

The George Stevens Collection at the Margaret Herrick Library of the Academy Motion Picture Arts and Sciences comprises one of the library's largest holdings — an appropriate distinction for the man who directed some of Hollywood's largest films just as the studio system was coming to an end — including *A Place in the Sun, Shane, Giant, The Diary of Anne Frank,* and *The Greatest Story Ever Told.* Yet Stevens remains a man difficult to know. He was soft-spoken, often scarce of words when working. A private person whose single passion was making films, Stevens's interior life remained largely hidden. This book, the beginning of my work on Stevens, is a biography of sorts that seeks to understand that interiority and to track it. I look at Stevens through dialogues about the cinema — often spoken by friends and colleagues, and Stevens himself. More than anything else I look through the lens of what he loved best — his films. I mean to place him squarely where he belongs: in the center of the always lively history and the culture of the American cinema. Influenced by its founding giants, D. W. Griffith, F. W. Murnau, and Frank Borzage, Stevens learned his craft swiftly in the early days of the industry. Perhaps more than any other director of his generation alongside John Ford, Stevens is a distinctly American artist, his films reaching for, in Stevens's words, the all important *pictorial* view of the American character and landscape. His best example, *Giant,* is a huge kind of American haiku, emblematic, iconic, displaying the characteristic Stevens frame that positions men and women in their all important relation to the physical environment. For Stevens that frame is fundamental. His films came first in his life. In a letter home to his wife written during World War II, Stevens wrote a poem in what he called "the spirit of Robert Burns," then recanted, saying that his job was not to write poems but to make "moompitchers." Perhaps, his "moompitchers" were poems after all.

xi

I want to thank George Stevens Jr., who carefully read chapters and provided comments, corrections, and offered insights into his father's life and career. I am indebted to Ned Comstock, archivist and brilliant overachiever at the USC Cinema-Television Library, who never stopped searching for and sending information on Stevens. I especially thank Barbara Hall, research archivist at the Margaret Herrick Library of the Academy of Motion Picture Arts and Sciences, who spent the good part of four years advising and pulling files for me from the George Stevens Collection. I thank also Val Almendarez, collections archivist at the Margaret Herrick Library, who provided valuable assistance. A thank you also goes to Dottie McCarthy in George Stevens Jr.'s office, who faxed and emailed unfailingly to get information to me.

I am grateful for close friends and colleagues who listened patiently to hours of talk on Stevens, bouncing ideas around and becoming unwitting Stevens scholars: Sandra Kumamoto Stanley, Harley W. Lond, a fine editor, Pamela Edwards, Virginia Crane, Gayle (G. G.) Golden, Bob Pincus, Miles Beller, Greg Rose, Linda Civitello, and, of course, Steven Gould Axelrod. Thank you also to Bruce Petri, an early Stevens scholar, for his constant encouragement, and to my parents for their babysitting duties and all-around support.

Also at the Margaret Herrick Library I warmly thank Linda Harris Mehr, director of the library, Stacey Behlmer, Faye Thompson, and Jenny Romero. Thanks as well to the library's Special Collections staff, who pulled files, photocopied and provided some well-needed comic relief on days when Stevens loomed especially large and seemed almost impossible to know. I also appreciate the help of the staff at UCLA Special Collections. I am especially grateful to Stevens's colleagues and other experts who took the time to talk to me: Jim Silke, Millie Perkins, Earl Holliman, Richard Schickel, Bob Thomas, Bob Hinkle, and Jane Withers. At the University of Wisconsin Press, my thanks go to my editor Adam Mehring, to my copyeditor Mara Naselli, and of course to humanities editor Raphael Kadushin.

Most of all I thank the late Ivan Moffat, who was there at the beginning of my research and with whom I spent many enjoyable lunches discussing his friend, George Stevens. Ivan was a constant source of information and generously read a draft of my first written chapter on *A Place in the Sun*. Sadly, he passed away before he could see this book. I am indebted to him.

PART I

The Early Years

1

George and Rex, Stan and Ollie

The film *is* the audience. Time and time again you sit in a room alone, and something is up there on the screen that can mean nothing. And in comes another, and there's a community of inter-action, awareness that another mind is in contact with the screen. The audience ... one among others ... brings [the movie] to life. The audi-ence *is* the film. And most importantly ... to be the audience as the film is being made is the cre-ative force of the film. That audience will define what the film is, whether it is and whether it isn't.

—George Stevens

Soft-spoken, intensely private, and undaunted on a movie set, George Stevens dominated the Hollywood studio system in a way that only a handful of directors have. For close to four decades, beginning in 1935 at age thirty-one, with his first important feature at RKO, *Alice Adams*, Stevens was one of the American cinema's preeminent storytellers and craftsmen whose body of work embraced nearly every film genre and helped to invent the iconography that defines the American experience at the movies. He put the cowboy hat on James Dean in *Giant;* he set Fred and Ginger dancing in *Swing Time;* he made Alan Ladd look ten feet tall in *Shane.* An idiosyncratic Hollywood player, Stevens was also one of the few directors who very early in his career commanded complete creative control of his films, often in opposition from studio front offices. As his career advanced and his films gained more momentum at the box office, Stevens ultimately became powerful enough in Hollywood that by the time he released (what he thought would be) his opus, *The Greatest Story Ever Told* in 1965, the film's choral supervisor, Ken Darby, said of him, "Stevens had enough clout in Hollywood to make you change your address."

Beneath the bravado and the cowboy hat, behind the dark sunglasses he wore so that others could not see his eyes or what he was thinking, stood a passionate yet paradoxical man who adored the audiences that came to see his movies but who could appear distant even to those who knew him. His silence drove Carole Lombard to distraction on the set of *Vigil in the Night* in 1939; he argued with (and won over) Katharine Hepburn on the direction of her character on the set of *Alice Adams;* later, the tales of his sparring with James Dean on the Marfa, Texas, set of *Giant* became legendary, if not entirely accurate. Yet he distilled from actors the performances of their careers and inspired in them a lifelong sense of gratitude and respect, even affection. In 1962 his name topped the short list of directors Marilyn Monroe wanted to work with on her last, ill-fated feature, *Something's Got to Give.*

Driven to perfection, Stevens uniformly shot more exposed footage than anyone else Harry Cohn or Jack Warner could think of. He was so intensely concerned with cutting a film that he would cloister himself in an editing room not to be seen for weeks on end. Eventually propelled to gigantic thematic proportions, his films grew larger by the decade until his aesthetic finally merged with the gigantic borders of the CinemaScope age during the last and most productive ten years in Stevens's career.

Born in December 1904, at the dawn of the American film industry itself, Stevens learned to crank a movie camera while still in his teens. In the 1920s, when he was shooting footage of Hal Roach's Rex the Wonder Horse on the terrain of Wyoming, Utah, and Montana, word spread among the cowboys and Native Americans on the set that Stevens was part American Indian, a falsehood he enjoyed since it appealed to his love of spinning an American tale and to his sense of himself as part of an American mythos that eventually found its way into his movies.

Two decades later, despite his successful years at RKO and Columbia during the 1930s and early 1940s, he turned his back on Hollywood in 1943 after he saw a screening of Leni Riefenstahl's *The Triumph of the Will* and understood the German threat. Stevens went overseas to head the U.S. Army's Special Motion Picture Unit for General Dwight D. Eisenhower and filmed American soldiers in action during the Normandy invasion, the liberation of Paris, and the Battle of the Bulge. Then, in the final days of the war, Stevens and his unit entered the just liberated Dachau concentration camp; the piles of human rubble that awaited him altered his view of human nature and changed his life and his art forever. His wartime experience defined his role as an American spokesman, as a cinematic Poet in the tradition of Whitman and Emerson—America's visual arbiter of a popular language, its representative speaker. In his wartime diary he wrote, "I see it is necessary for me now. Twenty-five years getting ready for this job. I am ready now." His words evoke the spirit of self-making voiced by Walt Whitman during the Civil War, the event that inspired Whitman to write great communal poems for the nation. Much like Whitman, Stevens wanted to create a language that would be a historical record for American soldiers and their families back home. He wrote in his diary that he wanted "to make the casualties easier to bear for those who have had to suffer bereavement." He saw his movie camera as a unique instrument that he would use to create a public record of the war articulated through what he knew best—the American film idiom.

When Stevens returned to the States after the war, his films became more serious, more personal, and more expansive. His canvas rapidly grew in scope as he expressed his cautious optimism for America, calling upon the contemporary urban and Western landscape as well as the frontier of a mythic past to give Americans a shared sense of this country's much needed archetypal experiences. He adapted Theodore Dreiser's novel *An American Tragedy* into *A Place in the Sun* before returning to the American frontier with *Shane*. Then he moved to the large Texas plain to make his epic tale of three generations of a Texas family, *Giant*.

Always an independent thinker, Stevens nevertheless worked successfully within the studio system, helping to shape it during the thirties, forties, and fifties as much as he was shaped *by* it. It was a system he understood and, when necessary, creatively manipulated to produce the kinds of films he wanted to make. Stevens repeatedly voiced his belief that movies produced within the system could also be works of art, things of beauty, and he successfully merged his poetic eye with his ability to appeal to massive audiences. A commanding presence in Hollywood, he had access to and control over these audiences simply because the masses always flocked to his films. These films were often unashamedly sentimental, unabashedly entrenched in the conceits of the seamless, iconic classic Hollywood narrative, and by the early 1960s he had become an icon himself, an arbiter of America's national language, the popular cinema.

Jumping Fences

George Stevens grew up simultaneously with the art form he helped to define. He was born in Oakland, California, on December 18, 1904. Serendipitously enough, his birthday predated by only months the opening of the first nickelodeon in the United States in Pittsburgh, Pennsylvania, in 1905. Stevens came from the theatre and spent his childhood on the stage — sometimes behind the curtain, holding scripts for his father, and sometimes in front of it, performing on stage when occasion called. No matter where he stood, from an early age he connected with the audiences that became so important to him later on. His father, Landers, a man described later by Stevens's friends as often histrionic, was the director and star performer of a Northern California theatrical stock company, at one point called the West Coast Defenders, which performed at the Old Liberty Theatre, among other venues. Life as stage performers was difficult, George Stevens's first wife, Yvonne, recalled. "It was a hard job because they changed the bill every week. . . . You'd do the two matinees a week, and then you'd give shows at night. And then you're rehearsing for the next week. So you didn't have time to get in trouble."[1] An advertisement in an Oakland newspaper on June 11, 1900, shows the company's populist bent: "Popular Plays for the People" played at the Dewey Theatre in Oakland, which listed a staff of eighteen people, not including the actors.

Landers Stevens was raised in San Francisco and came from a color-ful family. Yvonne Stevens remembered that his father, James, was "a handsome man who had a way with the ladies." James "may have been an attorney," though more likely, Yvonne thought, in the insurance business.[2] His brother, Ashton Stevens, George's uncle, was the famous one, a well-known Chicago drama critic who as late as 1939 still publicly championed vaudeville as a legitimate form of entertainment.

Landers was considered the handsome brother and began acting at age twenty in 1897. By age twenty-four he was an actor-producer in his own company. Any publicity was a good thing, so it did not hurt his no-toriety when he was mugged after closing the theatre one night and the incident made the local papers the next morning. As Landers was lock-ing up the Dewey Theatre and heading home, said a local Bay Area newspaper, an assailant attacked him. The newspaper story reported that "one of the two men" who attempted to rob him "struck him a powerful blow on the face at the point of the jaw, staggering Landers and nearly knocking him insensible." But "he managed to collect himself in time to draw a pistol and to beat down the assailant with a half-dozen blows on the face with the clubbed weapon." "It was the hardest battle I ever had," Landers told the paper. "While I was fighting the other man, whom I captured, [the first assailant] recovered himself and ran. I did not want to take a chance of killing him, so I did not fire."[3]

Landers met George Stevens's mother, Georgie Cooper, when she worked in the theatre in San Francisco. Born in Kalamazoo, Michigan, Georgie was the daughter of Georgia Woodthorpe, a classical stage ac-tress who was said to be the toast of San Francisco during the Gold Rush days and was thought actually to have come west in a covered wagon. Georgie's father, Fred Cooper, once ran a successful minstrel show. The Coopers lived briefly in Los Angeles around the time Georgie was seven or eight years old, where she played Fauntleroy at the Burbank Theatre, very near where George Stevens later began his career in the movies. The theatre was said to have been built by the father of actor Robert Stack and of course saw many acting troupes come through its doors. The Coopers must have traveled quite a lot; Georgie Cooper's sister, Edie Ogden Career, was named, as was the fashion back then, after the train station she was born in as the family passed through on their way to an engagement.

Georgie was fourteen and singing in a light opera company at the Tivoli in San Francisco when Landers first saw her. She began working in his stock company and they married in 1902. Their two sons had little choice about joining the family business, so George and his brother, Jack, older by one year, began acting on stage as the company performed a wide range of what George Stevens later called "modern" theatre — a mix of the classics, including Shakespeare, and more popular contemporary melodramas. George Stevens made his acting debut at the age of five appearing on stage with the tragedienne Nance O'Neill in *Sappho* at the Alcazar Theatre in San Francisco. Just being backstage during his parents' performances gave him an emotional rush he always remembered, especially, he later said, when he heard audiences grow quiet during a dramatic moment and explode into applause as emotion overtook them. Later, the scripts George held for Landers left an impression on him; he wanted to write them, and in a few years he would study them and practice playwriting.

With the two boys in tow, Georgie and Landers eventually took their stock company on the road, much of which George Stevens captured with a Brownie box camera his mother gave him for his ninth birthday. When the troupe toured the West Coast, Utah, Vancouver, and parts of Canada in 1914, George photographed local sights, capturing images of lakes, docks, cityscapes. In one particular shot, he caught a city skylight peeking through construction beams, creating a perspective he repeated several times in *Shane* when he shot fight scenes from behind wood beams and through the legs of bolting horses.

After the stock company faltered around 1920, Landers and Georgie set up a tent show in downtown San Francisco. The tent show was a lower form of stock company and a humiliating experience for them all. After spending time in San Francisco and then Boyes Springs, the family moved to Sonoma County, California, where George and Jack were enrolled in the Flowery School and then at Sonoma Union High School about fifty miles north of San Francisco. The Flowery School was an old-fashioned schoolhouse with eight grades packed into one room that used an equally old-fashioned stove for heat. According to schoolmate Henrietta Drake, at fifteen Stevens was already writing stories. His teacher, Mrs. Johnstone, who taught all eight grades, "especially enjoyed helping him and would have him stop by her cottage after school to encourage his endeavors," Drake said. That same year, when Drake was thirteen years old, her mother remarried and she went back to San Francisco to live. "At that time a theatre in the Mission Street District called the Wigwam put on plays each week, and, for a while . . . Landers [and Georgie Cooper] Stevens would perform there and we did enjoy seeing them."[4]

Landers Stevens stayed in the theatre as long as he could — until he saw his audiences dwindling and movie houses being built across the street from his theatre. He had little choice but to move the family to Los Angeles where he hoped to find work in the movies. In 1921, when George was sixteen, the family arrived in Glendale, just northeast of Los Angeles, where they stayed with relatives until they could afford to rent their own house. Georgie Cooper Stevens's cousin, Jimmy Horne (with whom George later worked) was already a successful director at the Hal Roach Studios. Landers also had friends in the business, including D. W. Griffith (known to the family as Larry), Alla Nazimova, Bert Lytell, and Hobart Bosworth, and eventually found parts in some Universal and RKO pictures.

After moving to Glendale, George had to drop out of high school in order to drive his father to acting auditions. That was when he started a photography business, taking and selling pictures of local residents and merchants. He also made a habit of frequenting the Glendale Public Library, where he checked out books to read and compensate for his loss of a high school education. Stevens kept a record of his self-education, noting his daily activities that combined efforts to keep his business afloat, chauffeuring Landers, staying close to family members, reading, seeing plays and movies, and, with the help of his cousin, Jimmy Horne, eventually breaking into the industry as an assistant cameraman.

Stevens's 1922 date book, written when he was seventeen years old, records a young man situated in his own business, close to his family, embarking on the most archetypal of American journeys, much like a young Benjamin Franklin or Jay Gatsby, fully engaged in the process of educating himself. While Stevens was cut off from a formal education, his date book reveals a young man already armed with a critical vocabulary, a knowledge of the theatre and storytelling, and an ability to understand what might compel an audience and what might not. He displays an interior life centering on literature, live performance, and the movies.

Stevens began the date book on Monday, January 2, 1922, writing, "Hard rain fell last night and this morning. Home all morning. Went around this afternoon and took a few pictures. Dined home. Developed pictures to-night and read Richard Haggard's 'Brethern.' It cleared late this afternoon." Stevens wrote steadily. For Wednesday, January 4, he commented about finding a room to develop his pictures: "Went to Astra this morning, engaged still room for one month at ten dollars. Cleaned it. Took Pop to Hollywood and Universal, home at five. Developed pictures and went to Ede's [George's aunt, Edie Ogden Career] for evening. Home at eleven and to bed." On January 5 he noted, "Went to Pasadena at night and saw the Smith-King Co. make a botch of 'Peg of My Heart.' I don't like the play." Then the next day he "cleaned Mrs. Garner's car, which we had been using to go to Universal. Went to T. O.&L. at night and saw Gloria Swanson in 'Under the Lash.' It was good. And fair vaudeville."[5]

Absorbing all kinds of narratives, Stevens again referred to Haggard's novel, calling *The Brethern,* "an interesting story with many dramatic situations" and a few days later, noted that he "Read 'K' by Mary Roberts Rinehardt. Splendid story. Later I read 'Ninety-Three' by Victor Hugo. Not very strong in its entirety but the last part is wonderful in its tragedy." He was impressed when he saw "a French picture, 'J'accuse,' one night, directed by Abel Gance . . . best foreign picture I have seen. It was splendid and required much thought." Then, on Monday, April 17, he wrote, "Some time this month I read 'The Count's Millions' and 'Barron Trigault's Vengeance,' by Emile Gaborian. Good story the latter being a sequel to the first not so vivid as two of his other novels I have read." Then, on Tuesday, April 25: "Read 'Notre Dame' by Victor Hugo. Thought it very fine story though not so strong as some of his other stories and less convincing."[6]

Stevens read heavily, sometimes consuming a book in one or two nights. In May he noted that he read *The Crooked House* by Brandon Fleming ("very good mystery story"); Maurice LeBlanc's *The Three Eyes* ("well told mystery throughout"); the play *Lilliom* by Molnar ("it is a beautiful play, almost a fantasy"), and Harrington Hext's *Number 87* ("a very interesting mystery story based on the supposed discovery of unusual power by Radio Activity. Entirely pleasurable and intelligent conversation of the characters is broadening to the mind"). To that he added

Anne Catherine Green's *The Leavenworth Case* ("It was a good mystery story . . . did not discover who murderer was until last of book. And was interested all through"), along with John Brinkwater's play *Abraham Lincoln,* which he considered "fine and interesting."[7]

A career in the movie industry seemed a perfect choice for a young man who liked storytelling. It was not long before Stevens started jumping fences from one studio lot to another to find work as an assistant cameraman in the new industry. As Stevens told Leonard Maltin in 1970:

> I was really a kid at the time. . . . I was in the theatre world, but looking for a job in the film business. There were no unions, so it was possible to become an assistant cameraman if you happened to find out just when they were starting a picture. There was no organization; if a cameraman didn't have an assistant, he didn't know where to find one. . . . And I learned this little bit about it; I was on a picture for four or five days. I had an opportunity to be on a set, and the assistant cameraman kept showing me things. One day I climbed the fence, knowing they needed an assistant cameraman. I told them I was an assistant cameraman. A couple of days later, I was one, but the first day or two it was pretty disastrous. I knew something about photography and I caught on quick.[8]

On Wednesday, July 12, 1922, after Stevens and his mother were quarantined for a week with small pox, which he recorded as if it were an ordinary event, he wrote that he got his break: "Started working at Warner Bros. studios as assistant cameraman." The picture was *Little Heroes of the Street* and Stevens worked on it until production ended on August 5. He mentioned that Floyd Jackman, whom he would work with a few years later at the Hal Roach Studios, was the cameraman, adding, "Wesley Barry was the star," and also that "Marie Prevort, Jack Mulhall and Philo Macullogh were in the cast. William Beaudine was the director."[9]

Stevens later said he jumped over a fence to talk to a man about learning to be a cameraman. He got the job, but when he told his father, Landers Stevens refused to let him work in the business, saying no son of his was going to be a "stage hand" — meaning an assistant to someone else — in the not-yet respected business of making moving pictures. The response was ironic, given that Landers himself, though a legitimate actor, came from the vaudeville stage, which was, if anything, condescended to by genteel society. Nevertheless, he thought movies were a distinctly lowbrow form of entertainment — not an unpopular opinion by far and shared by many. For this reason, the earliest film industry entrepreneurs sought to legitimate the burgeoning industry from the start, hoping right away to rescue it from its association with storefront nickelodeons visited by immigrants, the working class, the culturally disadvantaged riff-raff, as it were. The reason for this had to do with the movie industry's arrival at a time when nineteenth century views of popular culture were still held firmly in place; Landers's vaudevillian roots were not immune to certain prejudice. As Sumiko Higashi has written, "During the latter part of the nineteenth century . . . [there was] the impulse of the genteel classes to distance themselves from urban workers and immigrants . . . [and they] mapped out a *cordon sanitaire* for their own forms of conspicuous leisure. Consequently, performances of Shakespeare, opera, and symphonic music for the edification of the elite were elevated above popular entertainment. A sign of the increasing fragmentation of cultural production, the term 'legitimate' denoted stage plays enshrined in the pantheon of art as opposed to cheaper amusement such as vaudeville, burlesque, and the circus."[10] No doubt, such a means of rating entertainment would have determined Landers Stevens's position on the highbrow/lowbrow scale to be tenuous at best.

For this reason, "film entrepreneurs intent on escaping the lower-class stigma of storefront nickelodeons were determined to upgrade both production and exhibition." By the time Stevens entered the industry "the accelerating growth of the leisure industry meant that class and ethnic division reinforced by cultural consumption became less distinctive with each succeeding decade . . . commercialized amusement [in the twentieth century] became more democratic in the way the population accessed it — especially the consumption of movies, a visual form of entertainment that was more difficult to track down."[11] At this early date, Stevens was determined to enter into the business of making movies — a "democratic" art form at which he would excel by his ability always to balance popular, "democratic" cinema's two fundamental elements: art and commerce.

According to his 1922 date book Stevens was already working steadily by age seventeen and getting to know the new industry well. On Wednesday, August 2, he noted with some seriousness that "Will Hays, the man who is the head of the motion picture industry visited the studio and made a speech." His career also got a boost when he started "actual production of 'Michael O'Halloran' at Ince Studios on September 24 and worked for two weeks, ending on November 1." The entries started to get longer. Stevens secured much more work at the studios as the year went by. An August 6 entry says, "Left at 7 this morning for Keen Camp in the San Jacinto Mts. with Doubleday Productions [to shoot *The Flaming Arrow*]. Lester Leuneo is the star and his wife Francelia Bilington is the leading lady. Henry McCarty is director. I am working with Floyd Jackman [as assistant cameraman]." The production ended on Saturday, August 19. But on Wednesday August 16 he worked at the "Studio (Fine Arts, formerly the Griffith) today." He noted every job, and his work now left little or no time for his own business or for driving his father to auditions. For Sunday, September 10, he says, "Left at 7 this A.M. for Keens [*sic*] Camp with the Doubleday Co. Everybody in the Co. is the same as last picture with the exception of the leading lady who is Thelma Worth." For Monday, September 11: "Started shooting this morning in Finn Canyon near Idlewild." Thursday, September 21: "Finished the 'Devil's Gast' [*sic*] this afternoon."[12]

Soon Stevens began working for the Ince Studio, adapting a novel by Gene Stratton-Porter, whose novel, *Laddie*, would be the subject of his first serious film for RKO a little more than a decade later. "Started this morning with the Gene Stratton Porter Co. at Ince's Studio. We made some screen tests to-day." For Wednesday, October 4: "Worked on Stage in the studio all day. Irene Rich, Charles Clary, Josie Seggewick, young True Boardmant and others in the cast worked." For Thursday, October 6, he noted: "Worked all day in stream at Griffith Park. We took our shoes off and waded into the water to do our work," but also said, "Was interested in World Series game between Yanks & Giants but got no returns until on my way home. Game was tie." He was at the Ince Studio for the next week, working on the sound stage. On Friday, November 3, he wrote: "Went to studio at 10. Stayed all day. Went to Cinderella Roof at night with some boys from Ince's and photographed Madge Bellamy and some long shots, also made some screen tests." On Monday, November 27, Stevens wrote: "Started today with Beck Co. at Ince Studios [on *Destroying Angel*] as assistant cameraman. Andraie Barlataier is cameraman. Lea Baird is the star. Van Dyke is the director."[13]

Ince Studios had a colorful back story of its own in 1922. As Stevens told Kevin Brownlow in 1969, there was no shortage there of Ku Klux Klan members: "I worked at the Ince Studio . . . whilst carrying cameras and loading film and all of that, and I got to know a lot of people amongst the camera crew and the electricians and grips, and that back lot — and that studio, most of the guys I knew were members of the Ku Klux Klan . . . and Culver City was just loaded with this particular thing. This is the INCE studio in a community that was inclined along these lines, had many members. How much Ince had to do with it I don't know but I know a production manager of that company on his own was interested in it." The studio Klan members seemed to Stevens to be part of a larger phenomenon in the community. "Now I didn't know the Ku Klux Klan from the man in the moon and I'd been exposed to *Birth of a Nation*, you know, and the heroics and generally what I read in the papers, [and] the indication was that this thing [was] not a good thing. . . . I lived in Glendale at the time and I went out one night to the foothills, there was a tremendous parade of guys in white sheets with a man on horseback in the foreground . . . they were burning fires, and there must have been a thousand men in this parade."[14]

Klansmen provided only a small part of the local color of turn-of-the-century Los Angeles, still a small town and not yet the sophisticated metropolis the movie business would eventually make it. Working on Westerns as he did, Stevens did not have to travel far out of the city to experience a rugged landscape that was still gripped by its legendary past. During 1922 and 1923 he worked on numerous Westerns, including doing a stint as assistant cameraman on *The Virginian*, released by Preferred Studios in 1923.

By 1924, however, Stevens obtained steady work at the Hal Roach Studios, noting later that he went there just as Glenn Tryon replaced Harold Lloyd as Roach's partner. He was experimenting with film and on February 2 had written the Eastman Kodak Company in New York seeking information about Wratten neutral tint filters and later that year on panchromatic negative motion picture film. His apprenticeship at Roach changed his concept of storytelling in way he could not have anticipated and in fact shaped his imagination for the rest of his career.

The Hal Roach Studios: Rex the Wonder Horse

One of Stevens's first jobs at Roach was to assist cameraman Fred Jack-man on the short *Battling Orioles*, a comedy released on October 26, 1924, that concerned the misadventures of a once-famous but now old-aged baseball team. The short was directed by Ted Wilde and also Fred Guiol, who later became Stevens's life-long collaborator and friend. Now work came steadily. *The White Sheep*, which was released three months later on December 14, 1924, and written and directed by Roach, had Stevens again assisting Jackman on this comedy-melodrama about a small-town mayor and his three sons, all of whom love the same girl. But a larger force would supersede this kind of picture.

Stevens's work on *Black Cyclone*, released on September 27, 1925, was his first work with Roach to feature a beautiful black stallion named Rex the Wonder Horse. *Cyclone* was a Western melodrama that had Rex as an outcast colt that grows to become a savvy adventurer and gets involved with rival horses as well as a female horse he grows to love. Fred Jackman directed and Stevens and Floyd Jackman photographed the feature-length picture. As Stevens told Jim Silke, he loved doing these western films: "This was fascinating to me, it took me to outdoor places that I had never expected to be. I learned to do things really well that before I had only been able to do a little, like riding, riding broncs, and riding bare-back. I worked on a couple of pictures where we went out to Wyoming and Montana, then to Nevada near where Boulder Dam is now. We were there for six months. There were only two actors with us. It was very simple compared with the way we do things now. When we got off the train, we got pack animals, horses, and went back into the mountains and rounded up a herd of wild horses, and then we went to work photo-graphing the picture. . . . We did things with photography that had never been done before."[15]

Rex now figured prominently in Stevens's life. After working on *The Desert's Toll*, a Western melodrama released on November 14, 1926, that did not feature Rex, Stevens was back with the stallion on *The Devil Horse*, a handsomely mounted feature-length movie penned by Roach himself and directed by Fred Jackman. As Jackman's assistant, Stevens performed some high-wire tricks to photograph the beautiful Rex. At that point in his life the stints were exciting and left lasting memories of being in the Western outdoors.

Roach was the one who first cooked up the idea of using a horse to solve some serious financial troubles. He later told Kevin Brownlow that at the time, in the mid-1920s, the country was going off the Gold Standard and he developed a strategy for dealing with the problem of paying his stars when the banks closed for a time: "I said, 'Why be concerned with the stars? They're in the same position we are. You don't pay them. They're not the most important part of this industry. If you have to, you can star a horse.' This idea was passed around, and my distributors said, 'Why not?' I sent Chick Morrison to find the kind of horse he could train. This guy was the greatest horse trainer I ever saw in my life, a very intelligent man. And he found Rex, the most interesting horse I ever saw. It had a brain ten times better developed than the average horse."[16]

Rex, a registered Morgan stallion, had an interesting history before he appeared in movies. Because he displayed a violent nature when he was young, his one-time owner left him to wander free in Colorado. After many efforts and then a successful capture by cowboys (the stallion had already killed one), the horse was about to be destroyed when he was taken to the State Reformatory for Boys at Golden, Colorado. Chick Morrison decided to tame him by using kindness; even though Rex injured Morrison, the trainer persisted. As Roach told Brownlow, after Morrison succeeded in getting Rex to where he wanted him, "The next day, the guy rode the horse down the main street of Morrison, Colorado. . . . This horse had hardly had a saddle on before. The only thing that went wrong was that the horse went right into the bank on the corner. Thought it was a stall, I guess."[17]

Stevens later remembered working on *The Devil Horse*, the best known of the Rex series. As he told Brownlow, "We had our camp on the Little Big Horn River, Wyoming. The village was called Lodge Grass. This fifty-mile area was a Crow Indian reservation. The Crows had been what was called peaceable Indians, part of the Custer adventure. Every year, Indians came to this reservation for a powwow. Many brought their own teepees — which you see in the film — and this powwow was extraordinary. Throughout the night they'd beat out this rhythm on the big drums and dance, night after night, a variety of traditional dances."[18]

The Devil Horse is a fast-moving adventure yarn, not without its psychological undertones, that pits the beautiful Rex against a dreaded tribe of Indians. As a young colt, Rex, and his human, played by Fred Jackman Jr., are devoted to each other. But their bond is broken when Indians slaughter the boy's family and Rex is taken away with the tribe. Later the boy and his horse find each other and together help rid the area of the menacing enemies. The picture, even given its context of early twentieth-century racism and fear of American Indians, is nonetheless a series of high-spirited, easily watchable adventures evenly matched by the emotional depth of Roach's script that has Rex and Jackman Jr. bonded in a way that is romantic and even melodramatic.

While assisting on his Rex picture, Stevens also photographed with Jack Roach another Western melodrama, *The Valley of Hell* (working at Metro again), released on February 19, 1927. Then his work on *No Man's Law* found Stevens again assisting Floyd Jackman on another Rex adventure that has the stallion protecting a young girl among a group of outlaws. *Law* was released on May 1, 1927. Stevens then worked with photographers Winney Wenstrom and Earl Walker on the Western drama *Lightning* (Tiffany Productions), a story of horse wranglers based on a Zane Grey story and released on July 15, 1927, at the same time as *The Devil Horse*. During the same period he shot *The Girl from Gay Paree*, a farce concerning the adventures of a young girl in the big city, released on September 15, 1927.

Stevens was especially fond of these Western melodramas, particularly the Rex series: He told Jim Silke, "When I was a kid cameraman, the director of a Western was usually a western guy who could ride and do all those things. I remember the Eyemo camera we used. A hand camera. I remember standing in the back of a buckboard shooting over the horses. We were always doing stunts like that. It was part of the spirit of the thing." The men Stevens worked with left an impression: "these old western boys were pretty fine fellows. It wasn't that they didn't kiss the girl and only kissed their horse and didn't smoke: they were good men and the tradition was such that they wanted to be rugged, responsible. They had an integrity, and being a part of the company was like being part of a football team."[19] The series was an education in itself, especially because Stevens worked with Fred Jackman, who had earlier shot trick photography for Mack Sennett. "There were many things that hadn't been gone into in photography then," Stevens said, "It had been very harsh black and white. Trick work had been explored but there was not much feeling for the pictorial work. . . . We [Jackman, his brother, Floyd, and Stevens] used to send the film down to the depot; it went into Los Angeles by train. We had a little electric generator that we cranked with a rope to start our projection machine. When the film came back and we ran it, it was different from anything Fred had seen before. I was fooling with filters and the first panchromatic film, turning the sky black for night sequences, instead of just tinting it blue, and using long tele-photo lenses to bring the background up, things that a kid would do. . . . To me this was great."[20]

Laurel and Hardy

Stan was the story man. Babe was the golfer, and
Babe liked it that way.

—George Stevens

Though Stevens planned early on to write "play scripts," when he began working at the studios, particularly at Roach, he stayed with the "photo-graphic end of it," as he called it, because he wanted to be a director. From the beginning, though, he was equally interested in writing and photo-graphing shorts and could do both with facility. One lesson from this period stuck: he learned to put a story together on the spot. Of course, after Roach, when he moved to Universal and then to RKO, Stevens's trademark experience and way of working was to get hold of an un-finished script and construct it himself: doing daily rewrites, just in time for the cameras to roll the next day. It would later turn out that *Giant* was the only film he directed with a finished script in hand before shooting began.

While he got his full-scale education on the photographic end of the business working with the Jackman brothers, in 1926, just two years into his tenure at Roach Stevens began photographing the work of two re-cently paired Roach contract comedians, Stan Laurel and Oliver Hardy, which deepened his education in the business considerably. Stevens said to Eduardo Escorel in 1969: "When I was working on [early] comedies, I didn't care about comedy particularly. I was interested in the more se-rious work of the theatre. . . . And when I started working with Laurel and Hardy, I was fascinated by the whole ridiculous concept of the values they brought about — a certain amount of truth, a certain amount of buffoonery and considerable art — technique. So we certainly weren't talking about an art in those days. But we knew it was good. We knew what they were doing was worthwhile."[21]

The English comedian Oliver Hardy was already under contract to the studio when Roach snapped Stan Laurel away from Universal Pictures to work as a story man for him. Laurel wrote gags for a few months when several Roach executives decided he might be good in front of the camera. They paired him with Hardy in a picture called *Duck Soup*, which worked enough to their advantage that Roach now thought of them as a team. It took a while, but eventually the two comedians blended together with ease — and wit.

Stevens's first outing with Laurel and Hardy was the two-reeler *Slipping Wives*, released in April 1927. He worked with the pair, photographing them and sometimes writing gags with them, through 1931, entering into a new kind of apprenticeship that permanently, and profoundly, altered his view of moviemaking. He always said that even after he left Hal Roach comedies, Laurel and Hardy never left *him*. In a 1974 interview he talked about what he learned from the two comedians:

> In the fast-moving comedies, the only people who thought about what was happening were the audience, but in Laurel and Hardy's comedies, when something happened, the injured one thought about it, and the onlooker looked at him and thought about how horrible it was. They had the presumption to stop the hand-is-quicker-than-the-eye concept of comedy, which was Larry Semon and the Keystone Kops and all that hurried stuff. Before you could examine the situation, another object had crashed through the window, and it was time for the chase.
>
> But the beauty of the Laurel and Hardy shorts to me was their absolute deliberation, their great poise, their Alphonse and Gaston relationship with one another. The Laurel and Hardy concept moved over into other films considerably, with Cary Grant, Roz Russell, Irene Dunne doing the late take and even the double take. That had come out of the personalities of Laurel and Hardy, and the people that worked with them.[22]

Stevens revered the slow take, the pause, the deliberation — in short, all the conceits that characterized the duo's graceful brand of comedy, a comedy fully inhabited by flawed, sympathetic but still dignified human beings. By his own account, the gracefulness rubbed off on Stevens — and we see it, for instance, in the lyrical comedy scene in the police station near the end of *The More the Merrier* as Dingle (Charles Coburn) walks safely through the room without once looking up from his newspaper, and Jean Arthur's agility in keeping her head buried in Dingle's shoulder as he moves around, just so she will not have to face Joe, the man she loves.

It was as simple as working on a script and then going outside to make the picture, Stevens always said. Something large emerged from his work as cameraman and gag writer on the nearly three dozen shorts he made with Laurel and Hardy. In the small acts and accidents that passed between them — in the time that the "injured one thought about it" and "the onlooker looked at him and thought about how horrible it was" — the seeds of Stevens's own cinema took root. He found the relationship between "the one who is looked at" and "the one doing the looking" to be the beginning of important connections made, the start of a relationship between two human beings that, as Whitman might have said, contained multitudes. When Stevens later said that his films conveyed on celluloid "the human condition," he meant the sympathies, the fallibility, the courage, the dignity that passed between Stan and Ollie, even before the relationship extended to include their audience — to shared situations and emotions experienced by the two comedians and the spectators watching them. "Stan Laurel and Hal Roach both felt that the story was of paramount importance," Randy Skretvedt writes, "'You've got to start with a believable story' was Stan's credo of comedy construction; Babe Hardy echoed this with 'We did a lot of crazy things in our pictures, but we were always *real*.' Stan and Ollie were believable, human characters, and they needed to be placed in plausible situations."[23] The young Stevens absorbed all of this.

These stories created a bond between fiction and reality, between two characters on the screen, and then between the onscreen characters and the audience watching. One could not really go off without the other. Learning greatly from this period, Stevens's later aesthetic was shaped by this kind of bond. Moments of identification between human beings are created, and from them relations are formed between the characters on the screen, and between the characters and audiences. Without exception, in Stevens's cinema someone in the frame watches someone else in the frame, an act that is of course repeated as the spectator looks at the actors and crystallizes his or her relationship to them. When Spencer Tracy watches Katharine Hepburn try to cook breakfast in the last scene of *Woman of the Year,* all America watches. Spencer is the audience, Spencer is America.

Stevens's conception of real, believable people inhabiting real, believable stories has its roots in Laurel and Hardy's work. In 1928's *Two Tars,* for example, when Navy men Stan and Ollie take two young ladies out for a drive in their rented car they get into trouble on the highway. The modern world is, as always, too complicated for these childlike creatures and the highway is fraught with dangers. Stan and Ollie are, as usual, slow on the uptake when mishaps befall them — not because they are simpleminded or childlike (though they are) but because in their fallibility they are human, they are real. When Ollie gets into trouble with a gumball machine a perennial look of shame crosses his face. He looks not only around him and down at the ground but eventually at us, engaging the spectator in his predicament. We cannot look away and cannot help but be implicated in Ollie's misfortune. There is always one spectator who is in the same boat with him. Not only does the spectator look at him, so do others *within* the frame. Stan and Ollie take the two women in their car. By now the men are wearing the women's hats and the women the men's, establishing once again a connection between them.

When their car stops in a line of other cars, no one can move. Tempers flare and soon Stan and Ollie are embroiled in episodes of childish behavior with the other drivers. Bit by bit they take apart each other's vehicles; after each act of demolition the culprit waits to see the reaction on the other fellow's face before doing more damage. Stevens no doubt took the idea of the jalopy from this short and used it in *Alice Adams* when Alice and her brother drive in a borrowed jalopy to an exclusive party. The jalopy signals not only Alice's lack of money and social standing but, equally important, the connection this gives her to the real people in the audience during the Depression.

Another idea for *Alice Adams* evolved from a scene in *The Second Hundred Years,* directed by Fred Guiol and released in 1927. Stevens photographs Stan Laurel helplessly trying to get a brussels sprout off of a plate and into a spoon during a dinner party. In extreme close-up the vegetable escapes the utensil time and again. Stevens repeats part of the gag in the tragicomic dinner scene in *Alice Adams* when Alice's father drops a brussels sprout onto his plate and "maid" Hattie McDaniel takes a small broom and pan and sweeps the errant vegetable off of the plate. As a Laurel and Hardy gag the scene is simply humorous; by the time it is used in *Alice Adams* the sprout has a larger, tragic import, signaling the sadness and ineptitude running through the dinner scene as Alice Adams and her mother try to be something they are not so as to impress Alice's wealthy young suitor (Fred MacMurray). The audience as well as the family members, we imagine, share the close-up.

Laurel and Hardy's ability to create havoc at the same time they create community influenced Stevens profoundly. In a scene from *Double Whoopee* (1929), for example, Ollie stands outside a hotel with Stan, who is the doorman and calls cabs for hotel guests. First a cabbie rips a handkerchief at just the moment Stan bends down to look at something. Stan hears the sound and thinks he has ripped his pants, signaling just how precisely one character is implicated in or completes the actions of another, a scheme that works for Stevens in later comedies. There are elements of this visual ballet in *The Talk of the Town* in a scene when hounds pick up the scent of slippers worn by fugitive Leopold Dilg (Cary Grant) just as Grant slips them off and they are innocently picked up by Michael Lightcap (Ronald Colman), whom the dogs then go after; of course they are going after the wrong man. Also, in *The More the Merrier*, in just one example of many in the film, Mr. Dingle (Charles Coburn) puts his pants underneath a blanket on the bed and when he goes to make the bed unknowingly buries the pants. Later on Joe (Joel McCrea) gets into the bed and finds the pants. Then the pants are accidentally flung outside the bedroom window where they wait (outside the camera's range) until a later scene when Mr. Dingle finds them, not knowing how they got outside the window in the first place. Chain reactions connect individuals, implicating them in broad acts of compassionate fumbles.

These make for communities of participants who share in pranks and small catastrophes, as they do, for example, in the Laurel and Hardy short, *You're Darn Tootin'*, in which the cameraman shot the team hamming it up on a city street corner. The gag begins when Stan and Ollie hit each other for some misdemeanor one has perpetrated on the other; eventually their actions snowball and fifty or so more men and women are on the corner or in the street hitting each other and ripping each other's clothing. When one bends down another punches him and in turn is punched by yet another soul, creating a small nation of well-meaning but nevertheless angry pants splitters and head hitters. All the while, the action begins, as it does in *Angora Love* (1929), with one misstep inflicted by either Stan or Ollie on the other, followed by a sheepish look of concern and guilt from either one of the boys. But always they are "nice" boys, essentially childlike, not entirely smart, yet always optimistic. The optimism — the possibility of seeing the entire human race in the interactions of these two men — stayed with Stevens and framed his own essentially optimistic, forward looking and perennially romantic view of the world.

Stevens later said that he also actually learned to edit and to manipulate film — to cut pieces and to arrange it — when he worked with Stan and Ollie. "The Laurel and Hardy films influenced me . . . to be aware of how excitement can be created from the [use] of one piece of film against another . . . that almost any aspect of behavior, if it's arranged properly on the film and put together . . . has some interest to other human beings when they watch it . . . the comic with the serious. One relieved the other. One gave the other a kind of deeper significance."[24]

Then in 1930, just before he stopped photographing Laurel and Hardy on a regular basis, Stevens began directing later installments of Roach's *The Boy Friends* series. He improved the series by injecting energy into it but also came into conflict with Roach. Now that Stevens was a director, he wanted to move on to serious material. *The Boy Friends* comedies had little dialogue; he called them — along with the other comedies he made at Roach — "silent comedies that spoke," movies that "depended on situations and sight gags." "We were *inept* with dialogue," Stevens said, and the making of these movies was almost completely "improvisational." But he still recalled directing a scene involving the use of a glider that was more fun than anything else: "You know, we had no process shots, so how do you pretend this glider is up in the air? How do you get it up there in the first place? There was a cliff, where the top of Marina Del Rey [a Los Angeles beach] is now, that had an edge where we could move along. We got two big sticks, which they use to hoist girders. I hooked the glider on a hundred-foot one, and the camera on an eighty-foot one. We ran it along the edge of the cliff! It was absolutely terrifying, because when it would start to roll, you had the camera boom over you. At least the actor [Grady Sutton] had a glider!"[25]

But *The Boy Friends* series marked the end of Stevens's tenure at Roach. "I got fired from Roach," he told Maltin, "because my films had been turning out better than they had expected. Roach wanted to do a certain kind of picture, like the kind he had started that didn't work. I did gag pictures, because with gags you could get laughs with people who weren't so expert as comedians."[26] Tired of the gag stories, Stevens refused to direct one that Roach wanted him to do. "I hated it," he said later on. "It was the kind of comedy you see in 'The Nitwits,' the comedian falling into stuff and getting up. . . . It just bored me to death. There was nothing for the photographer to do, except if the comedian was slow getting off, then the cameraman could drop off speed and the comedian would get out a little quicker."[27]

Instead Stevens worked on something of his own (a habit that never left him), resulting soon enough in Roach firing him. The studio sent him a letter on November 6, 1931, terminating their agreement with him as of December 31 of that year. The studio regularly kept half of all employees' salaries in a fund, doled out to anyone who got fired, so Stevens promptly put the back money in a Culver City bank, and with his wife, Yvonne, pregnant with their son, George Jr., Stevens left Roach. Now at the start of the Depression, he was out of work for six months before former Roach manager Warren Doane convinced Universal to take him into the studio with Jim Horne, another former Roach writer-director and Stevens's cousin.

But Laurel and Hardy affected many facets of Stevens's life. It was "Babe" Hardy who had introduced Stevens to his wife, Yvonne, a Mack Sennett "cutie pie" as she once described herself at that time, and a personal friend of Oliver Hardy and his wife. Stevens and Yvonne met in 1928 and married on New Year's Day 1930. During the time they dated, Yvonne recalled, they would go to movies and more movies at venues such as the Carthay Circle Theatre, Grauman's Chinese in Hollywood, and Grauman's Million Dollar Theatre in downtown Los Angeles. She saw immediately how serious Stevens was about his career. "When we were first married [writing gags and directing The Boy Friends series], he'd be working all day, and then he'd come home and we'd have dinner and he'd just sit at his desk. We had a nice little apartment near the [Roach] studio, and he'd just sit there and until one or two in the morning. Then he'd get up at seven and go to work. That's the way he did it. . . . He'd pace up and down this hall, and he always did that, all his life. He just kept walking and walking and walking. Then he'd sit down at the desk again, and write. He was a hard worker." After Roach, she said, "George was out of work for six or eight months. I just couldn't understand it, because he'd go play golf every day. I thought, good night!" But in the movies, you don't go around knocking on doors. So Warren Doane had gone out to Universal, and that was how [Stevens] started [there]."[28] Stevens also kept his sense of humor during those months off, or so it seemed. Yvonne remembered a night the two were to meet in Hollywood to go have dinner at George's mother's house. George was a half-hour late, and when Yvonne finally saw him nearby, talking with two people before walking her way, she asked who they were. "Well, they were bums," he said, "and they wanted some money." When she asked what he said to them, he answered, "I told them to get out of the way. I'm working this side of the street."[29]

Laurel and Hardy's imprint on Stevens was permanent. They had invented a new kind of comedy, Stevens always said, and the three shared a reciprocal few years together, beginning with the time that Stevens's inventive use of panchromatic film saved Stan Laurel's career because it could register his pale blue eyes on film when other film could not. When he left Roach, Stan Laurel gave Stevens a parting gift, an inscribed copy of one of his own favorite books, Maurice Willson Disher's *Clowns and Pantomimes*. Stevens saw it as a kind of Bible to Laurel, a view of comedy from early on through the moderns.

Six months later Stevens ended up at Universal; as it turned out he did not leave comedy far behind — nor Rex the Wonder Horse. Almost twenty years later, in April 1949, Fred Jackman wrote a new version of *The Devil Horse* script, "written from memory," and sent it to Stevens, now busy trying to get *A Place in the Sun* into production. Stevens wrote back to Jackman:

> Brother, it was like a breath of fresh air. There was a perfect script. Nothing in it to keep a director from using all of his natural elements, the skill of the actors and the scenic wonders of the American West, and coming out with something really interesting. But, Jesus Christ, how things have changed. They have to put everything down for you in black and white now-a-days, and if it's anything that you care to shoot, or wish

to feel reasonably responsible for, you better put it down yourself. That's been my experience.

But kidding aside, Fred, the script I read here, *The Devil Horse* script, with simple essentials, has all that is reasonably required of an exciting motion picture, and it's not burdened with this superficial and non-essential pretension. Yes, of course, the script of a motion picture presented in its outline form places a burden upon the director. He must be a man with a sure understanding of his medium. He must be able to control all of these facets with a high degree of skill and also be endowed with imagination and resourceful creative powers. A director of that kind is in a position with no limitations upon him.[30]

2

The RKO Years

Remember back in the thirties when it was the thing to have a "social" message? [The film] had to have something to say about democracy, or the brave new world, or the fight against fascism. Our films [now] should tell the truth and not pat us on the back. Isn't there the slight chance that we might be revealing America as it is not? Would that be encouraging us in our own delusions about ourselves?

— George Stevens, 1946

Getting Serious

For Stevens in the first years of the Depression, work was as hard to find as were scripts not pinned almost entirely on visual gags and one-liners. But he kept working, and trying to get serious. When he landed at Universal in 1932 making two-reeler such as *Yoo Hoo* (1932) and *Should Crooners Marry?* (1933) under the Warren Doane comedy series banner, Stevens and his cousin, director Jimmy Horne, cooked up an ingenious plan to produce the pictures. Working as a team, often with Roach pal Fred Guiol, the three men switched back and forth — one writing and another directing, then turning it back around — continuously hiring each other in order to pick up whatever extra money they could. This way Stevens could experiment with what he called more "realistic" characters and situations, although he had to write them himself. In that early, brief time at Universal, Stevens and Guiol learned to write quickly and economically. Of her husband's work with Guiol during this period, Yvonne Stevens said, "George would say that the only two people he could trust were Fred Guiol and me. If he really wanted the truth, not that he would take your judgment, but least he'd get the truth from you . . . we were the only two, because by the time he was making it, everybody was yessing him to death. . . . But Fred, that was it . . . and it might not have been right, but that's what he thought . . . then George would think it over and then use his own judgment."[1]

While at Universal, Stevens also directed his first feature, the last in a series of George Sidney-Charlie Murray comedies, *The Cohens and Kellys in Trouble*, originally titled *Salt Air: A Murray and Sidney Comedy*. A spirited but ultimately gag-riddled tale of the misadventures of two caricatured men, Cohen (George Sidney), a Jew, and Kelly (Murray), an Irishman, the story follows their adventures when they reunite after a long time away from each other. Cohen is now a millionaire on vacation and comes to spend time with Kelly, the skipper of a run-down tugboat. But Kelly is also being pursued by an ex-wife out for alimony; she and a girlfriend show up and hound Cohen and Kelly throughout the story, which, save for Sidney's realistic performance, does not amount to much substance. Stevens shot *The Cohens and Kellys* from December 1932 through March 1933. Upon its release the comedy brought in laudatory reviews. Jerry Hoffman, writing for the *Los Angeles Examiner*, shrewdly said, "Should you ask, and I wish you would, the difference between one Cohens-and-Kellys picture and another is usually one year," but added that "George Stevens is entitled to much credit for making it a smooth comedy that runs along easily and entertainingly. This is his first directorial effort, and promises much for him with better material."[2]

Slapdash though *The Cohens and Kellys* may have been, it brought the recognition Stevens needed. But before he could benefit from it and sign a feature contract with the studio as it had promised, Universal shut its doors due to bank closures. Out of work again, Stevens at least felt confident enough about his earning power to hire an agent and contracted with Milton Bren of the Frank Orsatti Agency on Sunset Boulevard. By October 1933 Bren was in talks with RKO Studios to get Stevens a deal. On December 13 he signed a contract with the studio with a guarantee of eight months work to direct six shorts and one feature at a salary of $750 per week for the first year and increasing by $250 every year thereafter until the fourth year, when it would increase to $2,000 through the fifth year. Stevens stayed on with the Frank Orsatti Agency until February 5, 1936, when he signed with the flamboyant agent Charles Feldman, with whom he had a lifelong friendship and business arrangement until Feldman's death in May 1968. Feldman's first bit of business on Stevens's behalf was a settlement check he sent to Bren on October 19, 1934, for $1,500.

In September 1933 RKO loaned Stevens to MGM to direct a Laurel and Hardy segment of *Hollywood Party*, released in May 1934. Stevens's work with Stan and Ollie earned the movie its only good reviews. When he returned to RKO, a feature at last materialized. The studio needed a director for *Bachelor Bait* and asked Stevens to step in. He shot from April 30 to May 18, 1934, and the studio released it almost immediately. Also called *The Great American Harem* at one point, *Bachelor Bait* is a light comedy that touches briefly on the Depression (when mention is made of "everyone being out of work these days") before it supplies its audience with a leisurely paced series of misadventures. Stu Erwin plays a kindhearted man who, after losing his job as a civil servant in a marriage license office, opens his own business, Romance Inc., which becomes a successful matrimonial agency. When he sets up his secretary with a wealthy client (Grady Sutton) he realizes just in time that he is really in love with her. Much like the next few pictures Stevens directed at RKO, the mise-en-scène is relatively static and serves only as a backdrop to the comings and goings of the actors who run around in either a confused or agitated state. It could not have satisfied its director for long.

Stevens followed *Bachelor Bait* with two comedies featuring the popular team of Bert Wheeler and Robert Woolsey: *Kentucky Kernels*, released October 1934, and *The Nitwits*, released June 1935. Even the opening shots of *Kentucky Kernels* display Stevens's more expressive camera style, in part because he was able to work with more sophisticated material. The story opens with a young man contemplating suicide while standing on a New York bridge, ready to jump. Fog rolls in and covers the screen, giving it a rather soft, romantic quality. As much as he wants to jump, complications interfere with his efforts: a man walks by asking for a cigarette, then another walks by asking for a match. When he finally jumps he lands in a fishing net belonging to Wheeler and Woolsey, two out-of-work men living on a raggedy old houseboat and hoping to make a good catch of fish to sell and make their fortune. Instead, Wheeler and Woolsey embark on a slapdash, slapstick chain of events involving a young "Spanky" McFarland, a set of feuding families in Kentucky, and a love interest for Burt Wheeler. Scripted by Bert Kalmar, Harry Ruby, and Fred Guiol (from a story by Kalmar and Ruby), *Kernels* is packed with top-line action sequences and some rather sophisticated comedic moments.

Then Stevens segued easily — and happily — into the kind of serious material he wanted when his next RKO project came along. In October 1934 the studio began developing Gene Stratton-Porter's 1913 sentimental autobiographical novel *Laddie: A True Blue Story*. Stratton-Porter, it turned out, also penned the novel *Michael O'Halloran*, the source material for one of Stevens's first jobs as an assistant cameraman in 1922. *Laddie* was first assigned to fellow RKO director George Nicholl. An incomplete revised final script dated December 26, 1934, shows that it was reassigned to Stevens. Stevens's good fortune in getting *Laddie* was topped only by his getting *Alice Adams* several months later. *Laddie* was the kind of film that shrewd studio executives knew made good box office sales and therefore would be remade every once in a while. The story had been filmed by FBO in 1926 and would see yet another adaptation in 1940 as a vehicle for Joan Carroll and Tim Holt. A piece of pure Americana, *Laddie* is the sentimental tale of a young Indiana man, Laddie, inspired by Stratton-Porter's brother, Leeder, who tragically drowned when the author was still in her teens.

Laddie can even be viewed as Stevens's own unconscious autobiography — a fictional means of his pronouncing, cinematically, the parameters of his own character and preoccupations. At this point in Stevens's career, the property was closest to the kind of story that held importance for him, prefiguring not only *Alice Adams* but also *A Place in the Sun* in its portrayal of the American as essentially earnest and optimistic. *Laddie* is an idyll that recounts the idealized family life of late-nineteenth-century rural Indiana, focusing on the romance between the family's eldest son, a farmer named Laddie Stanton (John Beal), and Pamela Pryor (Gloria Stewart, loaned out by Universal), daughter of the neighboring farmer (Donald Crisp). Crisp's character disapproves of Laddie as a potential son-in-law because the young man is a simple farmer. Shot on roads and plowed field locations in and around Los Angeles and neighboring Chatsworth, *Laddie*'s mise-en-scène is romantically idealized, replete with vines and shrubbery framing nearly every shot. Lush and longingly looking back to simpler days, the sentimental film celebrates precisely those masculine (and archetypal) characteristics that in our collective imagination made America appear straight shooting and innately honest. Stevens could also have wanted his public to know that he also possessed these traits, or at the very least aspired to them. The Stanton family is large, loving, and entirely rooted on the farm. Their old-fashioned values embrace an honest Christian work ethic and a straight moral posture. Yet there is good humor and cheer in the scenes crowded with the family's working women, as if the very foundation of their lives depended on it. As for Laddie, when confronted by Pamela's father's snobbery he lets Pamela and her father know that he is "nature's noble man" — as if he were quoting directly from J. Hector St. John Crevecoeur's eighteenth-century tract on the American farmer. A man has strength and purity because the soil from which he grows possesses strength and purity as well. Laddie is proud of being plain, and proud of being a farmer. Of course, in the end his integrity wins the old man over and Laddie gets the girl.

Laddie premiered at the Circle Theatre in Indianapolis in March 1935 to wide approval from both critics and audiences. *Variety*'s critic wrote, "George Stevens has done a swell job of direction. He manages to get the full effect of the sentimental quality of the material without ever going maudlin, shifts cannily from comedy to the verge of tears and has gauged his pace perfectly for the mood."[3] The *Hollywood Reporter*'s critic called it "a box office knockout" and praised Stevens's ability to "achieve pathos without bathos, comedy without forced draft, and an artistic dignity belying its title and its origin."[4] In an important public mention, Louella Parsons wrote a glowing review in the *Los Angeles Herald*, especially praising what she termed the film's integrity; Stevens sent her a thank you note and a bottle of cologne in return.

Before *Laddie* opened, Stevens was back directing another comedy, *The Nitwits.* Also called *The Melodicks* and *Murder in Tin Pan Alley*, Stevens shot the film from February 28 to March 30, 1935, working again with Wheeler and Woolsey and joined by a very young Betty Grable. The story centers on three record company employees who are mixed up in a murder plot as a mysterious killer terrorizes New York. Scripted by Fred Guiol and Al Boasberg and based on a story by Stuart Palmer, *Nitwits* gave Stevens a chance to do some playful camerawork, including a song-and-dance number where Wheeler and Grable seamlessly twirl up and down several flights of stairs . The story is anything but original, but Stevens had the cast members moving around with a joyous, bouncy liveliness, energizing what would otherwise have been a familiar and ordinary Wheeler and Woosley comedy. The *Herald Examiner*'s critic wrote that despite its "hokumish" story, "it moves swiftly" and has a "lightness and sureness."[5] Though Stevens would later call *Nitwits* flimsy comedy, executive producer Pandro Berman had seen enough of Stevens's sturdy handling of drama or comedy to give him the true break he needed, *Alice Adams*.

Alice Adams

> I had this wonderful book, and all I had to do was not to ruin it.
>
> —George Stevens to Robert Hughes

Although he had cut his teeth as a serious director on the weepy *Laddie*, when Stevens directed Katharine Hepburn in *Alice Adams*, also in 1935, he entered the ranks of the important directors at RKO. Booth Tarkington's novel was prestigious material and a superior choice for Stevens, who was still looking for more serious subject matter. *Alice Adams* began as Hepburn's project, and at first she and Pandro Berman were undecided about who should direct. Hepburn was about to go with William Wyler, but after she and Berman tossed coins, with some bias in Stevens's favor, Stevens got the assignment. *Alice Adams* not only secured Stevens's future but also, at least for a time, raised the twenty-eight-year-old Hepburn's lagging box office numbers after *Little Minister, Break of Hearts,* and the singularly doomed *Spitfire* marked her as box office poison.

A shrewd commentary on small-town Midwestern America circa the early 1920s, Tarkington's novel tells the story of a social-climbing young woman who is also the victim of small-town snobbery. Alice's wants to be accepted by the town's prestigious families, but her father's lack of ambition and earning power keeps her low on the social scale. The fact is made painfully clear to her after she starts seeing but is ultimately snubbed by a wealthy young man named Arthur Russell. Alice must face reality and get a job to support herself.

Alice Adams had already been adapted for the screen by King Vidor in

1923 as a vehicle for his wife, Florence. In what would be its second screen treatment, the novel gave Stevens the chance to build on what he had already accomplished in *Laddie:* an ability to blend humor and pathos in a definitive piece of Americana. Stevens had read Theodore Dreiser's *An American Tragedy* by this time, the novel he would film thirteen years later as *A Place in the Sun.* In *Alice Adams,* Stevens already appears to aspire to Dreiser's examination of the nuances of the American character, also moving around comfortably in Tarkington's changing American urban landscape. In 1967 Stevens told Robert Hughes, "I had this wonderful book, and all I had to do was not to ruin it, and to dramatize it . . . and make a screen thing out of it, and not let the actress, Kate Hepburn, get in front of the story and demonstrate, and not let the director get in front of the story and demonstrate."[6]

Alice Adams was also Stevens's first serious opportunity to adapt a story from literature that reflected his lifelong preference for working with a novel, a play or even a magazine story rather than with an original screenplay. In 1971 he said, "it's so seldom . . . in my experience, that one ever comes onto a screenplay that is written for the screen that's adaptable to the screen immediately. I think there's a self-consciousness about the fade-in, fade-out, scene one, scene two, and three, and all those numbers — that technique which makes it very difficult to tell a story. I know I'd rather have the story in some prose form, any other prose form than the thing with the scene numbers in it."[7]

Hepburn and Berman's legendary coin toss proved lucrative for all concerned. Of course Stevens was affordable, receiving $11,050 for the job compared to Hepburn's $55,200. Hepburn had seen and liked *Laddie* and arranged for a quick meeting with Stevens who rushed to her house one night upon her request to discuss the project, even before he had time even to read *Alice Adams.* After he attempted to fake his way through a discussion of the novel, Hepburn reportedly told Berman the next day that Stevens was the dumbest man she had ever met. But she quickly changed her mind; during the shoot, which lasted from May 22 to June 29, 1935, most of the cast and crew knew that despite an occasional creative dispute Hepburn and Stevens were having an affair off the set.

Stevens later said that when he read Jane Murfin and Dorothy Yost's original script for *Alice Adams,* it looked nothing like the Tarkington he had just finished reading. So he set about rethinking the story. In script notes for March 21, 1935, he wrote: "Tarkington takes all of the simple things that people do for effect as part of their nature and exposes the motive that prompts them. They take on a great importance when analyzed, because of the fact that his characters take themselves so terribly seriously. We find Alice always acting, doing things for effect. Attention is called to them as we study them, where in another character they would probably go unnoticed."[8] Stevens understood Tarkington's gift for revealing his characters' often embattled interior lives to portray the American character in a decade still reeling from the massive economic and technological advances at the close of the nineteenth century. Alice comes from a family where change is slow to occur. She is struck by circumstances beyond her control that force her to labor under wish-fulfillment bordering on delusion. She wants to be accepted by those who snub her but is victimized by her father's lack of money, therefore, as her mother puts it, lack of "family." When Arthur Russell takes an interest in Alice, she believes she must lie to him about her family's social and financial affairs but ultimately is forced to confront her lies and face life squarely.

"This story is every girl's romance," Stevens noted, imagining how Alice could appeal to his audiences. She could be Everygirl, "sweet and likeable." From the start, Stevens's Alice is not Tarkington's Alice. Through Stevens's reshaping of Tarkington's story, Alice is transformed into an extension of Stevens's cinematic storytelling; she has just a bit of the romantic to her. In her discussion of Stevens's work with Hepburn on the film, Elizabeth Kendall writes that Alice is in part a creation of what Stevens knew to be true of Hepburn and that Stevens shaped Alice to Hepburn's own personality, bringing out a vulnerability to her character that (Kendall believes) directors had not yet tapped.[9] This may well be true; however, Alice Adams and Hepburn are but one moment in Stevens's body of work, that evolved from his days at Hal Roach. For Stevens cinema *is* the relationships born in the identification between two characters onscreen that then widens to include the spectator's identification with a character onscreen. The view informs his construction both of men and of women in the films. There must be something in these characters that the spectator wishes to possess and *wants* to identify with — perhaps a romanticized, more perfectly realized version of that spectator — at the very least there must be the promise for it. This aesthetic informed Stevens's construction both of men and women in his films. It is not specific to any particular decade in which he worked, nor does it evolve from any particular circumstance about that decade. It is the same before the war and after, when Stevens's view of the world and of movies became more serious, even urgent. When he wrote in his script notes that Alice lives "every girl's romance," he meant that there must be something in Alice, or something that *happens* to Alice, that an audience wants for itself. This is not mimesis, nor is it pure romance. Rather, it lies somewhere in between.

Jane Murfin's estimating script, dated April 1935, has Arthur in love with Alice at the end of the story. Though Stevens and Hepburn opposed it, this happy ending RKO wanted had been set in place even before Stevens came onto the project. After reading Murfins's script Stevens annotated it heavily before tossing much of it. Eventually he sat down with George Cukor's good friend Mortimer Offner, Dorothy Yost, and Hepburn herself and wrote a new one, taking a good portion of it, especially dialogue, from the novel itself.

Though Alice Adams lives in a small Midwestern town, Stevens gives her a large context: she is as much the simple, singular Alice as she is America's daughter, in this case a victim of towns hit hard by Depression-age economic hardship coupled with decades-old small-town small-mindedness. The story opens as Stevens's camera pans across the Midwestern town. The first image is a banner announcing the city of South Renford's ("A Town with a Future") seventy-fifth Jubilee. The camera pans right to the South Renford News building ("Circulation 5000"), then the Vogue Smart Shop, and then to Samuel's Five-Ten-Fifteen Cents Store. As the camera tilts down a black woman and her two children walk out of the front door just as Alice walks sheepishly and hurriedly away from the store and stops in the doorway of the Vogue Smart Shop next door, a better place to be seen. Alice opts for a bit of affectation: she takes a compact out of her purse and inspects it. She wants anyone looking to think she bought it at the Vogue Smart Shop, not the five-and-dime.

Alice walks into a florist shop hoping to buy flowers for the dance at Mildred Palmer's house that night, no doubt one of the few dances to which she has been invited. All the flowers are too expensive and she ends up going to the park to pick violets, stopping only when the camera also picks up the sign, "Do Not Pick the Flowers." Alice is short of money, and according to her mother, therefore short of "family." But the young Hepburn has a sweet, girlish voice; she infuses Alice with dignity, nobility, and almost, it seems, a bit of martyrdom. We can only imagine how Depression-age women in the audience wished they could be in Alice's shoes.

Hepburn rarely sits still and is breathlessly on the go. Alice goes home to show her mother her fresh-picked violets, singing their praises with just the slightest twinge of tragedy in her voice, which enlists her mother once more to her side: it is Alice's father who is the cause of his daughter's humiliation. He simply lacks drive and ambition. While Tarkington's Alice is manipulative and demanding of her parents, Stevens's Alice, upon returning home in these scenes, immediately thinks of her convalescing father and worries that her mother's demands on him to make more money will damage his health even further. She is kind and well meaning, an example of the best of Depression-age fortitude and of Stevens's lifelong preoccupation with uplifting rather than downtrodden characters. (Stevens would similarly alter Dreiser's Clyde Griffith in his interpretation of the character in *A Place in the Sun*.) To Stevens's mind, audiences would be hard pressed to find kinship with disheartened characters.

At the party later that evening, Alice's dress reveals no skin, unlike the other girls' off-the-shoulder fashions. The dress climbs right up to her neck to signal Alice's purity and naiveté, suggesting that Hepburn and Stevens created Alice to express an ideal of young womanhood no matter her poverty. (Hepburn reportedly was very proud of finding Alice's wardrobe at a Hollywood Woolworth's.) Later, sitting alone at the party, Alice conducts a series of small gestures and performances, pretending to converse with an escort who is literally not there in the chair next to her—just in case anyone looks over.

The scene is a visual feast for Stevens and Hepburn. Alice shows her discomfort by trying to appear nonchalant, the camera catching her in an assortment of poses and expressions ranging from poignant to desperate. A medium shot isolates her from the other party guests and captures Hepburn sitting in her chair, huddled close to the chair next to her, her arm draped across its back as if an invisible partner sat in it. She carries on a one-way conversation with this absent partner, crosses her legs non-chalantly and giggles as if responding to something funny that was said to her. The humorous and the tragic are simultaneous, soon broken up only by a sudden romantic moment later on when Arthur asks Alice to dance. As Stevens's camera closes in on Alice's hopeful face, the spectator cannot help but get caught up in the hopefulness. Alice *deserves* this happiness, this sudden change of fortune.

The simultaneity of the humorous and the tragic resurfaces in the film's centerpiece, the dinner sequence where Arthur comes to dine at the Adams home and Alice's pretensions blow up in her face. Stevens later said he had "an agonizing feeling about it. I know circumstances like that, a real agonizing thing for these poor people — sort of a major drama in which we put a light note in it to keep it from ever being too serious for the audience. I always like to do that in a serious scene . . . to definitely release a laugh so that I can go on and not get a laugh at the wrong time, which is most embarrassing." He described the emotional details of the scene as if it were a heroic battle: "I started to orchestrate it the afternoon when she started preparing the dinner, when everything was too warm, the kitchen was too hot, and you knew it was a bad day to entertain anybody — the omens were out that it's a sad day — and then it became valid as theatre because she was heroic. She dressed boldly and magnificently, and she was grateful, but the fates were against her, and she's setting a battlefield . . . that's going to lead to her own destruction, destruction that had to do with four plates of soup and some braided candles that were going to melt with the heat before matches were even applied to them. This kind of doom is settling over a young girl's aspirations, you know, and I thought that was a strong situation and I wanted to play it that way."[10] Stevens introduces a series of gags from his Laurel and Hardy days — the hired maid, Malena (Hattie McDaniel), who attempts to sweep into a small dust pan an errant brussels sprout that has fallen off Virgil Adams's fork; the close-up on the melted ice cream served to Arthur; Malena's maid's cap perpetually falling into her eyes; and Virgil's double takes at the sight as he futilely attempts to keep the front of his overly starched shirt from popping open. Stevens cuts from group shot to close-up to embrace both the humor and the pathos of the ill-fated evening. All the while, Arthur is observing these unfortunate events — as are we.

Alice's growing sense of futility and reality about her relationship with Arthur finally closes in on her (Stevens called it "a crescendo of suffering" in his script notes) until she is forced to confront the crumbling façade she has created and spill the beans to Arthur about her family's financial difficulties. After this confession, which she is certain will send Arthur running the other way, Alice is obliged a few minutes later to help her family out of a financial and ethical jam by telling old Mr. Lamb, her father and brother's longtime employer, who has accused her brother of stealing from him, that she is to blame for any dishonesty in their dealings with the old man. It is all her fault, she claims, because her mother and father have worked and scrimped so that she could have the nicer things in life.

In the novel, Tarkington rewards Alice for her honesty and her willingness to forfeit her fantasy of keeping Arthur by sending her out into the real world and into a secretarial school. The film, however, rewards her with the prize she has worked for so diligently — Arthur Russell himself. But this was not Stevens's wish, nor Hepburn's, since both director and star wanted to keep Tarkington's ending, with Alice climbing up those steps to secretarial school. Pandro Berman, speaking for the studio, argued for a romantic ending where the girl gets the boy. Both Berman and Stevens wrote long memos defending their positions. Stevens was right to assume that women in the audience would identify with Alice and would follow her anywhere, as it were. He wanted that "anywhere" to be the steps of the secretarial school. "Finishing with Alice going to the business college rounds out her character in that . . . she has learned to stand alone and not depend upon public approval, men, or social acceptance," Stevens said, adding that "she is heroic in her sacrifice" and furthermore that "she is deepened and broadened by her experiences." To this he added, "The ending is not tragic. When Alice goes up the business school stairs, it is as a woman who has found herself. She ascends into light, which means hope, and a burst of music symbolizing her own, inner triumphs. She is sacrificing nobly, even as Joan of Arc sacrificed for France. Alice is giving up her past, foolish dreams to meet life with head up, and a conquering look in her eye."

Berman and RKO eventually prevailed, enlisting the advice of George Cukor, who agreed with them, saying said that a realistic ending would not only be "bad box office" but would make it a bad picture "artistically."

Berman argued that a happy ending where Alice gets Arthur "does not leave Alice's character unfinished" because "Alice knows all along that she is pretending." He said that audiences "will feel that because of [her] suffering *and* the true worth in her manifested throughout the entire picture, she deserves a better fate than a stoic philosophy and a future as a typist — until, possibly, another man comes along." Berman believed, and probably rightly so, that given the romantic way Alice was constructed in the first place, a romantic ending would be the only logical ending.

Berman got his happy ending, though it was Stevens who basked in the glow of *Alice Adams*'s good fortune with critics and moviegoers alike. In the end Stevens also had his revenge. After he had had enough of the intensive studio conferences and disagreements over the film's ending, he filmed an additional ending showing Alice taking a pistol and walking, almost dazed, out the door, followed by a loud crack and a billow of smoke back onto the set. The pleasure of watching studio heads panic when he screened this melodramatic ending provided Stevens with at least some outlet for the frustration of directing the more inane one.

Golden Girl: *Annie Oakley*

> Well, I'd had *Alice Adams*, and it had come off
> very well. Now I could be a pain in the ass.
> —George Stevens, 1967

Though Stevens's next picture for RKO did not carry the same literary pedigree as *Alice Adams*, with *Annie Oakley* Stevens nevertheless had a sizeable legend on his hands. After the success of *Alice Adams*, he saw his star rise quickly at the studio; apprehending this new prestige, he surely was in the right frame of mind to tell the story of Annie Oakley, the crack sharpshooter from Darke County, Ohio, whose own star rose quickly on Wild West performance circuit in the late nineteenth century. Despite the diminutives that plagued her — Buffalo Bill called her "Little Miss," Sitting Bull referred to her as "Little Sure Shot" — Annie herself never shrank from looking larger than life in the spotlight once she got there. She was the epitome of Stevens's — and the 1930s much-needed — optimistic female. Early in her life she changed her surname from Moses to Oakley after a neighborhood in Cincinnati because it had a better ring to it. If anything, she possessed the cunning to transform herself into a frontier legend (at the time that the frontier was fast disappearing) and into a box office bonanza, the best audience draw in Buffalo Bill's Wild West Show. She was, in Buffalo Bill's words, "The Lovely Lass of the Western Plains." Oakley was also one of the relatively few women to secure a permanent place in American history books, a woman who, after all, claims to have been part of Buffalo Bill's ingenious plan to restage the entire Battle of Big Horn in Madison Square Garden in New York.

Annie was the ideal choice to be the first of many truly strong on-screen women in Stevens's body of work. She experienced herself as a mythical figure in her own lifetime, much of it no doubt owing to her own gift for self-mythologizing: along with biographies of her—whether fiction or fact—Annie wrote her own autobiography as well, a self-conscious demonstration of how aware she was of her celebrity. As a film subject, therefore, she was especially good for audiences during the Depression: the epitome of a self-assured up-and-comer who looks life squarely in the place where it tries to beat her down. Stevens had plenty of strong women in his own background, for one his maternal grandmother, Georgia Woodthorpe, who performed on stage (and became celebrated) during the Gold Rush days, even his mother, who with her husband put down then pulled up stakes as an actor, traveling up and down the West Coast. In Stevens's film Annie's love interest, Toby Walker, is himself a former vaudevillian as well. If audiences now needed a heroine who leaped from real life to the romance of "bigger than life," Annie was that subject.

On July 2, 1935, a news item in the *Los Angeles Evening Herald* reported that George Stevens would direct RKO newcomer Barbara Stanwyck in *Annie Oakley*, based on a fictionalized biography bought from writers Joseph A. Fields and Ewart Adamson. The studio signed Preston Foster to play Annie's romantic interest, Toby Walker (the name was changed from Frank Butler, Oakley's real-life husband). Melvyn Douglas signed on as Jeff Hogarth, Annie's fictitious friend and business partner, a part initially given to Walter Abel. A script was harder to come by than a cast. Stevens told a Chicago reporter soon after *Annie Oakley* premiered that when Berman assigned him the picture and he began shooting what was initially called *Shooting Star*, screenwriters John Twist and Joel Sayre had finished only four pages of the script. He was obliged to work quickly, putting the script together with Twist and Sayre as shooting went along. Yvonne Stevens later said, "They read over the script, and then if they had any suggestions to make they would write them out . . . then talk them over, and if George liked them, fine. Many times I'm sure they gave good suggestions. But essentially it would be George's way."[11]

Stevens took on the job of unflagging researcher, embarking on what became a career-long habit of uncovering realistic historical detail. He had his staff try to locate any of Annie Oakley's living family members. On May 13, 1935, RKO librarian Elizabeth McGaffey wrote to the County Clerk of Greenville, Ohio, to find names of Oakley's brothers and sisters and any extended family. Ten days later Annie's only living brother, John H. Moses, wrote back: "If your studio can reproduce some of the wonderful feats that that lady accomplished it will be a wonderful picture and any assistance I can be to you will gladly render." Oakley's own guns were shipped to the studio but ultimately were not used in the production.

Stevens's real challenge had more to do with shaping a screenplay as he shot the film, and giving the audience a sense of excitement in a story already told hundreds of times. He later recalled, "if you look at the picture, you will see reflections of lesser things gone by. I was continually developing things that would play with the audience, because the story was foretold, it was a foregone conclusion. But it was to be a first-rate film, modest in cost, but a feature in the 'A' bracket, so it was full of devices — with me depleting the store of whatever there was to give — to have a story that would hold on its own. There was an awful lot of chicanery going on there — reasonably honest chicanery — and we got by with that film nicely."[12]

Annie Oakley is essentially a romance that also recreates the spectacle of a life lived in the public eye. As befitting a legendary subject, the film opens with a preface: "No fiction is stranger than the actual life of Annie Oakley who came out of a backwoods village half a century ago to astonish the world." Annie is announced as a phenomenon of the Wild West show with which she traveled, something contrived, hardly believable, concocted by a slick public relations scheme. The inscription wills her to fiction.

But there is an alignment between the inscription and the real girl who rides into the frame. From the start, Annie (Stanwyck) is real—a hopeful, confident young woman, certain of herself and not shy about boasting of her talent as a sharpshooter. She rides shotgun in a wagon that pulls into the screen and stops in front of the camera, ready for romance. She comes to town to deliver game she has just killed and sells it to the local restaurant for a good price. When her wagon pulls up, it stops in front of a poster of Toby Walker, a former vaudevillian who has just joined Buffalo Bill's Wild West Show. Annie sees his face and pauses, uttering enthusiastically, "Ain't he pretty?"

As a way to exploit Toby and the Wild West Show, the show's promoters set up a shooting match between Toby and whatever local talent wants to compete. Annie rises to the occasion, but learns very quickly that if she wants to get her man, she must lose the match. This she does without a second thought and the real match is on: Annie competing with Toby and stepping down to give him the limelight. That is how you keep your man.

Annie and Toby play off the male-female competition theme. Then in requisite time they fall in love. A self-absorbed, egotistical man who habitually boasts about his shooting prowess, Toby is of course tamed and domesticated when he falls in love with Annie. As will become characteristic in a Stevens film, the woman improves anyone or anything she touches. Women are simply the natural bearers of law and order, and this without much effort. After all, when Annie first brings her game (and her guns) to town, one of the townsmen comments that with more sure-shots like Annie, "We'd have law and order in this country."

But Annie is before anything else a celebrity, and the film buoyantly reenacts the glamour of the Wild West Show, duplicating the spectacle of Annie, Toby, and Buffalo Bill's unique showmanship. Stevens films these scenes from a high distance, giving them breadth and transforming 1930s audiences into late-nineteenth-century audiences with the color and design of the Buffalo Bill's Wild West Show: spectacular riding stunts, the capture of Indians by cowboys on horseback, all circling the arena in colorful costumes and yelping to drum rolls and Indian calls. But an even more telling scene has one of the show's cast members reading a dime novel in which Annie and Toby figure as fictional characters, offering a smart commentary on nineteenth-century celebrity and on Annie Oakley's importance as a mythical figure. Along with Toby (or real husband Frank Butler), Annie is a central part of the myth (and the recreation of the myth) that links nineteenth-century America to contemporary audiences. Stevens would later revisit the idea of myth and its meaning for contemporary audiences when he directed *Shane*.

Annie Oakley was well received by critics and the general public and proved a bright spot for Stevens and RKO in the midst of the Depression. *Variety*'s critic wrote, "Stevens knows his way around in the herdheart whose preferences spell substantial grosses . . . a hearty human comedy, balanced with neat hokum, contrived from the show woman's life."[13] The *Hollywood Reporter* said, "Pleasingly different . . . a chapter of early Americana woven into a joyous romantic comedy . . . unforced laugh-maker. . . . Oakley's career followed with authentic detail."[14] The film proved that Stevens could make "hokum" work for him.

Off the Cuff: *Swing Time*

> Just make sure you get his feet in.
> — Hermes Pan to George Stevens

Yvonne Stevens said that by the time *Alice Adams* was in production it was "the beginning of the end for George and me." The marriage was unraveling. When she visited the *Alice* set she felt especially uncomfortable around Hepburn. "I always went to the studio . . . I made a mistake one time, and took his watch over . . . and she didn't even come over to say hello. . . . I really didn't suspect anything at that time."[15] Hepburn later confirmed that she and Stevens were having an affair during that time and also very early on during work on *Woman of the Year*. During the production of *Swing Time* it would also come to pass that Stevens and Ginger Rogers began a three-year on-again, off-again romance. In fact, on February 18, 1937, the *Los Angeles Herald Examiner* ran an item saying that Yvonne had filed for divorce from Stevens, claiming that he "preferred the company of his men friends to her own," staying away from her "for three weeks at a time, thereby depriving her of his company." She asked for $75,000 community property plus alimony and custody of then four-year-old George Jr.

Whether or not the reported filing was true (a similar item was printed ten years later in the *Los Angeles Times*, when the couple actually divorced) the flux of Stevens's personal life echoed the insecurity of the social world around him, made manifest by the lingering economic depression. This air of flux made it so that at the time he started shooting *Swing Time* a sense of the instability also crept into the aesthetic of his one true foray into the musical genre. Adding to all the uncertainty, Stevens, at only thirty-one years old, felt somewhat out of his element approaching the musical genre with two legendary hoofers the likes of Fred and Ginger. Also, when Pandro Berman handed him *Swing Time* (originally called *Never Gonna Dance*), it was another unfinished script, and he had to complete it off the cuff.

No other Stevens film in this decade bears as much of an imprint of the uncertainty of the Depression — and perhaps his personal life — as *Swing Time* does. Dance numbers, mise-en-scène, dialogue, and storyline look windswept and transient as if to say that very little in the world is permanent, everything can fly away or dissolve at any given time. It could not have helped much that he had something to fume about with RKO. Three months before shooting began in July 1936, Stevens's agent Charles Feldman wrote him on April 22 that he had met with RKO production head Sam Briskin who was "absolutely adamant that the following deal, which we have heretofore discussed, is the final and only deal: a retroactive salary (as of April 3, 1936) of $1,500 hundred per week with options leading to $4,500 per week starting April 3, 1942." Stevens signed but he was growing angry with RKO for working too hard for too little money.

As Stevens worked on the script for *Swing Time,* written especially for Astaire and Rogers's sixth pairing at RKO by studio writer Erwin Gelsey, the sense of impermanence shone through — and for good reason. When Stevens came aboard, Broadway playwright Howard Lindsay was hired to complete the script but quickly felt uncomfortable working in Hollywood. He left, leaving Stevens a note in his typewriter that he had taken the *Princess Alice* and traveled by way of the Panama Canal to get back to New York (in a later interview Stevens credited this fiasco, probably incorrectly, to the script for *A Damsel in Distress*). The studio then hired Allan Scott, noted for his lightning quick wit, and Ernest Pagano, known just as well for his lightning quick gag lines; the two sat down with Stevens and penned a script, with much help from Jerome Kern's music and Dorothy Fields's sophisticated lyrics. But then Rogers refused to commit to the picture until her salary rose to $2,635; which it finally did, after which shooting began just after spring 1936 and finished July 31.

The film's sense of tenuousness is evident almost immediately. The protagonist is an unusual kind of character for Stevens, at this point murky and ill-defined. After the starting credits roll, the camera finds its unlikely hero, John (Lucky) Garnett (played by Astaire), a dancer not so much in the middle of a dance routine as he is at the *end* of one. He dances offstage (runs, actually), setting up a precedent for the film: dance numbers always *ending* rather than beginning, with one or both of the dancers exiting out of the camera's eye, either stage right or stage left. At this early point, Lucky, who we are not certain is a dancer (and we never are), is also, it seems, a gambler. Lucky is a gambler in a movie all about life being a gamble, all about the possibility that in these tumultuous social and financially troubled times luck, money, even time, could run out at any moment.

Being a tenuous sort of fellow, Lucky is also about to run out on the most stable of American institutions: marriage. He is set to marry a wealthy girl named Margaret (Betty Furness) and is running offstage and out of the theatre to do just that when the story opens. But his gambling and acting buddies do their best to keep him out of that fray. They entice Lucky into a game of poker by claiming they have sent out the trousers of his wedding tuxedo to be cuffed, which is, according to them, the latest fashion. Without his pants Lucky cannot attend his own wedding. Instead he is left to play poker on the floor of his dressing room with the boys, a fraternity set up as an antifemale, antimarriage plot Stevens will use again, in *Gunga Din* and much later in *Giant*. It is an all-boys' club that emerged from the young Stevens's buoyant, even juvenile imagination.

The plan works. By the time Lucky gets his pants back (without a cuff) and shows up at his by-now canceled wedding, his bride and her father (played with much color and charm by Stevens's own father, Landers Stevens) offer him a deal of sorts. If he can make a living off this gambling that he loves so much and professes to be such an expert at, if he can raise $25,000, he can have another shot at marrying Margaret. Lucky sets off for the big city of New York to try his luck. But he seems more jubilant at suddenly being set free than at getting a second chance at marriage. At the train station Stevens sets up a shot showcasing Lucky's fraternity of friends, with him in the middle. He hops a train for New York with his good friend and shady gambling buddy, Pop (Victor Moore), in tow.

Once in the big city Lucky meets the girl of his dreams, working girl Penny (Rogers), and follows her into the dance studio where she works as an instructor. Eventually the two fall in love, even though Lucky does not tell Penny that he is engaged to another woman. Unlike Stevens's professionally stable women of the early 1940s films, Penny is a *girl* (as is Alice Adams) not quite sure about her future. A girl of her time, Penny is also pretty much down on her luck. When she first meets Lucky he makes her late for work, and her boss threatens to fire her for her tardiness. To make matters worse, Lucky follows her, pretending to be a dance student and then falls all over himself when she tries to teach him some steps. Penny is also unrefined and not particularly articulate. Lucky fares better than she does; he has more to say and sets off more of the plot's action leaving Penny to accept most of what happens to her. She does not move any real part of the story.

In keeping with Penny's down-on-her-luck circumstances, she believes that Lucky is indeed a terrible klutz and tells him not to waste his money on dancing lessons, whereupon her boss again threatens to fire her. Lucky feels guilty and suddenly remembers how to dance, surprising Penny as he sweeps her into a jubilant number, "Pick Yourself Up." Stevens's camera follows them in circular motions that mimic their movements — as if, even from a long shot, the camera's eye and the couple were one. It was no secret that Astaire and choreographer Hermes Pan worked out the film's dance numbers before calling Stevens in to shoot them. "Just make sure you get his feet in," Pan said.[16] Stevens moved the camera back when they needed privacy and looked down at them from high above using crane shots when they needed the huge dance floor.

Penny and Lucky make such a good team that Penny's boss sets up an audition for them at a swanky nightclub, The Silver Sandal Cafe. But Penny catches Lucky gambling in order to get the dinner clothes he needs for the audition and she barely talks to him again for a week, that is, until he woos her by getting into her hotel room and singing "The Way You Look Tonight" while she listens from the bathroom then, for visual effect, walks into the frame, her hair lathered into a Venus de Milo shampoo sculpture. But misunderstandings ensue and Penny makes plans to marry cafe orchestra leader Ricardo Romero (Georges Metaxa).

The film's dance numbers are its shining moments. Astaire's solo dance number, an homage to Bill Robinson, "Bojangles in Harlem," gives Stevens a chance to do some fancy camerawork, duplicating Astaire's real image onto a backdrop using three back-projected shadows of his figure. There are four Astaires, one real, the other three silhouettes, all four of them confusing what is real and what is shadow. Then in a stunning black-and-white wintery scene, Stevens moves Astaire and Rogers around the set while snow falls around them, and they sing a duet, "A Fine Romance." The song puts their frustration to music, each echoing the other's longing but each unable to voice in any other way. Stevens moves the pair from one point on the set to another, continuously reflecting each lover's inability to admit love for the other.

The snow scene sets the tone for the film's most glorious number, "Never Gonna Dance," with Astaire serenading Rogers as the two plan to part. Stevens gives the lovers a huge fantasy landscape, the empty nightclub, replete with a two-sided black staircase that almost embraces them when they dance. When the dance begins, Penny stands on the steps high above Lucky, who serenades her from below, the two evoking star-crossed lovers Romeo and Juliet. When the two dance around the ground, again embraced by the shape of the staircase, Stevens's crane shot opens up their physical and emotional space, giving them the room to express the largeness of their disappointment and sadness. They hold onto each other without actually touching, harmonious with each other in the thought of losing each other. The number's rhythm varies poignantly, simulating the lovers' uncertainty. Stevens often pulls the camera back giving them privacy, then moves to a medium shot to give their emotions more detail. The dance ends sadly, Penny twirling offstage and out of the left side of the frame, Lucky holding his arms outstretched as if hopelessly calling back what is now lost to him.

But even sadness is only temporary and turns to merriment in the end. Lucky and Penny shed their fiancés and find each other. Together at last — but who knows for how long — Penny and Lucky stand on the top floor of the nightclub before a huge window that reveals the enormous New York cityscape and sing a duet, integrating the songs "A Fine Romance" and "The Way You Look Tonight," each lover's signature song. Each sings the other's song, signaling their oneness. Still, the film ends on a transient note despite their unity before the city skyline. "The Way You Look Tonight" is a declaration of pure love, while "A Fine Romance" carries with it just enough doubt and inconclusiveness to mirror the tenor of the times.

Swing Time previewed in Santa Barbara, California, on August 4, 1936, and without much recutting opened in New York on August 28. Reviews were unanimously positive despite the shared view that *Swing Time*'s story line was minimal at best. The *Hollywood Reporter* wrote, "Supreme in the dance, in the personal appeal of its stars and in the class quality of its presentations, the series is this time enhanced by a record laugh-score and enriched by an air of irrepressible spontaneity."[17] Sharing that view, *Variety* said, "George Stevens directs brilliantly, scoring superlatively in every phase, keeping the comedy up to unflagging level of gay amusement in story, dance antic [and] character duels."[18]

Smokescreens: *Quality Street, A Damsel in Distress, Vivacious Lady*

Ironically, following the success of *Swing Time,* Stevens directed two pictures in 1937 that lost money at the box office and threatened to tarnish, though not too seriously, his steadily rising star at RKO. The Katharine Hepburn vehicle *Quality Street,* a remake of the 1927 Marion Davies film, lost $248,000 at the box office, followed by the equally disappointing *A Damsel in Distress,* a remake of a 1920 Pathe release. But it took only one sprightly romantic comedy, *Vivacious Lady* — shot simultaneously with *Quality Street* and *A Damsel in Distress* but released in early 1938 — to put the bounce back in RKO and Stevens's box office numbers.

Stevens actually planned to shoot *Vivacious Lady* first. In his date book (he called it "The Self Book") for March 12, 1937, he wrote, "The situation is rather tough on the 'Vivacious Lady' set-up. We have a starting date of April 1st. Must have a script complete to send Metro before we can get Jimmy Stewart as that depends on their approval. We need him." Two weeks into the shoot Stewart became ill and RKO suspended production until his return. But Stewart then went to work on an MGM picture instead and Stevens went on to shoot *Quality Street* and *A Damsel in Distress.*

Quality Street was probably the riskier of the two pictures. Adapted from the J. M. Barrie play, it is an exaggerated gesture of a story, a period piece entrenched in artifice and heavy staging that could have easily reminded Stevens of his early days on stage with his parents wearing period costumes. It was doubtful, however, that the story of an early nineteenth-century would-be spinster who masquerades as her own niece in order to win back her lover after he returns from war had enough in it to appeal to 1930s audience. This was another of Hepburn's projects; despite the success of *Alice Adams* her career once again teetered on the edge. With an outspoken heroine at its center, the play's subtle feminism appealed to Hepburn's independent, quasi-feminist sensibilities. Though Gary Cooper, Melvyn Douglas, Clark Gable, Fredric March, Walter Pidgeon, and Fred MacMurray were considered for the role of Hepburn's love interest, Dr. Valentine Brown, Franchot Tone won the part by the time the two-month shoot began on September 25, 1936, barely six weeks after the preview of *Swing Time.*

In the story, Hepburn's character, Phoebe Throssel, is a nervous young woman living on Quality Street, an avenue populated by similarly nervous older spinsters, each of whom, as the story opens, is seen flying to her window and fluttering madly when a hapless male (who happens to be the postman) walks innocently up to one of the dwellings to deliver a letter. Stevens plays the scene for broad comedic effect.

Though still young, Phoebe is a spirited bundle herself, possessed of breathlessness and exaggerated mannerisms. The drama begins when Phoebe, expecting her lover, Dr. Valentine Brown, to propose marriage to her, instead hears him tell her that he is going off to war. Disappointed but accepting of her fate to join the gaggle of spinsters living on her street, Phoebe goes on with her life and does what every good charitable woman should: she opens a school for children.

Ten long years pass before Valentine Brown returns. When he does, Phoebe worries that she has lost her looks. She is not the fresh beauty of ten years past; too much life has sucked her dry. This is a woman's sad confession about her worst fears about aging. But ever resourceful Phoebe decides to camouflage herself as her own niece, Livvie, who, naturally, is a duplicate of the younger Phoebe. Of course, Valentine seems to find her attractive. Phoebe-as-Livvie outwits him almost to the end, at which point he realizes the fib and confesses that he still really loves Phoebe despite the loss of her youthful radiance. Phoebe then comes clean. Hepburn's golden moments at the end of the film more than suggest her attraction to the play as she tells Valentine why she chose to masquerade herself: "You went to the great battles; I was left to fight the little ones," she says. "Women have a flag to fly as well as men; old maids have a flag as well as women. I tried to keep mine flying." The speech likely had meaning for Hepburn given her family's liberal politics and her mother's support for women's rights. With his own background of strong family women, Stevens could not have felt too much discomfort.

But audiences found little to recommend *Quality Street.* Preview comments were less than kind about its "artificial" qualities. "Would like Hepburn to walk like a normal person for a change . . . too 'slithery' . . . voice is artificial sounding, enunciation poor." Another said, "I am tired of seeing Hepburn in these silly simpering old-fashioned roles. . . . Let's have her in something modern, something that she can be herself in." When RKO released the film, the trade and newspaper reviews were not much more generous. The *Los Angeles Times* critic wrote, "Miss Hepburn . . . is treating 'Quality Street' as though it bore a dedicatory flyleaf. . . . It becomes what is known as a vehicle. Her Phoebe Throssel needs a neurologist far more than a husband. Such flutterings and jitterings and twitchings, such hand-wringings and mouth-quivering, such running about and eyebrow-raisings have not been seen on a screen in many a moon."[19] But the *Hollywood Reporter*'s critic saw it as Hepburn's "finest vehicle, not even excepting *Little Women.*"[20]

But the lengths to which Phoebe Throssel camouflages herself as Livvie in *Quality Street* were equally matched by Stevens's attempts to camouflage Joan Fontaine's less than sterling talent as a hoofer in *A Damsel in Distress.* Fontaine simply could not keep up with partner Fred Astaire, and Stevens faced a quandary when Astaire and Berman pressured him to fire her. After the success of *Alice Adams,* Stevens's status at the studio was on the upswing. "He wasn't D. W. Griffith, but he certainly was ahead of the Wheeler and Woolseys," Yvonne said.[21] The last thing he expected was a box office failure.

After *Swing Time* Stevens looked forward to working with Astaire again. Yet, after making more than a half-dozen films with Ginger

Rogers, Astaire wanted to make one without her. Stevens went along with him, though he had some misgivings. When British actress-dancer Jessie Matthews turned down the role of Lady Alyce in *A Damsel in Distress,* RKO turned its thoughts to various other actresses under contract. Stevens's March 12, 1937, date book entry sounded hopeful: "Papers blast forth this morning with the news that Lombard is going to do the 'Damsel' with Fred. I hope we get her. It should be a real winner of a picture with that combination." But RKO gave the part to a still inexperienced contract player, Joan Fontaine, who had had a small part in *Quality Street.* Yvonne Stevens recalled having lunch with Ruby Keeler at the time, who was "devastated" at not getting the part. It took little time to realize that Fontaine was in the wrong place — and in over her head. Stevens later said:

> This is Freddie's first picture without Ginger — and it's like Laurel without Hardy. . . . Freddie's a great worrier and he starts worrying about Joan Fontaine. I started worrying about Joan Fontaine ever since Ginger Rogers went to Big Bear to do her own picture. . . . As far as I was concerned [Fontaine] was in the picture, and we were going to do the best we [could], and somehow or other it's going to work out. Pandro and Freddie came down on the set and said, "Can we talk to you? We are very disturbed about Joan Fontaine. . . . we've got to make a change. . . . We've got to replace her." I said, "If we take this girl out of the picture she'll kill herself." They said, "Now, that's an exaggeration." I said, "It probably is. . . . I'll just say this: I'm going to stay here and you're not going to do it. You can't do it. We all made the decision." They believe they've made a helluva mistake. I've been shooting four weeks or so on this picture. She was a girl with problems, you know; she cried and all that. I said, "We've got to put her through this picture." So they all went back and they thought it over, came back with another plan — Al Jolson's wife, Ruby Keeler — somebody who could dance. I said, "I'm not going to take this girl out of the picture." Freddie was behind me. He said, "Go ahead, let's make this god dammed picture." And they were right. She was the wrong girl in the wrong spot. So she never knew that they wanted to take her out of the picture, or she would have collapsed.[22]

Stevens had to camouflage a dancer who could not dance within a story he thought "fragile" to begin with. But he adopted the attitude that he would get through the picture in whichever way he could. One way was to give Astaire his three solos and then two dance numbers with co-stars, George Burns and Gracie Allen. Hopefully, Fontaine would fall in gracefully without much showcasing.

The script for *A Damsel in Distress* was adapted by P. G. Wodehouse, Ernest Pagano, and S. K. Lauren from Wodehouse's novel. The project was a low-key song and dance romance that served as a vehicle for Astaire with a few minutes set aside now and then to showcase Burns and Allen's impeccable comic timing together, all of this encased in a George and Ira Gershwin score that includes "Things Are Looking Up," "A Foggy Day," "Nice Work If You Can Get It," and "Stiff Upper Lip." Astaire is Jerry, an American musical-comedy composer who travels to London and meets the aristocratic Lady Alyce (Fontaine), herself in love with another American man whom her family forbids her to see. When she escapes the castle one day with her butler Keggs (Reginald Gardiner) trailing her, she runs into Jerry and eventually falls in love with him instead. The extremely light storyline has Jerry constantly ousted from Lady Alyce's family's castle each time she invites him there, then switches locales to an amusement park, and into the British woods, as Stevens, cinematographer Joseph August, and choreographer Hermes Pan do their utmost to keep the action moving around Fontaine so that audiences are too busy to notice her shortcomings.

Two of *Damsel's* dance routines especially stand out. One is the episode that has Astaire, Burns, and Allen going to an amusement park and venturing into a fun house — which actually was an elaborate set built for the sequence — and traipsing in and out and in front of trick mirrors, long shoots, moving boardwalks, and hug turning disks. The stars are intermittently joined by a chorus of singers and dancers who help the trio perform the lively number "Stiff Upper Lip." Stevens's camera follows them like a shadow, sometimes staying back to expose the full effect of the topsy-turvy world of the fun house, then moving along in a roundabout mimicking the dancers' own movements.

Another dance number showcases the combined work of Stevens, Pan, and cinematographer Joseph August (a favorite of Stevens and John Ford) in an effort to deflect the spectator's view from Fontaine in her one dance number with Astaire. In that number the couple takes what is intended to be a light-hearted dancing jaunt into the forest surrounding her castle as Stevens, Pan, and August essentially transform it into a so-phisticated game of cat and mouse between Fontaine and the audience. Instead of putting obstacles in the way of his actors on the set (a device to make the actors a bit uncomfortable and ready for anything) Stevens puts obstacles and illusions in the spectator's path so he can take the attention off of Fontaine as she tries to keep up with Astaire. Stevens later remarked in his interview with Joseph McBride and Patrick McGilligan, "We did the thing on the crick with the fog; she didn't have to dance at all, he did all the dancing. And it was pictorial . . . we did what we could to make the picture work." The two are seen dashing around trees, hedges, bridges, and an assortment of foliage pieces, moving and darting about as much as possible over a creek and through the woods, the fog now and again rolling in and hiding them. Stevens intermittently obstructs the spectator's view of the couple by shooting them from behind tree trunks and other elements of nature, keeping these in the forefront as Fontaine and Astaire blend into the scenery in Stevens's long shots. Van Nest Polglase and Carroll Clark's production design and art direction gave him the additional atmosphere he needed.

But audiences saw through those trees when RKO released *A Damsel in Distress* in November 1937, giving Astaire his first box office flop — even as Hermes Pan won an Oscar for his funhouse sequence. After the experience of *A Damsel in Distress* Stevens abandoned his brief foray into the musical genre. Said *Time* magazine's critic, "Not so lissome a heroine as light-footed Ginger Rogers . . . actress Fontaine goes gamely but somewhat lumberingly through the curvets and caracoles required of her. Far more facile as an Astaire partner is, of all people, rumpish Radio Dunce Gracie Allen."[23]

Stevens now got back to work on *Vivacious Lady*. Though the picture incorporates one cheery dance number that critics noticed, it is little more than a light moment in a light comedy. *Lady* is essentially one long extended gag but so capably acted that audiences hardly noticed. James Stewart plays a small-town botany professor named Peter who goes to New York City, meets and impetuously weds a night club singer named Francy (Ginger Rogers), then brings her home but is unable to break the news to his stern, domineering college dean father (Charles Coburn). He is rightfully afraid that Francy just will not fit in with the small-town stuffed shirts at the college — at least not until the cast and audience work their way through a maze of humorous situations. Stevens saw *Lady* as a story about "inarticulation. . . . The boy and the girl had no-o business getting together — so the movie was really about the pleasant frustration of non-communication. . . . No-ow, to overcome this disbelief is the most difficult thing to do in films."[24] Stevens liked the inherent conflict and set out to make good use of it.

Stevens had gotten a copy of the story *Vivacious Lady* by I. A. R. Wylie back in September 10, 1936. Kay Van Riper and Anne Morrison Chapin produced a final incomplete screenplay by April 15, 1937, and more work was done on that. Though not credited, Stevens's friend Irwin Shaw and Anthony Vellier both worked on the script since Stevens wanted especially to play up the antagonism between Francy and Peter's father. Final screenplay credit, however, went to P. J. Wolfson and Ernest Pagano. By the time shooting actually resumed Stevens had impressed Pandro Berman enough for Berman to give him director *and* producer credit, although a studio publicity handbook for the film lists Berman as the producer and Berman himself later said that he liked to help young directors by giving them "producer" credit.

Vivacious Lady is little more than a light, good-natured piece of fluff with a superlative cast and dialogue intermittently witty and realistic. Stevens imparts Stewart with an earnestness and Rogers with a soft femininity that makes their onscreen romance believable. But the film's underlying artificiality and often-forced situations are played for laughs and little else. When Stewart takes Rogers home to Old Sharon University to *try* to tell his father about Francy, one gag has Francy pretending to be a university student enrolled in Stewart's class. But Stevens dresses her in black throughout most of the film, giving her a sexuality and sophistication that would hardly fit in with the town's erudite atmosphere. The audience is asked to believe that Rogers will fit in and yet at the same time viewers realize that she never will — a contradiction difficult to push to the story's borders. Rogers plays Francy as passive, consistently waiting instruction from her young husband. Stewart is equally passive, especially when he brushes up against the elitist and verbally wicked Coburn. Both actors and their characters are at the mercy of the next gag to come. *Vivacious Lady* has more than a few elements of the classic situation comedy to it, but the star quality of Rogers and Stewart lift it far above that. Stevens takes Francy and Peter seriously, and this creates characters who shine even in flimsy material. The cat fight between Francy and Peter's erstwhile former fiancée (Frances Mercer) benefits greatly from Stevens alternating between close and medium shots, giving it a vitality that characterizes Stevens's comedy style during this period and in the 1940s comedies to come.

Preview comments were superior all around, as were newspaper reviews upon the film's release in May 1938. The writer for the *Herald Tribune* suspected that "it is Mr. Stevens who has actually worked the trick of building a thin thesis into a beguiling photoplay. His direction is both imaginative and assured." Critics liked its "comic misadventures" and *Vivacious Lady* became one of the studio's strongest releases of the decade.

The more Stevens fell "heir," as he put it, to better or at least more high profile RKO scripts, the more he knew his worth at the studio. In 1938 at Berman's request he directed a scene from the Alfred Santell's *Having Wonderful Time,* an ill-fated Ginger Rogers vehicle, but at the same time thought more about actively seeking out more thoughtful material he had not yet seen from the studio. Though the worsening political situation in Europe remained far from America's doorstep at the end of the decade, Stevens became increasingly interested in the impending conflict and wanted to direct more serious, even political, properties. He read Humphrey Cobb's 1925 antiwar novel *Paths of Glory* and very much tried to film it. He later said:

> I really wanted to make that picture. I had a recollection of the First World War when I was a kid . . . and so, having read the book . . . I did very well in promoting [it]. . . . [RKO] got the book . . . and I went to work on the screenplay . . . and Berman . . . comes down and talks to me and says, "We can't make that story." And I said, "Why the hell can't we?" and [he later said] "the real reason is that France won't stand for it — and especially Hitler's rise to power." "Well . . . don't run it in France. You know this is a picture for the rest of the world," I said. And then the truth of the matter came out, that France would run no RKO pictures if we made "Paths of Glory" . . . and then a delegation from the studio came and said, "This is an anti-war picture . . . it's an argument against war. . . . This is no time to make an anti-war picture. . . . If somebody doesn't fight Hitler, what will happen?"[25]

Twenty years later, when Stanley Kubrick directed *Paths of Glory*, Stevens said he never went to see it because he did not want to go to "another man's wedding." He always considered *Paths of Glory* one of the important stories that got away from him. There were others also. Ironically, Stevens passed on *Winterset*, Maxwell Anderson's thinly veiled treatment of the Sacco-Vanzetti case (filmed by Alfred Santell at RKO in 1936), to get the opportunity to direct Hepburn in *Quality Street* in 1936.

Cowboys and Indians: *Gunga Din*

> When I was a kid in San Francisco . . . I could always tell from across the street whether I wanted to see [a] film. . . . If pictures were outside I would cross the street, but if I could see it all took place inside I didn't want to see it. You know . . . nothing but the ladies in costumes and love scenes and all that.
>
> —George Stevens to Jim Silke, 1964

Stevens's next feature at RKO was *Gunga Din*, an "outside" picture that almost turned into an albatross for the studio. Berman gave it to him in part because, from the looks of what the studio's originally assigned director Howard Hawks was doing (or not doing) on the set of *Bringing Up Baby*, it appeared that no one could have been slower and more expensive. Little did Berman know what he was in for. Little did he or Stevens know that *Gunga Din* would change Stevens from a director who came in on time and on or under budget to a director chronically late, chronically expensive, and chronically big at the box office.

Gunga Din had a production history with more byroads than the South Asian locale of the story that was adapted from Rudyard Kipling's writings.[26] RKO had been trying to make the film since 1936, when Hawks was slated to direct from a screenplay penned by playwrights Ben Hecht and Charles MacArthur. Eventually Berman decided Hawks would have to go after Hawks left and then returned to the studio. Production complications, including writer and casting changes, postponed the epic undertaking for several years.

The script itself had an entangled history. The film's title comes from Rudyard Kipling's much-loved poem narrating the bravery of (and the speaker's affection and admiration for) a brave native Indian water boy (*bhisti*) named Gunga Din. Din assists soldiers of a British regiment stationed in the northern part of India late during Queen Victoria's reign. In colonial India a bhisti furnished British soldiers in battle with water and provided help for the wounded, often risking his own life in the process.

By the time Stevens came on board, the script had already changed into various configurations during its long history. There originally existed a fifteen-minute silent visual adaptation of the poem alone. Then in 1928 MGM considered doing a feature adaptation. Irving Thalberg commissioned various scripts to be written but eventually put the project aside before he dropped it entirely. Then independent producer Edward Small made plans to produce a film based on the poem and in 1936 bought the rights from Kipling's widow for his Reliance Pictures Company. Small hired William Faulkner to adapt the poem for the screen; one of Faulkner's drafts has several British officers arriving in India to join the regiment and developing a friendship with a native named Gunga Din. Various versions of a narrative followed, all with different and often complicated endings.

RKO acquired the rights to the story from Small in the middle of 1936 when various writers were hired to elaborate and alter the story in development. Howard Hawks became involved at about the same time and began working on a new script along with Hecht and MacArthur. But Hecht and MacArthur borrowed a plot from their earlier success, *The Front Page,* and hoisted it on *Gunga Din.* In *The Front Page* one character tries to stop another from leaving the ranks; in *Gunga Din* two British soldiers try to keep their buddy, the third soldier, from getting married and leaving the regiment. But early in 1937, after two revisions, Hecht and MacArthur left the project. Hawks then made subsequent changes with RKO staff writer Dudley Nichols. Then, without any definite casting for the leads, Hawks left RKO in good measure over disagreements about his slow and costly handling of *Bringing Up Baby,* released in 1938. At this point Berman, now vice-president in charge of production, took over the *Gunga Din* project. Though he still considered Hawks a contender, he gave it to Stevens in April 1938. Stevens was thought to be the studio's most valuable director now, and getting the project spared him from directing another comedy, *Room Service,* starring the Marx Brothers.

Stevens agreed to do the picture only if he could take it outside on location — which would double its projected budget. It would now cost half a million to do, but Berman agreed to Stevens's demands. Stevens traveled up to an area around Lone Pine, California, with art director Perry Ferguson and came up with designs for three parts of the set: the town, the temple, and the parade ground. Then he and close friends and collaborators Joel Sayre and Fred Guiol spent time at Lake Arrowhead redesigning the script to he could shoot it at a location around Lone Pine — specifically in an area flanked by the Sierras, Mount Whitney, and the Alabama hills resembling areas in the Khyber Pass in India. The area was a popular movie locale, and had earlier served as the location for *The Charge of the Light Brigade* (1936) and *The Lives of a Bengal Lancer* (1935).

The Hawks-Hecht-MacArthur script took place inside the barracks and Stevens thought it would not work. If audiences were to be transported to India at the Khyber Pass, they should be able to see some of it. The shoot turned into a series of improvisations:

> Three weeks before we started . . . we didn't have a story . . . we didn't have an activity that took place in India . . . we needed something to give it validity. The three of us . . . came on this Cult of Thugee. We used that. We didn't know the circumstances of our story, we didn't know all of the principal characters, and so we left the city and went for about three weeks to devise an outline of a screenplay. I ran back and started setting up sets and ordering costumes. We knew the kind of picture we were going to make. I remember we ordered costumes for 500 Bengal Lancers and 500 52nd Gordon Highlanders. . . . We designed our sets, then went back and worked a few days in constructing more of the story, and arrived with a caravan of people on a Monday morning — we didn't have a first page of the script. And we set up a drill . . . in which the men are doing a Mounted Lancer drill afoot . . . and this was a prescribed drill in the annals of that military unit that they are supposed to be part of. And it would take a good deal of time, I was sure of that. And that gave us time to write the first scene of the picture, in the property truck, with a stenographer. . . . All the way through this film we don't know what we're going to do next week. . . . There's a great deal of vitality [that] comes from this, and we were enormously excited and pleased . . . with what we were doing throughout.[27]

Stevens's enthusiasm fueled *Gunga Din* and shaped it into a nonstop series of adventures. As he said at the time, "It has a variety of moods, movements, and it has a rather definitely arranged structure, to hold interest together."

Casting was yet another adventure. Initially, Jack Oakie was considered for the part of Cutter, the Cockney soldier in the group, and Cary Grant was cast as Ballantine, the officer whose impending marriage threatens to break up the fraternity. But Grant asked to switch parts, thinking Cutter offered him more opportunity to cut up and be humorous. Stevens agreed, and Fox loaned out Victor McLaglen to play MacChesney while Douglas Fairbanks Jr. was then cast to play Ballantine. For the part of Gunga Din the studio wanted to cast a young Indian actor, Sabu, but at that precise time producer Alexander Korda was about to star him in *The Thief of Baghdad* (released in 1940) and would not loan him out. It was Stevens's friend Garson Kanin who suggested the forty-seven-year-old actor Sam Jaffe for the part of Din. Jaffe had just been seen in the highly effective part of the High Lama in the film adaptation of James Hilton's *Lost Horizon,* and was given the part of Din. Stevens then cast Joan Fontaine as the young girl to whom Ballantine is engaged to marry. Despite Fontaine's unfortunate toe-tripping escapade in *A Damsel in Distress* she was better suited in *Din* as the shy, retiring fiancée who never gets her man.

Location shooting began in early July 1938 and continued for three-and-a-half months. *Gunga Din* marked a turning point in Stevens's ability to come in on time and budget as the film's slated sixty-four-day shooting schedule expanded into a one-hundred-and-four-day shoot. It was during this period in Stevens's career that he became affectionately known by his colleagues on the set for his characteristic avoidance of front office advice. Stevens would politely (and quite notoriously) *pretend* to listen to a worried executive about cutting back costs and moving faster and then simply revert back to his original plans. One of the more infamous episodes occurred during the *Gunga Din* shoot when Berman, concerned about Stevens's overextended tab and schedule, drove up to Lone Pine one Saturday afternoon to discuss the matter with him. According to legend, when Stevens saw Berman's car approaching, he took off (some say he went away with Ginger Rogers) for the weekend and left Berman his choice either to wait in primitive quarters until Monday morning or to return to Beverly Hills. Berman left.

Gunga Din cost almost $2 million to produce, making it the most expensive project in RKO's history. Upon its release at the end of January 1939, no immediate profit appeared; in fact the film took years to make money. Still, if "expensive" could ever be translated to mean "significant," then certainly *Gunga Din* was that — for Stevens's reputation and for RKO itself. It was big to begin with, running one hour and fifty-seven minutes upon its initial release but eventually trimmed to ninety-four minutes for its large-scale 1954 reissue.

Gunga Din's spontaneous if hectic mode of production gave the story an air of breathlessness, a sense of life as a series of fully lived boyish escapades. Its opening is serious and stately: a shot of a monument to Queen Victoria with the inscription "Regina Imperatrix: God Save the Queen," followed by a reading of one stanza of Kipling's poem, "Gunga Din." The lines introduce the story's erstwhile hero, the water boy who saves the lives of his British comrades yet loses his own in the process. Then more seriousness follows: "Those portions of this picture dealing with the worship of the Goddess Kali are based in historic fact." The studio did not want to offend religious believers or play wrongfully with old myths. It was not until thirty or forty years later, though, that Stevens expressed remorse about the film's bias against the bhistis and its complacency toward the British disregard for colonized peoples, an inequity still dismissed in the 1930s.

After the somber opening, the action begins with an act of vandalism when a group of Thugees destroy a telegraph wire the British put up then pose as pilgrims as their leader asks the British patrol if his group can travel with the soldiers to be safer along side of them. That night the Thugees strangle members of the British detachment. After this, all seriousness gives way to romance and adventure as the three heroes, Ballantine, MacChesney, and Cutter, enter the action and proceed to jump out of windows, run up and down stairs, punch out enemies, and generally destroy sets and scenery. The soldiers do battle with the enemy as the film's sheer joy and animation reflect a boy's adventure yarn. *Gunga Din* is purely a young man's film, reflecting the young man who directed it (Stevens was only thirty-four when he took his first big crew out to location for this picture). The story freed him from the more domestic stories he had directed and left him with a glorious adventure about three soldiers whose sole purpose in *Gunga Din,* beside fighting off Thugee assassins, is to keep one of their own from getting married, thereby avoiding breaking the bonds of their own fraternity. The home movies Stevens shot on the set show a smiling Joan Fontaine mugging with her fraternal costars, sitting on one actor's lap then moving over to Stevens's as he plays for the camera with Grant, McLaglen, and Fairbanks in tow.

At times the character of Gunga Din himself seems an afterthought to the action and focus on the three leads. Early on, following his inconspicuous entrance as the last in a line of bhistis who are taking orders and marching in the middle of the village on their way to assist the British soldiers, Din seems to disappear from the story. Later Stevens focuses on him in several scenes: when Cutter teaches him to salute and march like a soldier; when Din, using Annie the elephant, helps Cutter escape from a regiment prison; when he sounds the bugle to warn his British comrades that the Thugees are approaching and dies in the ensuing battle; and finally when he is eulogized and made a colonel just before the attending journalist (Kipling's widow did not want to evoke her husband the writer) recites part of the poem he has written for Gunga Din, and Din himself is superimposed onto the frame in the film's closing shot. The British commander decides to give Din corporal status, fulfilling the bhisti's great wish to be part of the regiment. Stevens later called the film a story about "the enthusiasms that develop from comradeship," and said of his three leads, "people are basically amusing and funny, and they're never more funny than when they take themselves seriously or heroically."[28] The character that names the story emerges from Stevens's sense of the joyousness of youthful adventure and bonding.

But the film was taken more seriously in India, where negative views of its treatment of Gunga Din emerged. In its February 1939 issue, the Bombay publication *filmindia* called the film "an Imperialist propaganda of the crudest, the most vulgar sort" that "depicts Indians as nothing better than sadistic barbarians." The writer Khwaja Ahmd Abbas particularly looked to Kipling's treatment of Din, saying, "the sacrifice of Gunga Din as sublimated by Kipling, was not the sacrifice of a friend, an equal, but that of a faithful servant. He served his masters with dog-like devotion." He said of the film, "All the British characters are honest, jolly souls while all the 'natives' are scheming, treacherous, unscrupulous devils. All but one! The solitary exception is Gunga Din, the faithful water-carrier — loyal unto death, despite the insults and curses that are invariably showered on him by his White Masters. He is always cringing before them."[29] In later interviews, though the question did not arise frequently, Stevens publicly lamented the film's attitude toward Gunga Din and the Thugees, but said also that *Gunga Din* was produced in the 1930s, during a historical time of widespread acceptance of such prejudice and criticism of British colonialism in India. For Stevens at the time, consideration of Din as a politicized being was simply a foreign thought.

Stevens captures Grant, McLaglen, and Fairbanks's free-spiritedness on film that matched his own during production, this before returning to women's material for his next four films. Looking back years later, Stevens congratulated even himself for being able to choreograph the huge operation — for example the final battle scene that required fifteen hundred men, several hundred horses, a series of mules, and four elephants. He tried the battles out on paper first, he recalled, then gradually reenacted the scene bit by bit, bringing in and rehearsing a portion of the actors and animals, adding to their numbers each time until he reached his full cast. Before that scene, he relied on spontaneity throughout the shoot, "writing a day ahead and then getting all those people in and doing the battle scenes which we did in one day. . . . I had a public address system that I kept on the ground," he said, "and I was on a horse and I organized the business from the horse using the P. A. system and moving around from one shot to another. We did that all in one day with a number of cameras. . . . I made the film long ago and I made it just in time. If I'd experienced another year, I'd have been too smart to make it."[30]

Variety called *Gunga Din* "a magnificent narrative poem spun into vigorous, ecstatic action" while the *New York Times* critic wrote, "All movies should be like the first twenty-five minutes of 'Gunga Din,'" and *Newsweek* called it "ambitious juvenalia" that "proceeds fast and seriously to combat on a mammoth scale."[31]

Stevens's exuberance over *Gunga Din* was quickly extinguished as he became increasingly frustrated with RKO soon after the film's release. The beginning of what would soon be the end of his relationship with the studio stemmed from his growing resentment that they were working him too hard and from his increasing desire to make more serious films. The war in Europe now encroached on America's psyche, just at a time when Stevens found two properties about war and the darkening political and social situation in Europe — Katherine Kressman Taylor's 1938 novel *Address Unknown* and Phyllis Bottome's *The Mortal Storm* (1937). He proposed the projects to the studio, but they were systematically turned down for being precisely what they were, anti-Nazi.

A month after *Gunga Din* premiered, Stevens was in New York staying at the Waldorf Astoria. On February 8, 1939, he and Berman conducted a conversation by cablegram about the two properties. In the first of three telegrams to Stevens that afternoon, Berman told him that he had had "lengthy discussions about them with RKO president George Schaeffer, who was "definitely afraid [to] commit . . . to any picture that is propaganda against anything. . . . He has every wish that we make a picture with regard to Americanism or democracy but [is] opposed to any specific movement against any other force." In a second telegram Berman reneged: "After serious thought believe if company would be willing to proceed with a picture that might be classed as anti-Nazi propaganda that we would do better to consider . . . Mortal Storm [which] has real body and great quality and is complete as a story of a family and of a love and of a regime."[32]

The Mortal Storm project never materialized for Stevens (it was later filmed by Frank Borzage), but in a final cable that afternoon Berman told him "Please read 'Sisters' by A. J. Cronin, novel about to be published . . . this is by author of 'Citadel' . . . definitely a picture possibly for Dunne, Lombard or Stanwyck . . . wish you would give me immediate reaction." *The Sisters* eventually turned out to be *Vigil in the Night,* his next and final film for RKO. But Stevens felt exhausted. Berman's telegrams prompted him to write out a long harangue for himself on Waldorf Astoria letterhead, condemning the studio for its treatment of him. Stevens was most at ease writing to himself, knowing he would be the only reader of his own correspondence: "Cannot do first-rate pictures — comparable in quality to those of the first rate directors continually without having an opportunity to refresh my imagination. . . . Since 1935 had taken four weeks off [November 1935]. Since that time have been continually occupied with studio work — and in such a manner that my work has necessitated a seven-day week." What little vacation time there was, Stevens wrote, "was terminated by Mr. Berman, expressions of urgency to make it possible to keep 'Having Wonderful Time' from reaching a new high in low quality film production."[33]

Stevens was upset that his "fine relationship with Pandro—was clouded by personal comment from him after completion of *Gunga Din* which contained no comment of approval or otherwise on shooting and writing." Instead, Stevens wrote, he received from Berman "caustic criticism on the fact that I was not cooperating on the plans of another photoplay. . . . This type of dealing makes it necessary for a person to watch out for himself." After letters back and forth between RKO and Charles Feldman, Stevens signed a new contract on March 3, 1939. But he would sever ties with the studio by the end of the year.

Women's Work: *Vigil in the Night*

When Stevens decided to take the assignment for *The Sisters,* he could not have moved further away from the masculine free-spiritedness of *Gunga Din* had he purposely tried. Originally a novella serialized in *Good Housekeeping* from May to October 1939, *The Sisters* was penned by A. J. Cronin, whose story *The Citadel* was adapted and directed by King Vidor in 1938. Its popularity was no doubt the reason for Berman's interest. For Stevens, here was serious material, albeit a bit melodramatic, but a property that at least aspired to a contemplation of world events, in this case the lives of two sisters who serve as nurses during World War I. He had by now begun to think more about the war raging in Europe.

The Sisters is the contemporary story of two English siblings, Anne the "good nurse" and Lucy the "bad nurse." One is conscientious and social minded, the other is selfish and immature and causes the death of a young child just a few minutes after the story opens. The first sister covers for the younger one and as a result loses her job and is forced to leave for a new city and a new hospital. There she meets a dedicated young doctor who is trying to raise money to start his own clinic. A series of tragic events befall them, culminating in their selfless aid to patients after an epidemic hits the city. The story ends on a stilted but hopeful note. In a time of expanding conflict in Europe, a story of female self-sacrifice and heroism could not have been more timely.

Vigil in the Night was not Stevens's first choice for serious material. But as adapted by Fred Guiol, P. J. Wolfson, Rowland Leigh, and Stevens, the film is probably his darkest work of the decade and his most somber look at women *and* the world. In his copy of *Good Housekeeping,* Stevens underlined several lines in *The Sisters* text that held particular importance: "There is nothing in the world so bad as a 'bad nurse,' a head nurse tells Cronin's heroine, Anne Lee. 'Nor so good as a good one. Remember that, Nurse Lee. Remember it all your days.'" He also underlined, "how pitiful was the death of a little child. How doubly pitiful a needless death." These are women's concerns of service, sacrifice, the sustenance of human life, and the tragic circumstances of death. Stevens incorporated them into the film when he began his eleven-week production on September 11, 1939. Once more casting against type as he had done with Barbara Stanwyck in *Annie Oakley,* Stevens cast the often-comedic Carole Lombard as the story's older sister and heroine, Anne Lee.

Vigil in the Night is an almost morbidly dark film, opening with the credits superimposed onto the image of a lamp's burning flame to suggest the "vigil" in the title. The focus is on women's vigilance in the night, the work of nurses. This image then dissolves into an exterior view of a hospital. Stevens's camera pans the side of the hospital until it finds an open window and looks into it, a set up he would use frequently in the coming decades. He moves into a close-up of Lucy Lee (Anne Shirley), who sits vigil over a sleeping child. She watches him for a moment, and then Stevens cuts to a close-up of a teapot whistling in the next room. Lucy leaves the child to go fix herself a cup of tea. By the time she returns the child is dead. The tragedy sets the tone: this is women's work requiring the highest order of sacrifice.

Lucy Lee may not be up to the task of nursing, but her older sister, Anne (Lombard), is. She rushes into the room just before hospital officials file in and takes the blame for the death. Because she makes this sacrifice she is fired from her job and travels to another city in England and takes a nursing job there.

Vigil in the Night sets up its symbolic parameters: there is a good nurse and there is a bad nurse. Women's work is *that* simple, that hyperbolic, that much civilization's bedrock: it is the burning light that must never extinguish. Within these boundaries and this symbology, heroine Anne Lee goes about her life and work of nursing the sick. When she meets a young doctor named Robert Prescott (Brian Aherne), she endeavors to help him raise money to open a new hospital. Men design the world;

women do its work. In one scene toward the end of the film, Anne gets a promotion and with it a new uniform. She looks like a nun, like a Madonna in fact. As *Vigil in the Night* celebrates women, it idealizes Anne more strongly as the story progresses, finally delivering her to the audience just short of sainthood. For all the bad nurses in the world, Anne's good works more than compensate for them. When an epidemic hits the city, children are rushed into the hospital, creating the need to open a separate wing. Anne is put in charge, and gradually her work draws other nurses to her, creating a community of women, including Anne's sister Lucy, who do the world's work of healing the sick, tending to the needy. But Lucy dies in the epidemic, the story's justification for the death she caused early on. After all, there is nothing "so bad in the world as a bad nurse."

Vigil in the Night is no love story. When Anne realizes how much she needs Dr. Prescott at the end of the story she tells him not that she loves him but, "Come, my dear Dr. Prescott, there's work for us to do." This may be a view of women in war. *Vigil in the Night* takes the small female battles and blows them up into life and death proportions. When Anne is told, "We're as close to war as we'll ever be," she responds, speaking for herself and the other nurses, "It's war and sacrifice *all* the time for us . . . our war never ends. You can't sign a peace treaty with disease."

RKO especially recognized the delicacy of the film's wartime context. Stevens's shooting script contains a closing scene that was later cut: a speech by Prime Minister Chamberlain played over the radio loud speakers that closes the story. Chamberlain tells the British people that he has a note from the German government stating that, "unless we heard from them by eleven o'clock that they were prepared at once to withdraw their troops from Poland, a state of war would exist between us. I have to tell you now that no such undertaking has been received, and that consequently this country is at war with Germany. You can imagine what a bitter blow it is to me that all my long struggle to win peace has failed." The studio ordered Chamberlain's speech cut partly because England was at war at the time of the film's release and partly due to its poor reception by preview audiences. Audiences were in no mood to take the subject of war into the theatre with them.

In spite of the film's somber tone, as well as its suggestion of war brewing at the time of its release, RKO marketed *Vigil in the Night* to a female audience and exploited its potential as a sizzling melodrama. Newspaper ads read "It takes a lot to make me love a man" along with "The world's most famous doctor rips the veil from hidden lives of those bitter women who know men too well — yet must somehow find love in the midst of terror, toil and disillusionment. . . . Revealed in this deeply moving story of two sisters and a doctor who defied an age-old code to find the love their Spartan calling would deny them." An advertisement in the *Showman's Trade Review* for February 17, 1940, a week after the film opened, displays an image of Lombard positioned with her head back, hair blowing and wearing a low-cut blouse, with text at the top that reads "I know men better than their wives do. . . . I see them stripped of the cloak of civilization. . . . I see the depths of terror in the secret places of their hearts. It takes a lot to make me love a man in the face of all I know about them."

Yet *Vigil in the Night* failed to bring in audiences, male or female, and eventually lost $327,000 at the box office. The *Los Angeles Times* film critic wrote that "the direction by George Stevens evidences authority, quality and, above all, repression." It could not have helped either that the *Daily News* called Lombard's performance "somnambulistic."[34] But by then Stevens had left RKO, with Berman right behind him.

3

The Women
The Early Forties

He was like the best cup of coffiee you ever had.
—Jean Arthur

At the USA Film Festival in 1971 Stevens was asked to comment on his prewar reputation as a "woman's director," working in the 1930s and 1940s with Katharine Hepburn, Barbara Stanwyck, Ginger Rogers, and Jean Arthur. "I didn't come by that activity by training," he said. "My interests had been in other areas — outdoor films and outside stuff where you could travel somewhere and see some things other than shoot over a chaise lounge in a boudoir at the handsome lady reclining there as she read beautiful dialogue."[1] Stevens was happiest outdoors, shooting the western landscape, meeting people with histories, much like his own, that were rooted in that landscape. But at RKO he hitched his career to sophisticated stories about women and kept riding with it even after he left the studio.

Studio publicity shots of the late 1930s and 1940s show a relaxed, easygoing Stevens, his shy demeanor of *Alice Adams* days replaced by a smiling, pipe-smoking man about town flanked by Tracy and Hepburn, or mugging with Jean Arthur and Joel McCrea on the set of *The More the Merrier,* looking as if a chaise lounge were not an unfamiliar prop. By the mid-1930s he had gained a reputation as a master of the sophisticated light comedy, and his finesse with the screwball comedy (a term he never liked using with own films) was about to bring him even greater popularity with audiences — and Columbia's front office. Hollywood consensus was that he had the magic touch with comedy, so much in fact that some of his colleagues — Hepburn most famously — could hardly understand or forgive his leaving those forms for larger, more serious subjects after the war.

Stevens looked to be in his element shooting in "boudoirs" among the chaises and, most of all, manipulating the "beautiful dialogue" of strong actresses Hepburn, Arthur, and Irene Dunne. After a successful decade at RKO, he was more settled artistically at the beginning of the 1940s, more in control of his craft in what would ironically prove to be the most tumultuous decade in his personal life. In the span of the next three years he would direct four commercially and critically successful "women's" films, then toss his career aside to go to Europe to photograph American soldiers in combat. When he returned from the war he sought out larger fictional landscapes than the interior of a boudoir. He would again go looking for the "outside stuff," as if his very being as an artist depended on it.

The 1940s began for Stevens on a less than positive note; in 1940 RKO released the expensive *Vigil in the Night* to box office disinterest. When contract problems arose there and he left, he went to freelance, but quickly landed at Columbia Pictures where Sam Briskin, then assistant to studio head Harry Cohn, worked out a satisfactory deal with Charlie Feldman for Stevens's services. The deal appeared noncombative on paper, and it proved financially and artistically rewarding. At Columbia he produced and directed *Penny Serenade, The Talk of the Town,* and *The More the Merrier,* all highly successful films that reached massive wartime audiences, especially women, and especially when they played at New York City's Music Hall Theatre, one of Stevens's favorite venues where films had long runs and the auditorium seated up to four thousand.

Even during this time of urbane, witty women's stories, however, Stevens never lost sight of the early Western days shooting Rex the Wonder Horse, but instead held them at bay. He told *Screen and*

Radio Weekly right after *Gunga Din* was released that all he ever looked for was a good story: "They all look alike to me. Motion picture stories, I mean. Not wishing to take any bows for so-called versatility, I'll qualify by saying that it doesn't make any difference to me what sort of story I'm called upon to direct, always providing the story has something to say. I look only for the basic idea. If in the situations the emotions are honest and the reactions natural, it doesn't make any difference whether the story is drama or comedy, slapstick or tragedy, musical or western, cops and robbers, or Indians and cowboys!"[2] It was simple, really. If the story had potential as an audience pleaser he took a second look.

Stevens signed with Columbia Studios on May 14, 1940, to produce and direct two pictures in one year. He always said that Harry Cohn "lured" him to the studio after realizing he was about to lose Frank Capra. So determined was Cohn to get Stevens that he agreed to a contract stipulation he also honored with Leo McCarey: never to talk to Stevens during production, never to come on the set. The way Stevens remembered it, "Harry Cohn wanted to bring me in. I told Cohn I wouldn't be able to make a picture with him at the studio there because I knew about rudeness and other misfortunes. And he said, 'I'll make an arrangement with you. You make a picture here and I'll never speak to you.' 'Well, that doesn't make any sense.' I said, 'you're a man of enormous experience, you know, and a reasonable exchange of conversation will be all right.' We never had a word of conversation. I made three films under that arrangement, and it always worked. I remember one day Harry Cohn walked onto the set, and he said, 'George, do me a favor. Please don't smoke in here; I've got a fire insurance problem.' And I said, 'Of course.' And I snuffed it out."[3]

When Stevens began shooting his first Columbia picture, *Penny Serenade,* Cohn became alarmed at the amount of exposed film he used but never told Stevens, who later remembered that he had total freedom on the film since Columbia was solidly behind it. But Cohn fumed when Stevens moved his offices to MGM for several months in 1941 to direct Hepburn and Tracy in *Woman of the Year.* Later Columbia extended Stevens's contract for another six months, and in July 1941 he signed for a third film. He shot *Penny Serenade, The Talk of the Town,* and *The More the Merrier* and then left for Europe.

"Like No Other Child": *Penny Serenade*

In July 1940 a fan of Irene Dunne wrote to Stevens after reading in a movie magazine that Dunne was to star in his upcoming production, *Penny Serenade*. Would Mr. Stevens consider having Dunne "sing at least three songs?" asked the fan, who had just seen *Roberta* and thought that the actress had a "lovely singing voice." As it turned out, Dunne sang no songs in *Penny Serenade,* but when her character played a Victrola to segue between narrative flashbacks and present time, she had women crying into their handkerchiefs so much that *Serenade* turned into one of the great American film weepies of any decade.

Stevens's first project at Columbia was actually to be *This Thing Called Love,* set to feature Cary Grant and, according to the trades, possibly Ann Sheridan. Serendipitously, Stevens was terminated from the project in June and by August began shooting *Penny Serenade,* a story he brought to Harry Cohn's attention. Its source material, Martha Cheavens's "The Story of a Happy Marriage," a short story scheduled to run in the August 1940 *McCall's* magazine, was a semiautobiographical tale of a contemporary married couple whose lives change profoundly after the death of their adopted child. The dark story was less a change of mood for Stevens, who recently finished *Vigil in the Night,* than for Dunne and costar Cary Grant, who had just wrapped McCarey's *The Awful Truth.* Stevens later remembered, "Cary Grant and Irene Dunne had been enormously successful in light, frothy comedy. . . . I had done something like that previously [and] didn't want to get involved again [in a comedy]. I guess I was in a mood by this time. And so these poor people became involved in my indulging myself with a story I got from Martha Cheavens. . . . But they became wholeheartedly engaged in it . . . it was shocking to the audience to see [Grant and Dunne] not having a fine time [but] relating to two levels of life."[4]

Two months before the story appeared in *McCall's,* Stevens had Cheavens's manuscript in hand and hired his close friend Fred Guiol to work on it. Guiol was put on the payroll on July 17, 1940, receiving $2,000 for the job and followed in August by screenwriter Morrie Ryskind, who received $49,000 and solo screen credit. He and Stevens worked for several months to restructure Ryskind's treatment into a workable script. Cheavens herself received $125,000 to come to Hollywood and oversee the production, if only to make certain that her characters were not seriously altered. It was not long, however, before the studio began to worry about money: notes comparing *Penny Serenade*'s budget (estimated at one time to be $839,229) and that for 1939's *Golden Boy* (estimated at $874,338) were useful ways to manage the anxiety that often set in after Stevens began his habit — learned to perfection during *Gunga Din* — of shooting from every angle he could muster on more exposed film than most other directors even thought of using.

Stevens made some small alterations to the story, changing the setting from Westchester County, New York, to the fictional California town of Rosalia. He also changed the characters' last name from Carey to Adams. But he never altered the story's central conceit. *Penny Serenade* was a woman's story driven by a woman's desire to be a mother and to keep her family intact in the face of ruptures that continually threaten to tear it apart.

Cheavers's story itself was not great prose; it was a sentimental tale aimed at female consumers. But these very features gave it some weight for the time. "The Story of a Happy Marriage" was timely as Americans heard more of war in Europe; it threatened the destruction of families and most familiar social structures. The story was also a holdover from a long-existing, very popular genre of fiction that American women had been reading for over a century — the emotionally charged sentimental novel. For much like the movie-going public in 1930s America, women made up the majority of the nineteenth-century book reading, book-buying American public that liked to read stories about themselves. The sentimental thread that ran through most of Stevens's earlier pictures — the sympathy he garnered for Alice Adams, the romance between Annie Oakley and Toby Taylor, and especially the sentimental view of nurses and womanhood in *Vigil in the Night*, all intricately linked to Depression-age social upheaval — spoke just as urgently for family upheaval descending on the American scene at the start of the 1940s. Steven was always drawn to the sentimental text and in the 1950s his popular films, *Shane* and *Giant*, revisit the subject of familial binding and its disruptions.

As *Penny Serenade* demonstrates, sentimentalism dramatizes the wish for familial and communal bonding just when that bond is threatened. It offers an "emotional and philosophical ethos" celebrating "human connection, both personal and communal," that also acknowledges the "shared devastation of affectional loss." In the sentimental vision, "the greatest threat is the tragedy of separation, severed human ties: the death of a child, lost love, failed or disrupted family connections." The sentimental valorizes connection as it creates "metaphors for a looming existential threat — the potential devastation of deeply experienced human connections."[5] There is no greater tragedy in the sentimental text, of course, than the death of a child, a tragedy whose prototype remains the death of the blond, blue-eyed Little Eva in Harriet Beecher Stowe's *Uncle Tom's Cabin.* The death of a child, the death of *this* child, causes heightened emotionalism and extreme rhetoric of loss, springing the story into action as the characters seek a bond to replace one that has been broken.

The deaths of two children motivate *Penny Serenade.* Though neither has blue eyes and blond curls, the idealized conception is nevertheless part of the film's rhetoric, which itself holds to the Western ideal. It is just the exaggeration the sentimental film needs. After the death of their own unborn child, when they begin to seek adoption, Julie (Dunne) and Roger (Grant) go searching for a child with curly blond hair and blue eyes. At the end of the story, after their adopted daughter Trina dies, they look to adopt again and do, in fact, find that exact child. With the evocation of Little Eva as ideal, along with its exaggerated sense of loss and reclamation, *Penny Serenade* is a pure example of American sentimentalism in the twentieth century. The film hinges on a dialectic between love and loss. The film's characters make repeated attempts to be a family but repeatedly run up against obstacles — not only by the tragic deaths of two of their children, but also by Stevens's camera and editing — as if he were intentionally adhering to "sentimental" textual conceits and mimicking the sentimental story's central trope: forming a pattern of rupture. The film's attempt to move forward and simply to tell a story is strategically interrupted by Stevens's dissolves, a frequent use of the iris lens, and by choppy movements back and forth in time.

The film's opening credits (with names and title written in a feminine hand) are superimposed on an elaborately framed picture of Dunne and Grant — as if the camera were framing the *idea* of an idealized marriage. But as the first scenes tell us, Julie and Roger have grown apart, become bitter, and then separated as the result of the death of their adopted daughter Trina.

In the first sequence, Julie walks into the frame and up the stairs of her apartment, but Roger is absent. The couple's friend, Applejack (Edgar Buchanan), is in the apartment playing a record, "You Were Meant For Me," a song whose lyrics tie Julie and Roger together, forming a bond: "You were meant for me; I was meant for you." Julie's first response is to ask Applejack not to play it. Her refusal of the now-too-painful song and the memories it brings is the film's first disruption of the marriage bond.

Instead, Julie asks Applejack to go to the station to buy her a bus ticket. After he leaves, though, she opens the phonograph album he had been looking at and plays the same song, intending to reminisce about her first meeting with her husband. But the reverie, the recapture of her emotional bond to Roger, is again interrupted when a scratch in the record causes the words to repeat. Stevens intends the disruption as a device, but also uses it as a way to segue way to a flashback of Julie and Roger's first meeting. All flashbacks belong to Julie, as does the story, and she plays the record and recalls the scratch in the record. In the flashback, Roger happens to be walking by the record shop where Julie works and hears the very same scratch played over a loud speaker onto the street. Jarred, he turns and looks inside the shop and sees Julie sitting there. He walks in and their romance begins. Stevens also uses the device of the iris fade in and out to interrupt the narrative and to move the story between past and present tense. The flashbacks revolve around Julie standing at the phonograph in the couple's apartment and recalling memories. She either puts on a record or takes one off to signal a recollection, disturbing the spectator's sense of connectedness, although that is the effect Stevens wants.

In an early flashback, Julie and Roger play out conventional male-female roles of the time, intended of course to ensure strong audience identification as well as pleasure. Though he loves Julie, Roger resists the idea of marriage because he is a man; though Julie naturally wants to get married, she hides her feelings for Roger, not wanting to look as if she cares about him. She is, of course, concerned that he will think she is trying to trap him. In a charming scene at the beach, which Stevens plays with heavy emphasis on visual, symbolic cues, the couple is eating fortune cookies and breaks them open to find their fortunes. But in the midst of this scene a little boy walks into the frame, passes their table, and drops sand on Roger's lap, interrupting the fun he and Julie share. Might it be a forewarning of events to come?

Then, after getting back to the issue at hand, marriage (the bond), they read their fortunes. Julie's reads, "You will get your wish — a baby." Roger opens two cookies: the more disturbing one reads "A wedding soon," and then the more conventional, more comfortable "You'll remain a bachelor." Yet not long after the couple marries, their happiness is jeopardized when, after they move to Japan where Roger works as a reporter, she discovers that he does not have a head for money and cares little about financial security. The future suddenly seems a big risk. Still, a larger disruption is on its way: Julie finds she is pregnant but loses the baby in a massive earthquake (Stevens considered having her break the news of her pregnancy to Roger just as the earthquake hits, but changed his mind — his first impulse was to go for the very dramatic).

After Julie loses the baby she is told that she cannot have any more children. Using a sentimental trope, this fact is the central rupture that pushes the story forward: all characters, all events seek to find union with the knowledge of this tragedy. The loss motivates the couple to adopt a child; it motivates Roger's emotional appeal (a scene Stevens added to the story) before the judge when he and Julie stand to lose their child, Trina, because the newspaper he runs shuts down and they have no income. Later, after the couple also loses Trina — the very crucial "death of a child" — it appears that the marriage might not survive the tragedy. This kind of a death is too great a blow to the family bond, to the human connection.

Penny Serenade traverses a path of continual loss, even though loss is itself interrupted by occasional gags and humorous sequences, such as when Roger and Julie bring baby Trina home and try to get her settled in bed and get some sleep themselves. In another long sequence Julie hopelessly tries to give Trina a bath but fails miserably until Applejack takes over and shows her the ropes (a sequence prefiguring *Woman of the Year*'s final sequence when an increasingly humiliated Hepburn tries hopelessly to make breakfast for Tracy but makes only a mess of the task he can accomplish much more easily than she). In 1940s America, such reversal of male-female roles created a howl in the audience and therefore achieved the emotional bond with the onscreen characters that Stevens intended.

In Cheavens's story, Trina's death is told to the adoption agent, Miss Oliver (Beulah Bondi) simply as part of the narrative. But Stevens changes the moment into the cinematic: Julie sends a letter to Miss Oliver, who reads as the camera creates a strong visual bond between the words on the page, Bondi's saddened face while reading the letter, and simultaneous close-ups of Roger and Julie sitting in their living room with nothing to say to each other. What marriage will survive such loss, the audience asks. The rationale, for the sentimental text, of course, is that the death of the child, especially one "like no other child," in Miss Oliver's words (and delivered with each baby she shows the couple), is the metaphor for a looming existential threat in Europe and America in 1940 poised to disrupt the affectionate bond and to break apart the family and the society it holds together.

The death of a child is no ordinary death. It is "a rupture like no other rupture" and communicates to Stevens's wide audience, or "as wide an audience as possible," that the ties that bind stories and their audiences are, for Stevens, the very ties formed by the communal experience of movie watching. Roger and Julie suffer the death of their adopted child yet are given a chance to reconfigure the family — to adopt another child, another "child like no other child." For Stevens's audiences, the sentimental reaffirms the possibility of bonds, of family — and therefore culture — at the start of a war where the threat of arbitrary rupture is everywhere. Going to the movies serves to offset that threat.

Bonding with the public was almost immediate. *Penny Serenade* previewed in Santa Barbara, California, on March 14, 1941, getting two more California previews in two months, one in Inglewood and one in Huntington Park. On March 1, Columbia publicity director Lou Smith sent a memo to David Lipton telling him that he "saw *Penny Serenade* last night in rough cut, about two hours and forty five minutes." Eventually it was trimmed by forty minutes. "Make no mistake about it," he said, "this is a truly great picture. It's a tear jerker yet has some fine light moments. Superb performances by everyone." He also said, "I cried three times during the showing and everyone around me was mopping up too. . . . Instead of having the actors jump off cliffs, this one will have the audience jumping off. No matter what other product comes along, this is Columbia's big picture for the year; we might as well recognize it. *Red Book, Life, Look, Woman's Home Companion, Ladies' Home Journal* all have press screenings."[6]

After visiting the set during shooting, columnist Harrison Carroll wrote in his syndicated column, "Behind the Scenes in Hollywood," for December 18, 1940, "With the world in the glooms, Hollywood producers are rapidly being overcome by nostalgia. Almost every studio is making a picture about 'the good old days.' . . . Over at Columbia 'Penny Serenade' . . . turns back the clock [as] I watch director George Stevens shoot a scene of a New Year's Eve party in 1928." But studio exploitation focused strictly on romance: an ad in the *Hollywood Reporter* read "Remember the tune everyone was singing . . . the night we fell in love?" Most reviewers were moved: *Variety*'s critic wrote, "customers are going to have . . . [a] fine time sniffling and weeping. . . . The characters are young home folks and could be duplicated in an instant from any local phone book." The *Hollywood Reporter*'s critic added, "No audience can remain unmoved by the human, down-to-earth story, and no woman who sees it will remain dry-eyed."[7]

A Body Like Leni Riefenstahl's: *Woman of the Year*

Stevens did a complete turnaround with his next film, *Woman of the Year*. By the summer of 1941 industry talk confirmed that Stevens was "one of the hottest directors in town," a view that was widely held in the industry and that stemmed in good part from his comic touch and his sympathetic portrait of women. *Woman of the Year* altered that portrait. When MGM released it in 1942, women as well as men in the audience cheered for a helpless Kate Hepburn making a fool of herself in the kitchen in the film's final sequence. But as decades changed, *Woman* earned increasing disdain from female viewers who objected to its treatment of Hepburn's character.

Stevens directed so many films about women before he left for Europe, it is surprising that feminist discourse has not caught up with him or contemplated his body of work in any serious way. Were this to happen, there would no doubt be some serious but also playful debate about how women fare in his films, especially those he directed during this period: *Woman of the Year*, *Talk of the Town*, and *The More the Merrier*. While he still gave these women a humorous edge, an increasing awareness of the war in Europe and then America's entrance into it complicated social conditions and individual lives and found its way into Stevens's movies. *The Talk of the Town* contains debate about the letter of the law; *The More the Merrier* has Jean Arthur taking patriotic action, albeit humorous, to ease the housing shortage in wartime Washington, D.C. Even in these last three films, with *Vigil in the Night,* Stevens's women are more complex, more connected to the world conditions than an Alice Adams or an Annie Oakley, even a Penny or a Francy. As society became more problematic so would fictional characters, including women, follow. But *Woman of the Year* presents Stevens's most complex woman to date, and if Stevens and feminism were ever to meet up, the discourse might now have a good time with this film.

One of the most pervasive and satisfying ideas to emerge from feminist discourse in the last thirty years is the notion, suggested by Annette Kolodny and Nina Baym for American literary studies and fine-tuned for cinema studies by Laura Mulvey and Teresa de Lauretis, that in Western literature and art there is essentially a prototypical narrative, perhaps even only one that dominates — that is the narrative of the working out of the male, "Oedipal" journey. As the theory goes, and to distill only its basics, narrative itself is driven by the male's desire to complete a mission of self-discovery. In a journey patterned after Oedipus, the male's goal is to complete a process — to get someplace — that ends in the discovery of his self-identity. According to Roland Barthes, "The pleasure of the text is . . . an Oedipal pleasure (to denude, to know, to learn the origin and the end) . . . every narrative [is] the unveiling of the truth." As this male completes the journey, his narrative — the story within which he travels — finds satisfactory closure. But that which drives him and makes the trip necessary is the capture of self-knowledge, self-definition. The hero is the mover of the narrative, its center and its term of reference, its "consciousness and desire."[8]

So then, the story — *a* story — belongs to the male, not the female. Along his way to self-discovery, however (and especially in the movies), he meets the female whose function in the narrative is to do one of two things, maybe both: to provide her body as the landscape upon which to complete his journey *or,* as is specifically relevant to the specular nature of the cinema, to offer her body (unknowingly) as obstacle — that is, as a spectacle at which the camera and spectator like to gaze and that complicates his journey and the male's narrative. Her body threatens the completion of his journey. He must tame, slay, her power, her body, in order to complete himself and his journey. According to de Lauretis, after Laura Mulvey, "The legends of Perseus and Oedipus . . . make it clear that their threat to man's vision, and their power consists in their enigma and 'to-be-looked-at-ness' (Mulvey's word), their luring of man's gaze into the 'dark continent,' as Freud put it, the enigma of femininity. They are obstacles man encounters on the path of life, on his way to manhood, wisdom, and power; they must be tamed, even defeated, so that he can go forward to fulfill his destiny—and his story." Subject identification, therefore, is predominantly male in classic Hollywood cinema, and in turn the female spectator is "other." There are two positions, "male-human-hero" on one side and "female-obstacle-boundary-space" on the other."[9] The ideal viewer is, of course, male. The female, as the object of the male gaze, does not move the plot but is instead the representation of "difference" to be slayed or tamed by the male subject in his need to define himself and complete his journey and narrative. The great example of this second view is Hitchcock's *Vertigo* wherein Scotty (James Stewart) must remake the (sexualized) body of Judy (Kim Novak), his threat, in order to return to the past and unlock the puzzle of the death of the "unreal" Madeleine (Novak).

According to this paradigm, the female body exists in the narrative essentially to service the psyche of the male who is on his way somewhere important. The female body (selfhood) is second-rate goods. For this reason film studies have always read with celebration those 1930s American films where a female embarks on her own journey of self-identification. She is Claudette Colbert as the runaway bride who moves a narrative of her own in *It Happened One Night*. Whether or not she actually achieves self-identification on her own and without Clark Gable's push is debatable. But at least she moves across the country, even if only by the terms of her own good looks.

Within this scheme, feminist film criticism has its favorite classic directors with whom to argue for the way they position women in their films in classic Hollywood cinema as bodies to be objectified, codified, and generally either abused or gazed at (which amounts to the same thing). As the discourse has it, Hitchcock abuses; Hawks and Sturges do not (Hawks like his females *male*); Ford idealizes women (unless she is Maureen O'Hara, who gets punched in *The Quiet Man*); Sirk identifies with them; Curtiz gives them a darkness and Cukor caresses them; Wyler pushes them around but for their own good.

Until now, however, feminist discourse has not bothered with George Stevens, which is unfortunate since in his films of the 1930s and 1940s especially he so often fully identifies with the female and perceives her to be a signal of the way society operates: she indicates how well things are or are not going. Such identification would potentially prove solid ground for critical discourse to take up with Stevens, so why should it not?

Stevens first demonstrated his identification with his female characters when he placed *Alice Adams* on a crowded dance floor in 1935 and examined (and understood completely) her humiliation and wish that life would hand her some notice, some acceptance by others. After *Alice Adams* he reinforced his identification with his women, especially Annie Oakley's conflict between loving Toby and wanting to compete with him; again in Anne Lee's wish to be a good nurse and not a "bad one" in *Vigil in the Night*. Few male directors have spent as much time as Stevens constructing the female form and character on film.

But *Woman of the Year* shows a lapse in Stevens's generally fond regard for the female character. Instead, his camera takes a persistent pot shot at her, insisting that she ultimately acquiesce to the demands of her partner, Sam. If she refuses, she is humiliated, scorned and made to suffer the consequences. Stevens's camera (and no doubt the audience for which the camera is positioned) takes an almost perverse pleasure in debasing the body and the spirit of Tess Harding (Katharine Hepburn) by first calling attention to and gazing at her (yes, sexualized) body only then to punish her for it.

But there is a reason, and it might have been larger than even Stevens understood. The extent to which his camera debases Tess Harding might just be a way of acting out a larger dance between pro-American sentiment and anti-Nazi sentiment as it played out in this country just at the start of U.S. involvement in the war. Since the late 1930s, America had kept a worried eye on Europe and on its increasing occupation by the German army. By December 1941 we were also at war and Stevens, like many other directors, began to prepare himself to go overseas. He was about to give up a lucrative job, and as his friend John Huston later said, Stevens knew exactly how much he would put his career in jeopardy by doing so. But Stevens was exhilarated by the thought of making a difference, of defeating the body of Nazism. He was caught up in these feelings, and while directing *Woman of the Year* his camera became an extension of himself.

Stevens always credited his decision to go overseas to one important night when, sitting alone in a Hollywood screening room, he saw what he afterward called the film that changed his life: Leni Riefenstahl's *Triumph of the Will*, the 1935 Nazi propaganda documentary covering Hitler's 1934 Nuremberg rallies and widely regarded as one of the best pieces of propaganda ever produced. Stevens felt so enthralled with Riefenstahl's film — her presentation of the "perfection" of the German race in the German "body" — that he saw that body as a threat and wanted to join the fight to eliminate it, to participate in its defeat (George Stevens Jr. remembered that his father enlisted right after he saw *Triumph of the Will*).

At this very same time, however, from August to October 1941, while America thought about the war in Europe, Stevens was in production on *Woman of the Year*, a story that focused on the sexual and very competitive relationship between two writers, Tess Harding and Sam Craig (Spencer Tracy). The couple spar, then marry and fight it out to see who wears the metaphorical (and for Hepburn, literal) pants in the family. Along the way the film takes delight, first in establishing Tess's sexuality and "looked-at-ness," then in turning around to slay her for bringing sexual pleasure to Sam, to Stevens's camera and, by extension, to the audience. The story has its very overt political agenda: to level all that Tess, a political commentator with strong ties to Europe, and her body signify, that is the threat to America by anything European, anything related to foreign governments or citizens, anything having to do with "otherness" at a time when war seemed imminent and traditional American values needed to be shored up, protected and secured.

As the back story has been handed down, Hepburn had passed over Cukor to direct her in *Woman of the Year* because she wanted a more forceful, "masculine" director. Hepburn said Stevens agreed to direct the film because he believed he owed her a favor for her choosing him to direct *Alice Adams*. Stevens later remembered how he became involved with *Woman:*

> [Katharine Hepburn] had the script written by Garson Kanin and company . . . he did [work on it] but it was under the table. Mike Kanin and Ring Lardner got credit for the original story and Gar was quite influential in the original story, as you could see if you read the original story, and never knew either one of the other guys. So he had nothing to do

and was very helpful on it. [He] got the team together, the family to-gether and they wrote the script.

Kate brought the script out to me and asked me to read it and it was forty pages short of a conclusion. It was about one hundred pages. It was never concluded until we got down there shooting it. So I read it and it was really good. It's very rare to read a script that you can shoot. So I called Kate and I said, "This is great." And she said, "I'm coming over." I said . . . "What do you want to do with it?" I said, "Bring it to Colum-bia. Let's do it." She said, "You missed the point." I said, "What is the point?" She said, "I've already promised Louis B. Mayer because he's been very helpful to me. So I've come to persuade you to go to Metro." I said, "I can't do that. I'm making pictures with these people down the street." She said, "Oh these people are difficult to solve." So I went down to Metro to do the picture while Harry Cohn burned.[10]

This might have been the time, as Stevens remembered it, when "Louis B. Mayer came to me . . . because I wouldn't go there [to MGM]; he came with his car three different times to take me to dinner, to tell me to come to his studio. And I told him, 'L. B., some day you'll make this proposition to me, offer me that kind of an arrangement, and when I take it, I'll be too old and too tired to do the work that I'm doing.'"[11]

But as Stevens went to work reorganizing the script, he was also readying himself to join in the fight to save democracy, readying himself, as was the rest of the country, to express his patriotism. Unconsciously he was preparing to go overseas. Within the context of a feminist dis-course, he was preparing an agenda for himself and the country to com-plete a journey of self-discovery — a discovery of a very masculinized battle (as marketing tests later revealed, women in the audience for *Woman of the Year* enjoyed Tess's defeat no less than men). Stevens would locate within himself and within his America as well the hawkish mood and fervor needed to support the war and defeat the enemy. He had just seen the German bodies of Leni Riefenstahl. These "bodies" had to be devalued and challenged by shoring up a set of American val-ues to take to Europe.

As Stevens geared up and readied this "American" identity he simul-taneously directed *Woman of the Year*, a film that collapses the figures of Leni Riefenstahl and Tess Harding. The film's visual clues, no less than its antifeminine ideology, confuses one for the other. Tess Harding is a threat to Sam and to his American values. Her first appearance in the film is as a sexy woman straightening the seam of her hose. The camera sets Tess up for defeat by confirming her "otherness" as a sexualized body-as-obstacle and then punishing her for it until she is no longer a threat. Tess's power is sexual and political, each dangerous to the less (but smugly) sophisticated Sam whose Oedipal job it is to locate and to demonstrate his own American muscle — a simple, powerful American self. Riefenstahl's "body" figures as the "European" Tess in *Woman of the Year*. When Stevens contemplated the "perfection" of those German bodies in *Triumph of the Will*, he could not help but consider their "otherness," their almost sexual perfection, their *threat*. As he later said, he felt a strong attraction to Riefenstahl's film no matter how much it simultaneously repelled him. The "foreign" bodies belonging to Leni Riefenstahl's camera and to the anti-Americanness implicit in the character of Tess Harding had to be defeated in this American film.

Years later Stevens met Riefenstahl and he told her that when he saw *Triumph of the Will* in 1941, he thought that the German army was the "strongest and most invincible army in the world" and that was why he wanted to go fight against them. He said he did not realize until later that seeing them in her film made them appear better than they really were. "I think all film is propaganda," he told Riefenstahl, and hers was the best example he had experienced.[12] It is doubtful, though, that Stevens even remotely considered *Woman of the Year* his own piece of propaganda for the war effort.

Woman of the Year is organized around Sam Craig's success in taming Tess Harding, the object of his affection but also the greatest obstacle to the journey Sam must complete to define his (and America's) unbeatable strength of self.

The film opens with credits superimposed over a figure of a woman resembling the Statue of Liberty. But she also has wings, with which she could easily fly to any of the cities or countries depicted in drawings behind her: New York, Moscow, Beijing, Paris all give the female an international, global context — an otherness, as it were. There is no mistaking that the story is centered on a strong, international woman. After the credits roll, the camera opens onto a shot of a busy New York street and rests on a speeding newspaper delivery truck displaying advertisements for two columnists who write for "The New York Chronicle":

political commentator Tess Harding and sports writer Sam Craig. The camera finds Tess's ad first, which reads, "What Do You Think?" and beneath that line, "Tess Harding Tells You Daily in The New York Chronicle." From this, the camera cuts to several newspaper headlines that establish Tess's prominence around the globe: "Tess Harding Feared Lost in Convoy," evoking powerful celebrated women such as Amelia Earhart or even internationally known nineteenth-century transcendentalist writer Margaret Fuller who drowned crossing the Atlantic from Europe back to the United States. The camera halts on another headline, "Tess Harding in Talk with Churchill," shoring up Tess's status as a powerful political voice, and finally it settles in on two advertisements positioned side-by-side, one for Tess and one for her rival, Sam Craig. Here the camera closes in on Tess's ad first: "'Hitler Will Lose' says Tess Harding," then pans left to an ad for Sam: "'The Yankees Won't Lose' says Sam Craig in The New York Chronicle." They share the side of a truck but the scale is tipped in Tess's favor; she carries more weight and is better known — an American who travels in Europe. Sam is simply an expert in baseball. Tess is European and Sam's obstacle; she is America's obstacle. The agenda: to cut Tess down to size. This is war.

The camera begins chipping away at Tess in the film's opening sequence. Sam walks into a bar and begins eating and drinking with his cronies and then establishes his American take on the world. He and the other men listen as Tess, whom Sam has yet to meet, is interviewed as a panelist on a radio show — a voice with no body but powerful nonetheless. She expounds on the war in Europe. "Ever met her?" one of the men asks Sam, who quips, "I understand she don't talk to anybody that hasn't signed a non-aggression pact." She is asked about baseball and replies in a condescending tone, "I don't really know anything about American sports," then suggests that baseball ought to be abolished while the war is on in Europe so that Americans can spend their energies paying attention to the right things. After this Sam cries in a loud voice, "We're concerned with the threat to what we like to call our American way of life: baseball and the things it represents as part of that life. What's the sense of abolishing the thing you're trying to protect?" Tess, it appears, is a threat to baseball, to Sam, and to America. He fires back at her in his column the next day, calling her the "Calamity Jane of the international set."

Tess is un-American; worse, she is a threat to Sam's ego. After his column appears the next day, Tess retaliates with her own. It is time for a truce, and Tess and Sam are called into the editor's office. When Sam walks in, Tess is already there. A medium shot on Sam's face lets the spectator see what he sees, even though the camera must swing down before coming back up in order to catch it: a full shot of Tess sitting on the edge of a desk, her left leg stretched out as she straightens the seam of her stocking and, from what we and Sam can see, she is enjoying it. The camera caresses her leg. She takes pleasure in her own body; moreover she finds pleasure in seeing that Sam's face lights up as well. Now Tess is a triple threat. She is famous, respected, and worse, she has a body that both the camera and Sam enjoy. Sam the American has his work cut out for him.

After promising to "make up," Sam and Tess walk out the editor's door, she ahead of him and walking faster as she realizes he is gaining on her. She ducks into the stairwell to hide just as he turns the corner to follow her and surprises him. She reminds him that the sports department is downstairs and that he seems to be on his way upstairs—obviously where her office is located. They stand on a stairwell taking turns at being either one step above or below the other. Their burgeoning competition resolves itself temporarily when Sam takes her to a ball game, and the script and the camera take turns at humiliating her. She knows nothing about baseball and Sam smirks condescendingly each time he has to explain a play to her. Worse, she wears a large hat that blocks the view of the unfortunate male spectator behind her: Tess, her body and her hat, are obstacles even to the completion of this brief journey to watch a baseball game. The camera loves her hat but the spectators at the game do not. The script will give this smart aleck her due.

Tess invites Sam to a party that night at her apartment. Once there he realizes that he is the only American and the only guest who speaks English. Of course Tess is fluent in each language spoken. The next day, when he visits her in her office, Stevens reaffirms Tess's function in the narrative as object and spectacle. Sam opens the door to talk to her but Tess does not see him. She is sitting behind her desk, her back to him, speaking on the phone in a foreign tongue with her legs propped high up on the bookcase behind her. Sam does not particularly seek out her legs; the camera does that for him.

Sam calls Tess "the girl without a country" and says that the day he took her to the ballpark was the day she "came home" and that it was fun "being with the people." Later, Sam is alone with her in her apartment, one furnished with ornately curved wood furniture, evoking the roundness of the female form. Stevens (who later recalled that he had to fight to get the lighting he wanted) gives the room stark contrasts. As Tess walks around she casts shadows of herself onto the walls. Stevens positions her in front of a huge self-portrait that reaches toward the ceiling. She asks Sam if he would like "a glass of milk." But there are two of her in the room, the real body and the painting that is the representation of her body. She asks Sam if he likes the painting. He responds that it is "beautiful" but "a little too high to reach," to which she says, "I'm not." In another part of the room a bust of her head, cast in plaster, stands forthright next to the wall. Tess and all her replications are everywhere.

Once her body is established as dominant for the camera, the film gives Tess one magical moment before it sets out to humiliate her either by taking her power from her or by punishing her for owning it. After Sam and Tess realize their attraction for each other, he takes her to his favorite bar. Sam stands at the bar in a reverse mirror shot; when he moves away, Tess, who stood behind him, is now revealed, as if she appeared by magic and is herself magical, certainly loved by the camera and by Sam. But then it is on to business. Sam's American dominance must be established before Stevens and American soldiers go to war. But all of this is for Tess's own good. She needs to come home to America. As its representative, Sam evokes Crevecoeur's American farmer, inherently, natively good because he grows from good "American" soil. It becomes especially urgent to tame Tess as her European ties become stronger when it is learned that her friend Dr. Lubbek, a Yugoslavian statesman, escapes from a concentration camp and is headed for Tess's apartment.

But as with a neurosis that resists its cure, Tess's power increases the more Sam tries to push it down. She arranges their marriage date before he knows about it. On their wedding night back in her apartment, which Sam resists moving into, Tess lies on her bed waiting for Sam when all of Europe enters instead, blowing up in the camera's face. Instead of Sam, Dr. Lubbek unexpectedly arrives at Tess's apartment and enters the bedroom. Who is in her bed, the "foreign" Europe or America? The slapstick scene is the film's crisis, a contest between America and this "foreignness" of Europe. Dr. Lubbek's friends invade the apartment after his arrival, and in defense Sam invites his friends as well.

From here on, Tess is seen wearing pants instead of the short skirts she wore in the film's first scenes, a signal that some change has taken place — for better or worse. She is less the spectacle in pants, and for good reason. The camera now implements its most strategic hit: an ill-fated attempt to transform Tess into a wife and mother. By this time the spectator is convinced that she will fail at both. The narrative's intention to overcome its obstacle first must neutralize the female body's "looked-at-ness." She cannot be sexualized if she is a wife or mother. Therefore the course becomes clear: she will need to fail at all three by the time the script and the camera are through with her.

Tess is not good as a wife; she is too independent and unable, it seems, to comprehend what it means to be part of a couple. She fails at one of her two greatest challenges — the one that defines "American" values as Sam conceives of them. But Sam still needs to complete this narrative to fulfill Stevens's drive toward identification with his country. Until Tess can be brought over to Sam's side — and that might be Uncle Sam — he cannot secure his American values, which of course include a wife, nor can Stevens imaginatively topple the "body" of the German army.

It is beginning to look less likely that Tess will settle down and acquiesce to Sam's agenda for her, so the camera, in collusion with the script, prepares her for motherhood instead. Since the spectator knows she will fail at this as well, it appears as one more humiliating punishment. She tells Sam that she wants to adopt a child, and in characteristic manner she has gone ahead and brought home a Greek refugee boy on a trial basis and without consulting Sam. It is a kind of goodwill public relations gesture on her part, but in the end it is short-lived. Tess also fails at motherhood. She discovers that she has been voted "America's Outstanding Woman of the Year," an ironic title given the kind of loathing the script has for her. She decides it is all right to leave the young child alone while she and Sam attend a banquet in her honor at which she will receive her award. Sam tells her she has no heart and after she goes off to the banquet alone, Sam returns the child to the orphanage. Of course Tess eventually sees that she has erred. She attends her widowed father's wedding — alone — and realizes she loves Sam. But

Sam leaves her and refuses to return. He will not rest until he has neutralized his and the story's obstacle: the woman who has a body (and *is* a body) but "has no heart."

The final humiliation comes. Sam returns to his own apartment that he had left to move in with Tess. She later follows him there to tell him that she wants to stay married; she wants to be a wife and she is willing to give up her career (she has already forfeited her sexualized body). In the film's final and longest sequence, Tess is in Sam's kitchen — now in *his* territory, not her own — where in a series of comical disasters that build slowly (Stevens said the bit came from Laurel and Hardy comedic deliberation) she attempts to cook him breakfast as proof of her serious intentions and to offer herself as a sacrificial lamb.

Sam is asleep in bed and Tess decides to surprise him when he awakens. She finds a cookbook inscribed to her by Sam's mother indicating some of Sam's favorite recipes. Tess now enters the sanctity of American motherhood and she is visually out of place. Her dress straps fall down repeatedly. She cannot make coffee, waffles, or even toast. She cannot coordinate the meal even though she can enter into international peace talks. The scene depends on sight gags that help the scene peak slowly. Tess makes a spectacle of herself in a way that her body never could. She is a spectacle of disaster — to the camera and to Sam, who eventually wanders into the kitchen, sits down and watches every mistake Tess makes. His deadpan face resembles Stevens's own, Hepburn later recalled.

Oedipus has his story of self-identification handed to him on a platter from Sam Craig's kitchen and his hard won makeover of Tess Harding. She is on her knees while he sits above her in a chair. She begs him to take her back and he at last agrees. Sam asks her, scoldingly, why she must always go to extremes. At his suggestion she should change her name to Tess Harding-Craig, a woman leveled and ready to be an American wife. This is a happy compromise, it would seem. Yet it is Sam's idea, not Tess's own solution to her dilemma.

Nor was the film's ending the solution that screenwriters Ring Lardner Jr. and Michael Kanin had in mind. According to production files, the original ending was not cruel to Tess but instead more of a compromise between she and Sam. But preview audiences showed disdain for the original ending, which had Sam moving out of Tess's apartment and going on a drunken binge. Wanting to help him, Tess covers for him and intends to write a feature that night on a world championship fight that Sam was scheduled to cover for the newspaper. She interviews the fighter, meets his wife, and when she realizes how happily married they are, she repents and wants to return to Sam, who at last arrives at the fight. Tess tells him she is willing to quit her job to be a dutiful housewife and all is well.

Yet Stevens, producer Joseph Mankiewicz, and studio head Louis B. Mayer agreed, "it was not enough that Tess Harding grow in the relationship." Mankiewicz later said, "The average housewife was going to look up at this beautiful, accomplished goddess up there on the screen . . . and, well, hate her guts." Accordingly, Mayer agreed that a new ending should be written. Mankiewicz added, "Now women could turn to their . . . husbands and say, 'she may know the president, but she can't even make a cup of coffee, you silly bastard!'" Hepburn hated the ending but audiences loved it and she acquiesced.

In later interviews, Stevens claimed he wrote the sequence along with Fred Guiol. "I had to put something on at the finish," he said. Stevens hated the ending all along and was proven right when at an early screening the audience reportedly walked out shaking their heads; later he called it buffoonery but recalled that he had nevertheless wanted to do it all along. He remembered also that during the production he threatened twice to walk off the set if the studio used the original ending. But Hepburn and Tracy convinced him to stay.

Yvonne Stevens thought that Stevens probably was the funniest man on the set. "If there were only two or three people in the room, George was the funniest man that you ever saw in your life, and when he'd do an imitation of Jimmy Cagney, people would be rolling on the floor. But I remember [on the *Woman* set] there was a bit that Spencer Tracy had to do . . . there was a lot of slapstick in *Woman* . . . so George told Tracy about it, and Tracy didn't quite get it. So George said, 'This is the way you do it.' The lights were on, and George got up and did this scene. Well! Everybody just died at the way he did it. So Tracy called him over, and he said, 'Don't ever do that again,' because Tracy had to get up and do the same scene . . . and it wasn't as funny."[13]

Reviews in the Hollywood trades praised the film and confirmed Stevens's mood. *Variety*'s critic called the final sequence "for the women.

It shows the wife's . . . inept efforts to cook a simple meal when she returns, contrite, to try to be a good wife and house woman. In these scenes every woman in the audience will feel superior to the actress on the screen." The critic for the *Motion Picture Herald* added, "[the] conversion of the fame-stricken wife to the home-loving husband's ideals of domestic solidarity is arrived at earnestly and in convincing manner."[14]

MGM's press book for *Woman of the Year* infantilizes Hepburn herself in its promotions. The view of Tess/Hepburn asserts her "personhood" one moment and presents her as a model for women who want to be dutiful American wives the next. One of the books contains a page with the headline: "Hepburn — Woman of a Thousand Faces: She Expresses Herself Without Words in 'Woman of the Year.'" Below these lines sit ten photographs of Hepburn, each one labeled according to expression: "Intrigued," "Interested," "Assertive," "Questioning," "Angered," "Frightened," "Downcast," "Flirtatious," "Worried," and "In Love!" Another advertisement reads, "Tracy Kayos Hepburn in Five Rounds." Still another features a page including placement squares within which advertisers could place their products. Above them, a paragraph addresses merchants specifically: "Names . . . big names . . . sell your merchants on the value of cooperative motion picture advertising. There are none bigger or more influential than Tracy and Hepburn. None that are so popular with masses. You also have a title, which, in a merchandising sense, can be applied very flatteringly to housewives — as indicative of their shrewdness in buying and marketing. Layout below is merely suggested." A paragraph below this targets the movie patrons, suggesting that they be thrifty with their money and buy wisely. The advertisement reflects the economy of a country just entering the war: "Be the WOMAN OF THE YEAR . . . In Your Own Home! The First Step Is To Shop And Save! Now is the time to buy wisely and economically. Save on every purchase you make. Anticipate your needs for the future. Like Katharine Hepburn you can be the 'Woman of the Year' in your own home. A little foresight will make your husband just as proud of your domestic ability as Spencer Tracy was of Katharine Hepburn's success as a career woman. Buy now and make your husband's income go farther!"

Another press book includes a suggestion that newspapers run an advertising campaign to "Exploit Marriage vs. a Career Among Local Working People." The campaign's message is bolstered by another advertisement asking the question, "Would You Give a Wife Like Hepburn the 'Brush-Off'?" Below that a paragraph suggests an exploitation theme targeting movie patrons: "Tracy and Hepburn continue their respective jobs after marriage. Eventually, she becomes a gadabout, more interested in being a successful career woman than in establishing a home. It's only when Tracy threatens to walk out that she becomes a good wife. Ask men in a newspaper, theatre or radio contest what they would do with a wife like Hepburn."[15]

The press book reflects not only the economic concerns of a country at war at the time MGM released *Woman of the Year* in February 1942 ("Now is the time to buy wisely and economically"), but also heralded a reconfirmation of traditional American values to hold together a country literally split apart as men went off to war. Studio publicity departments aimed these press books specifically at women, given that they were more sophisticated in the advertising apparatus of the film industry. As Mary Ann Doane has said, "By the 1940s, the system of tie-ins and press books was fully in place and the machinery had attained a fairly sophisticated form. . . . Audience analysis confirms that women were fully immersed in the discursive apparatus surrounding the cinema — fan magazines as well as news columns and articles on or by stars in women's magazine."[16] The press book was a studio's most creative means of involving advertisers and exhibitors in efforts to confuse the distinction between the spectator's reality and the film's fiction. This is fitting given the collapse in *Woman of the Year* of the world at war and the fictional war between the sexes. Fittingly, it was around this time that FBI files kept on Stevens (albeit lighter than files kept on fellow directors such as Frank Capra and John Huston) noted that he represented the Directors Guild (he was president) at a September 1942 meeting and had connections to the "Communist fronted" Hollywood Theatre Alliance.

Disorder in the House: *The Talk of the Town*

While *Woman of the Year* diverges from Stevens's otherwise sympathetic view of the American woman in the 1940s, *The Talk of the Town* and *The More the Merrier* return her safely back into his sympathies, and back into the light, humorous domestic setting. It may have been Hepburn's angular body and wise-talking attitude (competing with the male ego) that inspired the good-humored yet nevertheless punishing mood of Stevens's camera and pen in *Woman of the Year*. It may have been the aftermath of their second brief affair just before filming began, or simply a reaction to the aggression contained (or that appeared to be contained) within Hepburn's rather feminist views. Stevens, of course, never got another script like *Woman of the Year* to work and to rework, adding his own touch of retaliation and vengeance. By the time the film premiered, America was at war and his path was unclear.

With *The Talk of the Town* and *The More the Merrier* the very soft and less threatening Jean Arthur receives pampered treatment in two vehicles produced during a time in which Stevens knew he would soon be off to war. As he later said, he was not certain what he would find in Europe; he felt freed up to have a good time on the set because he had no idea of when he might return. In good measure both *The Talk of the Town* and *The More the Merrier* were morale boosters during wartime, and both draw the viewer's attention to an interior domestic setting into which contemporary, divisive, and often chaotic social issues are thrown. The result is partly a throwback to Stevens's early days with Laurel and Hardy, comedy with an often-frenzied mise-en-scène and a camera that slides gracefully from one humorous situation to another.

The Talk of the Town concerns a young woman, Nora Shelley (Arthur), who plans to rent her New England cottage to a renowned law professor, Michael Lightcap (Ronald Colman, whom Cohn also was not allowed to bother on the set). Lightcap intends to rent the house for a year to write his book. These plans are complicated when an alleged arsonist and murderer named Leopold Dilg (Cary Grant) shows up at the cottage door seeking shelter just prior to Lightcap's arrival . Nora cannot turn Dilg away and lets him stay in the attic, telling Lightcap that he is her gardener. Eventually Dilg and Lightcap meet and come to respect each other — though each has a radically different view of the world — while Nora becomes romantically involved with both men.

Much like *Penny Serenade* and *Woman of the Year*, the action in *The Talk of the Town* occurs inside a home (this home's furnishings were especially cozy, and the film won an Academy Award for set decorations), but the "family" that resides inside is an extended, nontraditional one, similar to the gathering of roommates Jean Arthur, Joel McCrea, and

Charles Coburn in the upcoming *The More the Merrier*. Just when families experience upheaval in wartime America, the social world intrudes
on them, bringing chaos to the very bedrock of American institutions.
Appropriately then, when Michael Lightcap arrives before he is expected, he tells Nora that "there is a nervous, impulsive quality in you
that I find in my students — a disease of the age," as he calls it. She responds with, "Yes sir," feeling infantilized by Lightcap, a stalwart representation of the law, the ultimate patriarch. The "nervous, impulsive"
quality of Nora Shelley's voice and manner stems not only from Jean
Arthur's impeccable gift for sexy verbal shenanigans but also from writers Irwin Shaw and Sidney Buchman's word frenzy. Couple these with
Stevens's alternately breezy and frenetic pace, and *The Talk of the Town*
became a visual and verbal feast for those who could take their minds off
the war and think while they watched the show.

A nervous and impulsive "disease of the age"? Indeed. Shooting began on *The Talk of the Town* on January 19, 1942, just some six weeks after
the Japanese bombed Pearl Harbor and America became fully engaged
in the war. The war loomed for Stevens and his crew during the four-
month shooting schedule, which ended on April 8. Columbia marketed
The Talk of the Town with a campaign that belied the seriousness of the
world around it, instead focusing on the magical world of movie making
that churned out comedies to deflect popular angst over the war. One ad
read, "The most lovable guy the police ever wanted for murder! The
nicest girl gossips ever went to town on! The most amazing pupil a girl
ever taught that life and love are much more fun than books!" Another
read, "You'll take them to your heart . . . as they take you for a most exciting trip into a world of romance, drama, comedy." An additional ad
only slightly hinted at the story's dramatic content: "Comedy so gay . . .
drama so thrilling . . . love so exciting . . . it will be the talk of your
town!"[17]

Beneath the humor in Columbia's marketing lay Shaw and Buchman's witty war of words that audiences surely knew had roots in the
seriousness of the times. Stevens took the script and choreographed
around it a humorous, and very physical, series of mishaps, delivering a
movie perpetually hanging between humor and drama — or, according to
the script, somewhere between the law and human frailty. He later denied that the film purported any "legal philosophizing" whatsoever. He

would deny publicly his attraction to the world of the intellect and channel "thought" into visual expression.

Fred Guiol joined Stevens as an associate, and Stevens also agreed to take Everett Riskin on as producer, though *The Talk of the Town* was still credited as "A George Stevens Production." It was also reported in the trades that Riskin would also work with Buchman on finishing the script. Sizable changes were made to Shaw's first draft treatment and screenplay, which follows Michael Lightcap closely before he arrives at Nora Shelley's house and has Dilg entering the story much later on. Along the way numerous titles were considered: *In Love with You, You're Wonderful, A Local Affair, The Woman's Touch, Morning for Angels, Scandal in Lochester, The Lochester Affair,* and even *Nothing Ever Happens.* Even the shooting script mentions four: *Three's a Crowd, The Gentlemen Misbehave, Mr. Twilight,* and *Justice Winks an Eye.* Arthur and Grant shared top billing over Ronald Colman, though Arthur was paid only $50,000 for the film (it was said she was in Harry Cohn's doghouse from previous rifts), while Grant received $106,250 and Colman $100,000. Arthur turned out to be one of the few actors who liked Stevens's slow, meticulous pace, shooting from every angle, and even his time-consuming care in setting the stage for an upcoming scene. Late in the production tempers flared only briefly when it was reported that Grant thought Arthur was trying to upstage him in the courthouse scene.

The story draws a line between Lightcap's strict interpretation of the law and Dilg's more indulgent humanity. Stevens mimics the divisiveness by opening the film in both lightness and darkness. The first few minutes are dark and heavily stylized, depicting a town's quick indictment against one man, Dilg, wanted for arson and murder after allegedly setting fire to the town's mill and inadvertently killing the guard who was inside the building at the time. A somber looking Grant is caught in close-ups that are more a portrait of the downtrodden than the criminal, cloistered in dark shadows broken up only by obscure streams of sunlight pouring in between the bars of his jail cell. Stevens's shooting script calls for Dilg to be only "half seen" in these shots. Stark newspaper headlines move along the frame in a rapid visual narrative, spelling out his crime and subsequent capture. After he is sent to jail Dilg escapes into more darkness as a severe thunderstorm complicates his move to safety when he sees Sweetbrook, the nearby home of Nora Shelley. All the stark darkness of the outside world rapidly melts away when he enters the softness of Shelley's environment.

But with Lightcap's arrival events become gleefully chaotic as characters frantically move about and mishaps parade in and out. The film cannot decide if the three are an extended family or a romantic triangle. In either case, the three are vehicles for an often-divided treatise on the American scene. Lightcap is the pillar of reason and logic, a professor of law who believes firmly that life is lived by a set of unwavering principles. The law stands above "small emotions" and the "loose thinking of everyday life." On the other side is Dilg, the fugitive who is really Everyman and believes in the "human side" of life and the law; he calls himself the "everyday garden variety of human experience" and even disguises himself as the house gardener to hide his true identity as a fugitive. He is the wronged man and later described as the "only honest man" in town; so no wonder "they want to lock him up." The clear division struck in this house reflects the outside world. The fact of war, having now arrived at the country's emotional and psychological shores, also sends strife into a larger "American house" — a culture and society torn, yet nevertheless energized by a patriotic mood. As a friend, Nelson Pointer, wrote to Stevens in September 1942, *The Talk of the Town* is "courageous . . . and can go a long way toward discouraging blind passions. It dramatizes one of the basic things we are fighting for — a decent social contract."

The Talk of the Town is a microcosm of a wished-for, idealized version of the world, a fiction where warring sides find a solution. Dilg absorbs some of Lightcap's rhetoric and beliefs just as Lightcap relaxes his stringent code of ethics. He even shaves his beard, an affectation he used as a way to hide from the "humanity" Dilg represents. The shaving scene is an oddly sentimental moment; as Lightcap shaves, Stevens's camera closes in on the face of his African American assistant who watches the deed with tears in his eyes, as if Lightcap's actions carry the weight and the consequences of upsetting delicately balanced social codes and behaviors. But battle lines and warring parties eventually crumble into disarray. The "law," in the form of the town's local police and justice system, intrude on this extended family and into this house like clockwork, obscuring the film's reach for a balance between desire for law and humanity. During one breakfast scene Nora tries desperately to hide the morning newspaper with Dilg's picture plastered front and center on it so that Lightcap cannot know his true identity. Lightcap picks it up and Nora screams out (in close-up) a sexy, frantic "No, no, no, no, no, no," to stop him, as if to finally let out all the frustration, sexual and otherwise, that she has held in from the start. She runs over to Lightcap and throws two sunny-side-up eggs onto the picture of Dilg's kisser right on the front page. The chaos is almost too much for this woman too.

As if to drive home the sense of division and disarray, Stevens filmed two endings for *The Talk of the Town* and essentially let an audience poll decide which he would use. (The film's title was chosen in the same way.) In one ending Nora marries Dilg; in the other she marries Lightcap. According to production notes, audience opinions ranged from the logical to the outlandish. On the side voting for Dilg, one fan wrote, "Grant needs her more than Colman. The professor has his law career to fall back on and so won't suffer by loss of the girl like Grant would — who has nothing." Another wrote, "Colman's beard arouses suspicions and makes him unsympathetic." "Arthur has done enough for Colman by making him beardless and modern — he should be able to carry on from there and get himself another girl," another suggested. "Colman is such a well-established, gracious loser — fans enjoy seeing him suffer," said another. Still another signaled a sign of the times, "While there are men of draft age on the screen the girls should marry them — later on the mature men will have it all to themselves." Fewer sided with Colman, one writing, "Grant is too weak and play-boyish to make a permanent husband." Another said, "Grant got [Barbara] Hutton in real life, so let Colman get Arthur on screen," and still another opted for some realism, "Send Grant off to war without Arthur to stay true to life." Of course Grant gets the girl in the end, but not until the movie's very last scene.

Stevens's shooting script includes a deleted scene that shows Dilg and Nora married. Dilg addresses a crowd of people in the park and complains that the park benches have been removed. Where will America's citizens be expected to sit if there are no benches, he demands to know? Just then a policeman strolls by as Nora keeps a playful eye on her husband and the story ends on a note of humor.

The romantic comedy found a strong female audience early on. Even before he finished shooting, Stevens received a letter from a women's organization, the Centerville Women's Club, requesting that Ronald Colman's beard to be sent to them after he shaved it off. They wanted his razor as well.

"Damn the Torpedoes, Full Speed Ahead": *The More the Merrier*

As Stevens moved closer to leaving Hollywood, he directed his last Columbia film, *The More the Merrier*. The most lyrical film of the period, *The More the Merrier* concerns a young woman, Connie Milligan (Jean Arthur), who decides it is her patriotic duty to do what she can to ease the housing shortage in wartime Washington, D.C., and rents out half of her apartment to an older gentleman, Benjamin Dingle (Charles Coburn). Though Connie is engaged to Mr. Pendergast, Dingle thinks Connie needs a boyfriend and rents out *his* half to an army officer named Joe Carter (Joel McCrea). The two men gang up on Connie in a good-natured way before Connie and Joe do what American moviegoers expected them to: fall in love.

Stevens recalled the production's precarious beginning:

> We had a little script and we rehearsed it with Joel McCrea and Jean Arthur and Charlie Coburn. They sat in the room and they read it. And Joel — this was a break for him. This was a Cary Grant part [but] Cary's not available. Coburn will be great in the picture, or damn good . . . [but] Joel is just not for this. . . . He's been playing Western guys, and he talks a little bit like a school boy reading his lines — it was really an ordeal. I said, "Oh God, I'll never do this again." It was enough to discourage any of us from continuing. And Joel went home and his agent called up and said Joel wanted out of the picture. And Jean Arthur is a hero. She had lots of things she'd be a nuisance about but by God if there's something to do, she'd do it. . . . We went to work . . . because the thing was right, the time was right, . . . so full of life [with] that situation is Washington. . . . There was something about the times . . . you know you might as well have some fun because you might not be around too long.[18]

The More the Merrier reflects the rather breathless milieu that produced it. The film is a fluid series of physical and verbal gags that run smoothly enough to appear operatic. Stevens crams each scene, and each shot, with action that is rhythmic, lyrical, and urgent. In one early scene, Dingle sneaks up the front steps of Connie's apartment building, escaping the eyes of those already in line waiting to rent half of the apartment Connie has advertised. He colludes with Stevens's camera and comic sensibility to fool those people around him. The world is a crazy, urgent place where lives have come unhinged and a dingy (as in Dingle) yet good-hearted kind of energy is loosed upon the audience.

The script is credited to four writers: Richard Russell, Richard Flournoy, Lewis R. Foster, and Frank Ross (Arthur's husband at the time). But according to Arthur's biographer, John Oller, the script had a far more interesting origin than that. Supposedly, Arthur and Ross went to New York in mid-1942 since Arthur was on suspension from Columbia for having rejected too many scripts. There the couple met friend Garson Kanin, who was in the Army and stationed in New Jersey. Kanin needed money and offered to write a script for Arthur. She and Ross would pay Kanin $25,000 for the script that they could offer Cohn for nothing. After a subsequent weekend visit to bustling Washington, D.C., Kanin and a new friend, beginning screenwriter Robert W. Russell, came up with *Two's a Crowd*. Not able to pass on a bargain, Cohn eventually let Kanin read the story to him on the phone. Cohn liked it just from the opening scene and agreed to take it.[19]

Columbia gave Stevens *Two's a Crowd* in June 1942, though it contained a different ending in which all three occupants of the apartment — Connie, Joe, and Dingle — still share their crowded quarters. Connie finally admits to Joe that she does not want to marry her fiancé, Mr. Pendergast, and wishes someone else would ask her. She and Joe admit that they love each other. After they kiss, the script reads, "Joe and Connie. They smile like they're never gonna stop." In Stevens's ending, Connie and Joe actually marry, but only after a long series of mishaps. Even then they cannot admit that the marriage is real until Dingle plays his last trick on them and they fall into each other's lives for real.

Numerous titles for the film were tested on audiences. *Washington Story, Love Is Patriotic, Too, Full Steam Ahead*, and *Come One, Come All* each lost to *Merry-Go-Round*. But an interoffice memo reached Stevens asking him not to use that title because "certain quarters in Washington" believed it "indicates frivolity on the part of Washington workers" and that the appearance of "military uniforms in a night club might reflect on various branches of the service." In addition, Joseph Breen's office, the Production Code Administration, provided other censorship stipulations, among them, there should be "nothing suggestive of homosexuality" (Coburn and McCrea share a room and spend some time in the bathroom together); bathroom gags should be minimized; Dingle should not be seen "entering the bathroom when Connie is in it" (this would eliminate Connie's "unacceptable" screams); there should be "no indication that Dingle is sitting on the toilet"; Joe should "not be seen strictly in his B.V.D.s"; and Connie should never be shown in "night gowns [or] play suits." It was also suggested that the studio send the script to the FBI for approval since the organization figures prominently in the story. Breen also sent Cohn a letter in October 1942 informing him that use of the song "Damn the Torpedoes," which also figures as a motif, was denied because of the repeated use of the word "damn." Nonetheless Dingle utters the phrase repeatedly.

The energy in *The More the Merrier* threatens to run rampant but is repeatedly tamed in the nick of time. Stevens juxtaposes the disorder in Washington (crowds of people, lines of traffic) with the orderliness imposed by the city's monuments that signify power contained. With Dingle's recurring (and altered) phrase from David Glasgow Farragut, "Damn the Torpedoes. Full Speed Ahead," the energy could easily go astray were it not also contained by the lyrics "full speed ahead" that moves it straightforward.

Order and disorder share space throughout the story. When the story reaches its romantic crisis as Connie and Joe return to her apartment late at night and sit on her front steps, the story collapses (sexual) tension and orderliness. Connie talks about schedules but is overcome by the chaos of sexual feelings for Joe. As they get closer the camera follows, almost forcing them together on the steps; Stevens cuts from a long shot, to a medium shot, and finally to a close-up of their kiss. Later, after they admit they love each other (trying to create order, a bond) chaos intrudes again. They lie in their respective beds, in separate rooms, but Stevens's camera and editing put them close together as if they were lying in the same bed. Nothing is settled, however; they are brought together only to realize the war will inevitably separate them. Just as in the social world, the world of the film is ultimately an ambiguous one. Connie and Joe want to be together but know that the war separates everyone — an irony given that if it were not for the chaos created by the war they would never have met.

Yet in the scene near the end of the story where Connie, Pendergast, Joe, and Dingle end up in a police station, Stevens's camera creates a graceful visual orderliness; its energy stems not from the dialogue but from the actors' physical gestures and movements. Dingle hides by reading a newspaper while crossing the room and Connie, having fought with Joe, then hides behind Dingle's shoulder to "shoulder" herself from him and Pendergast. Stevens's camera moves from one character to another, just as the characters themselves move, giving them a silent, poetic rhythm, without the need for language. That balletic energy repeats in the film's very last scene as Joe and Connie walk in and out of their respective rooms only to realize soon enough that they are standing in the same room. Dingle has his own plan and has had the wall between them removed. He fulfills his life's credo, again in collusion with Stevens's camera, that says in these crazy times people must "damn the torpedoes" and move "full speed ahead."

Studio exploitation acknowledged the war while it also tried to make light of it. A proposed publicity stunt for *American* magazine in January 1943 (as Stevens was leaving for Europe) had a pictorial spread, a "shot of Stevens and a bevy of girls on [a] Washington rooftop set" of the film. Predictably, much of the publicity stressed Arthur's playful sexuality, positioning her on a blanket wearing a scanty two-piece bathing suit. She asks, "Do you think it's wrong that I shared my bath and kitchen with two strange men?" and "Can they put a ceiling on that old feeling? Don't give it another thought. . . . They'll never ration romance!"

Knowing Stevens was going into the service, the cast of *The More the Merrier* gave him a going away present: a saddle with his name engraved on it. That month, January 1943, as he was finishing editing, he made the papers when he underwent an emergency appendectomy. Critics held out open arms for the film, praising it widely. Stevens was already in North Africa when *The More the Merrier* was nominated for an Academy Award for best picture, and Stevens for best director in 1943. Coburn took home the Oscar for best supporting actor. In 1944 Stevens won the New York Film Critics Award for the film but by then was fully engaged in photographing the war, uncertain if or when he would return to direct films again.

On February 1, 1943, Harry Cohn sent an interoffice memo to Duncan Cassell: "George Stevens is leaving at the end of the week to enter the Service of his Country. Anyone to whom you assign his office must take it with the understanding that he will vacate it when Mr. Stevens returns." It never happened.

4

Toluca Ville
The War Years

Then at the break of day we were off and three
hours later after a ride that Yakima Canutt would
have wanted $500 to do, we stood under the
Eiffel Tower, but not for long.
—letter from George Stevens to Yvonne Stevens, France, 1944

Stevens left Los Angeles the second week of February 1943 to serve as a
major in the U.S. Army Signal Corps, which was responsible for photographing Allied activity during the war. He first covered combat cleanup
in the North Africa campaign, then, headquartered in London, he shot
footage while in the European theatre and photographed some of the
war's strategic operations, including the invasion of Normandy, the liberation of Paris, the Battle of the Bulge and, finally, the liberation of the
Dachau concentration camp. Stevens remained in Europe until the end
of 1945. The war was the adventure of his life. Certainly the experience
of covering and being part of the Allied victories in Europe changed the
way he saw human nature and made being a film director seem all the
more urgent after he returned home.

Stevens left ample evidence of his three years in the service, mainly providing the government with a cinematic record of Allied activity in North Africa and Europe. He also created a personal record of the war — not only in the color footage of his expeditions that he shot on the 16mm Kodachrome film he brought from Los Angeles, but also in his journal and diary entries, and his letters home to his wife Yvonne, to his mother, and to his son, George Stevens Jr. Much like his fellow directors who enlisted, among them John Ford, William Wyler, Frank Capra, and John Huston, Stevens was overage to serve in the war. Nevertheless, from the start, he wanted to be in on the action; euphemistically put, he wanted to be on location, not on a sound stage. As he later said:

> I quit the film business. . . . I wanted to be in the war. I didn't want to make films at that time. I had an opportunity to go overseas right away if I'd go in the Army at a certain time. Soon as I'd finished *The More the Merrier*, I previewed that picture two nights in a row, and then I cut it and left it. I was in North Africa when the picture opened, never heard about it until I was in England some three months later.
>
> I figured if I'm a civilian, I'll make pictures, but in the Army I'm not going to. . . . And when they told me I could get a commission, I put in for combat photography. I was accepted to head up a unit, and I was sent over to North Africa. Then I was sent up to England to prepare for the invasion. I was to get the special photographic teams together, which I did. I was continually getting into a position in which I was going to be sent out to Pinewood with a moviola to put a film together. Well, I just controlled my fate in order not to get into the cutting room. I was a planner for the films on Overlord and laid out the idea of how the story be put together. . . . They got this British guy, [director] Carol Reed, and Gar Kanin to take over the film developing end of it, and I was over on the other side; if they wanted film, I would get it for them. My job was to catch the scent and be at the right place at the right time. But they used to ask us for certain things — Carol Reed came over and told us what he'd like to get, and they — John Huston and Willie Wyler — put the damned film together. I shot film for Frank Capra particularly, very important films [*Why We Fight*]. They'd tell us what they wanted, and we'd go out and do it.[1]

On January 8, 1943, Stevens received his letter of "temporary appointment," which read, "By direction of the President you are temporarily appointed and commissioned in the Army of the United States, effective this date. . . . This commission will continue in force during the pleasure of the President of the United States for the time being, and for the duration of the war and six months thereafter unless sooner terminated."[2] Stevens was sworn in as a major on February 18, 1943, and left Los Angeles that week. His son, George Stevens Jr., recalls his father's departure:

> We all went to New York and stayed at the Waldorf Astoria. It was meant to be for a short time but he got pneumonia and had to go to the hospital at Fort Jay [just outside Manhattan]. He was sick for a while. My mother used to take the train out to visit him and take him fresh pajamas and things. . . . Then we went to Washington, D.C., and stayed at the new Statler. Dad did some business at the new Pentagon, planning his work and getting orders. . . . I remember us being in the nice dining room at the Statler and there being a ruckus at the maître d' station. Dad rushed over there. It seems Irwin Shaw was going to tear the guy apart because he wouldn't let him in the dining room. Shaw assumed it was because the man was anti-Semitic. The fact was they allowed only officers and Irwin was a new private first class. Dad got him in. One day we went to Washington National Airport and saw him off as he got on a government DC-3. I remember my mother and I went and sat in Lafayette Square across from the White House, very sad indeed.[3]

Stevens's bout with pneumonia saved his life, causing him to miss an ill-fated flight out of the country that crashed killing all its passengers.

According to his passport, Stevens arrived in Egypt on April 13. Four days later he traveled to North Africa and stayed until June 15. He went to Algiers in early June to coordinate a documentary film covering the Allied troops' cleanup operations and the task of processing thousands of captured German prisoners. "I remember over in North Africa," Stevens said, "right at the finish of the campaign, at the end of May, I got tanks and engineers and all kinds of stuff together. They didn't have what they needed to put an American film together on the North African campaign; and we shot already blown-up villages being blown up more, staged stuff like tanks and jeeps going through villages — they'd always scream when you went through the village in jeeps — and we took tanks and ran them through the water like they did when the British Seventh Armored Division cut off the Germans. We shot that for them, and learned a little bit about how to live in the Army."[4]

On May 7 British troops from the east and American soldiers from Algiers completed a pincer attack that won a final German surrender in Tunis and more or less completed the war in North Africa. The Americans had captured German General von Arnim, who had replaced Rommel. The event led to Stevens's meeting with General Eisenhower and left a lasting impression. Stevens said:

> I flew down to Algiers . . . [to] a little sub-action going on at a Bonn Peninsula, and it happened to be my opportunity to meet General Eisenhower. . . . I had problems in what I was doing. . . . Combat Photography . . . and guys in the staff arranged it for me to give the od man a pitch, and I knew how to do it, too. So I'm curious about von Arnhem, and I'm sitting there across the table from Eisenhower. . . . I've been properly introduced . . . so I'm terribly curious, and I said, "General, did you talk with General von Arnhem when he went through Algiers?" . . . and he looked up at me and he looked me right in the eye and he [said] to me, "I'm here to kill Germans, not to talk to them." When I used to see the campaign star for Eisenhower for President and all these stories about him, I remembered what a horse's ass he was . . . [it was] simply a rebuff to me, to keep me in my place, but in the fashion that everybody is totally stupid or he only has to be a little bit smarter to overwhelm their stupidity. . . . "I'm here to kill Germans, not talk to them." I'll never forget it.[5]

After Stevens left North Africa he arrived in Persia on June 30 and stayed until August 20. He began keeping a journal while there. An entry for July 4 shows Stevens in a characteristic posture, using a journal as a means of self-discovery: "All right. I've been on this job six months now. Two months here, four overseas. Needed that experience to discover what difficulties might be encountered in getting my job done under conditions new to me. The principle parts of the operation were remarkably simple. Two points need authorization. Local officers should not attempt to take over the job and add it to their own Kodak battalions. Transportation must be given to the unit. Some wheels and an airplane." He noted that there were "legions of signal corps photographers all over, ten good news reel photographers," and wrote that some of the hierarchy and regulations bothered him: "Officers in charge are absolutely incapable of this kind of work in most cases, and smother operations by capable men because good work would set a standard they could not keep up. . . . Most commanders won't have signal corps men if they can help it. Film is being shot but no picture is being made. Signal corps once had [a] group like this; took it apart, no one wanted to run it. Now starting all over again."[6]

Stevens recorded in his diary entries that he went out to Maison Blanc in the desert and put the cameras behind the tanks where he could get out and shoot. He thought about the implications of his job as a photographer in the war and what it meant for him. He began to perceive his mission in more and more grandiose terms. He saw himself as a crucial link between what was happening in the war and how Americans back home would understand it. He now viewed himself self-consciously, seeing his job as a responsibility to families back in America to report the war, record it for posterity: "If you have bought a two bit war stamp this is your show. This is what you are getting for your money. Civilian morale builder. No more strikes. Show the war." Stevens thought of himself as "a liaison between the men who fight and those who serve at home" and called his work "civilian orientation," a way to "prepare the civilians by sharing the soldiers' experiences, for resuming [the] relationship with men who have been away." He wrote with compassion: "Make the casualties easier to bare for those who have had to suffer bereavement. Construct a celluloid monument to those who have been the ones to go. . . . Gave up my personal film projects of ~~the highest possible caliber~~ to make films for the war dept of the highest possible character. I see it is necessary for me now, to give you information — I thought you must have when you brought me into the Army. Twenty-five years getting ready for — this job. Now I am ready. ~~Ten years~~ Early years as a cameraman on the most formidable outdoor projects. Director-writer-producer of the top flight screen creations." Stevens's sense of mission, capabilities, and what he might accomplish grew more and more defined. But he also felt frustrated at not being the one in control, not being able to realize fully the potential he felt within himself: "The great American ability to make movies — lost in our war effort. No position or authority established for our men. We have to go back to the end of the line — along with majors and *wait for someone higher up to tell us what to do. We are never told because no one higher up presumes to know what to tell us.*"

In his frustration, Stevens wrote, "We should have gone to Panetilerria and filmed destruction of guns and gun emplacements — showing great damage done by our fire power. [Lieutenant Colonel Melvin E.]

Gillette was off without me seeing through his eyes." Prevented from doing what he considered to be his mission, Stevens believed that much of what the Allied forces were accomplishing in North Africa was going unrecorded because of the lack of organization from the higher ups, and at this early stage, the Signal Corps' lack of mobility.

By the second half of 1943, Stevens detected a downward spiral in the war spirit. "Politically the war is going stale," he wrote. "People at home and in England are more and more turning their thoughts toward the resumption of normal peacetime activities — England vacation this year — Show no vacations with troops. Air raid precautions being relaxed, in London campaign against the blackout. So far unsuccessful. More and more everyday think the war is almost over. The men who are fighting this war have not gone stale. Everyday their presence on the scene of conflict, reassures them that they are engaged in a brutal struggle." He returned to his sense of purpose: "When I am put on the ground to make a film, I have to do a good job. I cannot go off on an expedition and not make a film. These amateurs can stay out on a job indefinitely, no picture comes from their effort and so long as they keep a pleasant social relationship with their local command their job is accepted as well done. Men called in from the industry to do special works have been commissioned to do that work and are given authority to do it."

Stevens left Persia on August 20, 1943, five months after entering the war. Frank Capra, for whom Stevens shot footage in North Africa, later recalled his version of Stevens's move to London:

> He's not an easy man to push around; he certainly wasn't easy to be pushed around by his superiors . . . and none of us were but we wanted to get the job over with. . . . First place I sent him to was Iran with a group of people . . . we wanted to get actual film of our help to Russia. We were sending them lend lease material to the tune of about eleven billion dollars but nobody knew it, and I wanted to get it on film. But the Russians are too smart; they wouldn't let anybody photograph their film, they wouldn't let anybody near their border, so this group of people with George at the head of 'em, they were dying of doing nothing, so George left there. He left the gang into another man's command and . . . went down to Libya someplace. . . . He was trying to get to London. . . . They stopped him at Libya and said, "Where are you going there, Major?" And he says, "Well, I'm going. . . . " So they say, "No, you can't

leave here, you're in my district and you can't leave here without my permission." Well, that didn't mean much to George. He left on the next plane.[7]

Stevens flew to New York and stayed there and in Washington, D.C., from September 15 through October 26 before flying to London where he received orders from General Eisenhower to organize a forty-five-man Special Coverage Unit (SPECOU) in London in preparation to film the invasion of Europe. Stevens's unit was linked directly to the Supreme Headquarters' Allied Expeditionary Force (SHAEF), and from then on would have plenty of supplies and almost complete freedom to move around the European theatre. Among his group were writers Irwin Shaw and William Saroyan, British writer Ivan Moffat, cameramen William Mellor, Jack Muth, Ken Marthey, and Dick Hoar, as well as Columbia Studio soundman Bill Hamilton and Hal Roach assistant director Holly Morse. Stevens had "Toluca" printed on his jeep to remind him of Toluca Lake back home in Los Angeles. That meant a lot to him, Ivan Moffat later said. He traveled around Europe with the name of his neighborhood right by his side. Throughout the next two years Stevens and the men in his unit would hand each other the camera, often taking turns capturing the images Stevens sometimes sent home to be developed.

Stevens's London notebook entries provide a lively picture of the period when he was putting his unit together just before heading out to cover the invasion of Normandy. He spent a good amount of time in London with Shaw and his friend Saroyan, whom he particularly requested to be part of his unit. Some of his entries capture his private moments taking in the life of a city hit badly by war but coping with great stamina, even nobility. At one point Stevens shared a penthouse and later was responsible for keeping Saroyan out of the army barracks and in private lodging. Stevens's notebook entries show his love of observation and his acute understanding the people he watched. In an undated entry, written in late December 1943, he recounts his admiration for the British citizens after spending an evening at the Coliseum Theatre at Christmas time:

> [In London] At 6:05 Solo [Stevens's spelling, an affectionate reference to Gene Solow, a war correspondent who traveled with Stevens and

remained a close friend after the war] and I arrived at the Coliseum Theatre in the blackout to see the Christmas Pantomime "Humpty Dumpty" put on by the present King of the panti producers Emile Littler. This is one of his eight companies and of course the best. . . . Air Vice Marshall (Butcher) Harris and his family occupied the stalls next to us. His three children were delightful to watch; their enjoyment was so keen. Particularly the brown-eyed blond little girl about 5 years old who was enchanted by it all. The Air Marshall had many a good laugh himself and but for his uniform you might have thought him to be a jolly baker whose entire thoughts were devoted to the pleasures of his family and fireside. . . . Not the man whose air legion has made him the terror of the 3rd Reich. Even as he sat amused at this simple legend being acted out, his fierce work was going on. I'll bet there were no fairy tales being performed for children in Berlin this night.

At the end of 1943, Stevens flew home to Los Angeles. Later he wrote to his friend and war buddy Joel Sayre that "I flew home and on the second day that I was there I got a telephone call from Anatole Litvak for me to return to Washington by the night's plane. Yonnie and Georgie were considerably upset and so was I."[8] On February 7, 1944, back in England, Stevens wrote to Yvonne, "It is so difficult to write about oneself and be sure you have kept security first. I am in perfect health. Second, miss you and my boy more than you can know. Third, working endlessly on difficult job, for me much discouragement but do our best to do good job . . . the main thing I am looking forward to is for this to end successfully. . . . Wish Hitler was in hell and am glad to help in any way to put him there." Then, on March 15, he wrote to her that, "These have been dreary months, these last, and if it hadn't been for your letters ~~life would have been nothing~~ there would have been nothing to think cheerfully about, because you know that I find much [of] this difficult to believe in fundamentally."

Stevens thought about his son, George Jr., now thirteen, to offset the depression setting in from being away from home for so long. He wrote to Yvonne on April 30, in response to a letter from her:

> I have thought much about what sort of job George should try and get for the summer. I could not think of anything that would be best. My conclusion is this. He should get a job. What sort of a job it is at this time I do not think is important. It will be his first job and whatever it is that

will be . . . [of] importance as good experience. He will, I believe, benefit
. . . no matter what his first job is. He will have to learn to get along with
his boss and do things that are not designed for his pleasure. He will get
from it the satisfaction of personal accomplishment, the realization that
he as a person can do something himself, independent of the parental
organization, which has made all things in his young life possible so far.
He will earn some money, a portion of which should be designated for
the community welfare. By that I mean his home, which has taken care
of him, should benefit somewhat from this new found earning power,
no matter how small it is. This I hope does not have to be told to him,
but I will pass a guarded hint along to him in a letter. I say guarded hint,
because I'm sure important things like that are much better if they come
from him as already part of his character development. Rather than a bit
of police work. All this is meant for is to call attention to the important
fact — that each person must learn to pull his weight in the brat. . . . You
are the Supreme Court to him; your decisions should be based on judgment and wisdom so that he will respect those decisions, because from
that pattern he will develop his own code of conduct. And a boy must
learn to decide things that effect other people in a code of fair play — not
one which is governed by the pleasure of the one deciding. . . . I don't
think you need advice on how to do what you're doing but I just want
you to know I am interested too and feel very far away.

To Stevens, the battles found in Europe paralleled the moral battles
faced everyday in one's life, and he wrote home accordingly.

On the morning of June 6, 1944, Stevens began his great adventure. He
and his unit were on the HMS *Belfast* as the Expeditionary Forces
landed on the beach at Normandy in the early morning. He covered the
trip with his own 16mm color film. The photographic unit was not
allowed on the beach until a few hours after the main assault. Then
Stevens and his men landed at the small town of Burners, at Juno Beach.
Afterward they camped at the small town of Carentan, a town midway
between the American beaches of Utah and Omaha. They witnessed the
greatest in-pouring of material they had seen so far in the war.

On June 23 Stevens made his first journal entry after Normandy. He
noted road hazards for men walking on foot. "Signs that reveal Presence
of Mines" included a long list: "Disturbed or Discolored soil or grass. . . .
Bits of paper, string, crushed cigarette pkg or butts. . . . Foot Prints. . . .

Small Depressions or mounds. . . . Little Puddles of water. . . . Pegs or markers. . . . Vehicle tracks showing that traffic has deviated from a straight line for some reason." But he closes the entry with a little humor, a limerick he calls "Picturesque Speech": "Little slivers of memory sticking into you. / The sailor came in with the tide and went out with a wave. / My troubles always come in the large economy size."

Stevens and his unit were summoned on July 4 to the Allied Army's headquarters in France. At the send-off the unit found itself in the company of commanders in chief of the Allied land forces: General Montgomery, General Omar Bradley, and General George Patton. Stevens and his special coverage unit went with General Patton's American Third Army. They moved west, heading to Brittany from Carentan through St. Lo, and witnessed extreme devastation — ancient towns destroyed and large numbers of civilians killed. After fierce resistance, hundreds of German prisoners were rounded up. The Third Army arrived at the port of St. Malo on August 18. The town had just been liberated the day before their arrival, though the Germans held out for another two weeks.

Then Stevens and his unit moved out of Brittany with American troops and headed toward Paris. Along the way they passed numerous villages that had been liberated and were throwing flowers and good wishes to the troops as they passed by. The men crossed the Seine some thirty miles outside Paris.

On August 23 when General Eisenhower agreed to let the free French army liberate Paris itself, Philippe Leclerc led units of the Second Armored Division into Paris and Stevens convinced him to let the photographic unit drive with them. When they arrived, Stevens set up his cameras at Montparnasse Station in the heart of the city where German General von Choltizt would surrender to Leclerc. After the ceremony took place inside the station Stevens convinced the two men to let him record the scene with better light in the street outside, which they did. General Charles de Gaulle also attended the ceremony.

Stevens always described the day he and his unit drove into Paris as the most exhilarating day of his life. The footage shows him driving into the camera's view in his jeep, Toluca, with a broad smile on his face. In a long letter to Yvonne, written on September 1, he described his elation at being part of the liberation of Paris:

Dearest,

There is so very much to tell to you that I really don't know where to begin. First, from the time that I wrote the last letter to you, until two days after the fall of Paris, I did not at any time have my clothes off. I think the time was about two weeks. The days and nights all ran over themselves and became pretty much one thing, the struggle to get to Paris. We had a small party of our photographers in jeeps along with the armored column. With the responsibility of getting in first thing and photographing the activity. That we did, but the doing and the two weeks before were the most exciting, the most unbelievable time of my life. . . .

The morning that we came into Paris was the wildest thing that I have ever seen. The civilians lined the streets and went mad as the Tanks and armored cars came in. They stood in the streets and cheered as the shooting went on all around them. Our jeeps brought in the first cameras and I believe the first American flag, which we got from a Frenchman just outside the city. We were only eight or ten miles out, where we halted about two AM and waited for daylight and the artillery fire to cease. Then at the break of day we were off and three hours later after a ride that Yakima Canutt would have wanted $500 to do, we stood under the Eiffel Tower, but not for long. The Jerries were up in it and the French resistance was fighting them from the ground below and it was too hot for some lonesome jeeps. More of a ride through town then we holed up in a railroad station, stood off the last attack the Nazis made before they surrendered. They brought the Jerry general and officers for the surrender.

The shooting went on for a couple more days, German snipers and the few bad French who were fighting with them. . . . There is much I could tell you and will in further letters but I do hope you and Georgie have seen the newsreels that carried our film. We have heard that the films of the liberation of Paris were the best ever taken of anything like that. We are completely exhausted at the moment and hoping to get a chance for a few days rest but time and us marches on.

Two months later Stevens sent home packages with souvenirs he picked up in Europe. "The belt is from a German," he wrote in a letter in late October 1944. "Many of us wear them with our field uniform. George might want to have it cut down and wear it with his. The green spotted silk is a piece from one of our invasion parachutes. I have been wearing it as a scarf; it makes a very fine scarf. Many parachutes were left on the ground and many of us made nice soft silk scarves out of the pieces."

On October 7, at Reims, about to load up "to Brie to Verdun, the Hq of the 12 Army group," Stevens wrote in his journal that he visited the Pommery Grem Champagne factory and watched production of wine and champagne: "As we passed by rows and rows of Magnum bottles stocked in the caves, I stopped and looked at one bottle and wondered — for who was it destined? For a wedding? For a romance? Would it excite some poor mortal into an act that would change the whole course of his life? Then I looked at all of the bottles and wondered, what was their destiny? When and where would they be opened in 1947 to perhaps 1967? What a story if one could just sit in that dark cave and foresee. A delightful movie could be made on the pattern of 'Tales of Manhattan.' Why would a Frenchman like Duvivieir do a story like this about a tale coat, when in his own France there was this situation so provocative to the imagination?" Stevens could apply his story sense not only to the little romantic fantasy he imagined but to the uglier reality in which he found himself:

> Above us Mons. Floquet opened some 37 for us. He showed us pictures of the last war with Reims destroyed by a shelling and much damage to the cellars. . . . He told us about the battlefields between here and Verdun in the chalk hills had not lost their scars. We drove to what had once been a village at TANURE near Sommefry. Miles and miles of trenches criss-crossed the chalk hills. Some greens have grown to hide the scars. But everywhere you looked it was this weird irregular lacework of old trenches completely pock-marked by shell craters. Some pillboxes remain, some barbwire and occasionally a part of a weapon. How many died here? Three crowded military cemeteries we passed all within a few miles of one another. The villages here abouts, are new villages. Something rare in France, where every[thing] is so old. New tile and new stone and cement, that is new since 1918. Overhead American bombers were returning throughout the afternoon. We stop on "Hill Americans" famous to the Rainbow Division and watched their sons return, those that did return, from carrying the coal to Metz.
>
> Enough contemplation for one day. We drove on in the evening, it was very cold and we put on our army great coats and stopped beside the road to Verdun and had cheese from a K-ration and cut a loaf of "du pan" that Sgt. Hamilton had donated.

But heavy fighting lay ahead, even though from the streets of Paris it might have seemed as if the war was over. On December 16 the Germans attacked American troops along a sixty-mile span between Belgium and Luxemburg in an attempt to recapture the port of Antwerp in southeast Belgium. The six weeks of heavy fighting was known as the Battle of the Bulge. Approximately nineteen thousand GIs were killed. The hard winter, the coldest on record in Europe, depressed Stevens, despite receiving presents from his family, which one of the members of his unit recorded on film.

In mid-1944 letters from Hollywood began to arrive. Stevens's colleagues updated him on the climate of the wartime movie industry and asked him about his future plans after the fighting was over. The letters must have seemed like documents from some other very surreal world. His agent, Charlie Feldman, wrote him on May 27 that "war pictures have been taboo in Hollywood for the past year. The production companies insist that the public does not want war pictures, but looking over the grosses, the largest grossing pictures are those with war backgrounds." His friend Dave Epstein wrote in July: "Seriously, George, the class of pictures they have been making is better left unexplained. These birds are in for an awful jolt when this war is over. They have been reaping a harvest at the box office with the lousiest crap imaginable. Exhibitors keep warning them to come down to earth, but they are swimming so deep in big grosses they can't hear any complaints." Then David O. Selznick cabled Stevens: "If you haven't any plans for yourself after you leave the service I'd like to suggest you get in touch with me as I think I have something very exciting to offer you." Feldman wrote again in October:

> Though you have been out of circulation, not a week goes by but that some producer calls me in, attempting to discuss with me a possible deal for you upon your being released from the service. Sam Goldwyn is very, very anxious to have you. Jack Warner says he will make a most attractive proposition, if you are interested. Darryl feels you belong at his studio. Naturally, I advised these tycoons that I don't know what your plans are nor your disposition and that no undertakings of any nature can be made until such time as you return. . . . I tell them that I feel quite sure . . . that George Stevens Productions will have to be set up in a most independent manner and under the best possible percentage terms and

guarantees ever dished out. . . . I will try to give you the trend of the industry. . . . There has been so much independent production going on that it is absolutely impossible for an independent, unless he is working through one of the major companies, to get studio space. . . . All the studios have tremendous backlogs of pictures . . . there are about forty pictures in New York waiting for release.

In January 1945 Stevens returned from Paris to London after putting in two weeks of work with Garson Kanin and British director Carol Reed on their British-American film project, *True Glory*, which won the 1945 Academy Award for best documentary. Stevens planned the project. The next phase of the war would feel devastating.

From Nordhausen to Dachau

By spring the Allies were advancing once more into Germany. On March 24 they mounted Operation Varsity, as twenty-two thousand parachuters and glider men supported land forces crossing the Rhine. Once across the Rhine, Stevens and his unit moved with the American First Army as it advanced into Germany. They had gone 150 miles in less than three weeks and on April 11 reached Nordhausen, one of the Germans' most secret installations located under a mountainside and comprised of forty miles of tunnels housing the largest underground factory in the world. At Nordhausen the Germans produced the V2 bombs that blitzed London. Locating that site and all of its intricacies provided good material for the master caption stories Stevens and Moffat wrote to accompany the footage they sent back for newsreels. At Nordhausen the two men collaborated on a master caption story called "V-Weapon Underground Factory and Slave Camp," which was sent as an accompaniment to the footage his unit filmed for Americans back home to see. He dated it April 15, 1945:

> The accompanying material shot at the Nordhausen underground factory for the mass-production of V-weapons may be considered as stark an example as could be found anywhere of the utter German indifference to human life reaching a very high peak of brutality side-by-side with a supreme example of technical perfection in the science of mass

destruction. The factory itself lies bomb-proof in a series of vast tunnels and amphitheatres hewn out of the interior of chalk-hills at an estimated cost in slave-labor of some 25,000 men working day and night for fourteen months. . . . Near the mouth of the factory, on the open hillside, lies a system of barracks that formed the prison quarters of several thousand slave-laborers of whom inestimable numbers have lost their lives through starvation and torture while the process of building went on. . . . The crematorium had been swept clean of all but the mass of smaller human bones that still lay concentrated in the neat pile of ashes at the foot of the furnaces where the Germans had burned the amputated bodies of the dead slaves. . . . So completely without record of their past lives had these creatures been left that of two thousand-odd men and women and children it was possible to identify but four men by name and nationality.

Though Stevens would have thought it impossible to imagine, the sights that awaited the unit at Nordhausen still did not prepare them for what they encountered at Dachau.

On April 15, Stevens and his unit reached the Elbe River, where Allied forces were ordered to halt. On the west side of the river stood American soldiers — Bradley's Twelfth Army — and on the east side stood the Russians. At Torgau the two came to an emotional face-to-face for the first time. Two hundred and fifty miles south lay Dachau, just outside of Munich. Stevens and his unit headed for the camp. As he later recounted: "I was ordered to make a link-up with the Russians up at Torgau, and I got a signal up there, back from the divisional headquarters . . . to get everybody I [could] that's available to me . . . that they were sending my Paris unit, that had sound recording cameras — the only ones in existence at the time — down to Munich. . . . And this Army that came up from the south, which was the 69th Infantry division that liberated Dachau — and so I have to get down there. . . . So we just loaded up our jeeps with weapons. We had a 50 caliber in each jeep, and each jeep's equipped with one Tommy gun, and we had engewehrschutzes, which is that little German hand machine gun. . . . So we put three schtzes in a jeep and a Tommy gun, and a guy standing on the back with a 50 caliber, and we'd just taken off down across country."[9]

The Allies liberated Dachau on April 29, 1945. Stevens reached the camp two days later on May 1; with him were three other officers and fifteen enlisted men. They remained there about a week, long enough to hear Truman and Churchill's declarations of victory in Europe on May 8 and long enough to record scenes that Stevens later said could never be described in words, only in pictures. His footage captured survivors along with those who did not live to see VE day. He jotted down on the back of a photo of the freed inmates, "There were 38,000 people in the camp when we got there and 6,000 cases of Typhus."

It was reported that when the surviving inmates at Dachau were freed they joined American soldiers in killing the Nazi soldiers who had been their torturers. All in all, American GIs shot almost one hundred and twenty two German SS right away; Dachau inmates themselves killed forty or fifty. Stevens snapped a poignant photo of a dead German Shepherd dog and wrote on the back of it that the dog had been stoned to death by the former prisoners and now lay dead next to his water bowl on the cement in front of a bungalow doorway. Ivan Moffat filed several caption reports on Dachau. For May 2, he filed a "Master Caption Story: Bodies Lying by Railway Track at Dachau," writing that "the Nazis made a serious attempt to evacuate the Concentration Camps in the path of our advance, for obvious reasons. . . . Two large transports of prisoners were taken from the notorious camps at Buchenwald and Sachsenhausen and sent south in boxcars and open cattle-trucks for confinement at Dachau." In another caption story, "Life at Dachau," Moffat reported on May 4 that "Conditions at Dachau at the time of our entry were so appalling, the numbers involved so great—over 30,000—that no instantaneous check to the high mortality rate was possible. It was a question of isolating [the] area so as to stop the spread of typhus to other areas as much as it was one of evacuating the inmates to better and healthier quarters, even if this had been possible from the point of view of numbers."

Moffat reported that "photographs show the bodies of those who have died during the morning lying outside the living-huts awaiting removal, whilst the inmates—utterly indifferent by now to the sight of death or the need for elementary measures of precaution—are seen squatting within a few yards of the row of corpses and cooking a meal. This was the case not in just one or two barracks but along an entire row of blocks. . . . To the inmates, death was the absolutely normal and permanent feature of their intimate surroundings. . . . It is not surprising to see occupants cooking beside the typhus-ridden bodies of their room-mates — they were obliged to sleep in the same rooms and even in the same *beds* as those who died during the night."[10]

Stevens later said the shock of Dachau only added to the shock of Nordhausen. He saw the crematorium after the burning had stopped; bodies were stacked up outside of them. "The Poles hated the Jews worse than the Germans did. It's a sad thing to say, but it has discouraged me tremendously with all backgrounds — the better the Christian, the better the Anti-Semite; and the Aryan Germans are wholesomely, exuberantly, schmaltzy Christians, where the tears come down for the Savior. The Poles are all trained in it. And it was an easy thing to do, to have the so-called destroyers of their god identified as Jews. Also, it justified the whole goddamned terror, to have this kind of a belief. They wanted to have it, and they had it." These were words Stevens could hardly believe even as he uttered them. They were images he photographed and then wanted to refuse; they ended up in storage for years afterward. "Doing this kind of work . . . you don't talk about these things, you don't say 'Jesus, I saw this,' — even war correspondents, you just file it. So I'm look-ing at it. I'm looking at these people — who are they? And what? In the boxcar. And you say 'Jesus Christ, how do you get to, how does one have to be confronted with this?' This cannibalism — I never heard anybody ever talk about it. . . . And into Dachau we go, inside the wire. I never read anybody that in any way states what it means — the horror of it. That people can be subjected to it and survive, and that people can do it. That's the awful thing, that people can do it, and that people can abet it. They should get themselves struck down or killed."[11]

Like the others, Stevens was ill-equipped to make sense of the images at Dachau, so he filed them away somewhere in his psyche and moved on. After Dachau the unit made its way to Berlin. On the way the men took a departure to Berchtesgarten, Hitler's vacation home in the Alps. There Stevens took a few mementoes, one being, he said, a brick that he later used when he built his barbeque in the backyard of his home in Toluca Lake. He also took a sampling of Hitler's flatware. Then in July, finally at Berlin, where the Russians had given them clearance to enter, Stevens's unit split up and his men went their separate ways. Stevens at-tended the Berlin Conference of the Three Allied Powers as a U.S. del-egate in Berlin on July 13, 1945. In September he was in France. On the back of a photo taken of Stevens and several men in his unit he wrote, "Major 'Dick' Cahoon and I at Dachau on the morning of May 2nd. . . . Those nice coats we have on belonged to the Nazi S.S. Guards at Dachau. We liberated the coats, as you can see. Poor little Toluca has no nice coat and is quite cold."

In February 1945 Lieutenant Colonel George Stevens and the SMPCU received a commendation from General Eisenhower for its "outstanding service in connection with the military operations of the Allied Forces." Stevens stayed in Germany almost until the end of 1945 preparing concentration camp footage with writer Budd Schulberg for *The Nazi Plan*, a documentary Stevens directed and Schulberg wrote that was presented as evidence at the December 1945 Nuremberg War Crimes trial of Herman Goring and twenty other Nazi leaders. He said, "and then I got out of Germany."

He returned to the United States on the *Queen Mary*, along with seventeen thousand other men, thirty-two of them bunking with him, in what they were told was Winston Churchill's state room. He arrived in New York and couldn't get a room at the familiar Waldorf-Astoria due to overcrowding. He did, however, manage to visit with Charlie Feldman, who was staying at the Sherry Netherlands, to run into Joan Fontaine, and to take in a performance of *I Remember Mama* with Barbara Bel Geddes, which would become his first postwar film. Before he left the city, he tried to see the Notre Dame game out at Yankee Stadium. He could not get in, but he walked around the stadium a couple of times listening to the crowds cheer. "So I came home slaphappy to be home, to put on civilian clothes. You go to restaurants and see people you used to know. I see my boy, we play football, we play games, and we do all of these things."[12] Already back in Hollywood, Stevens was demobilized from the United States Army in March 1946 with the rank of Lieutenant Colonel.

"Moompitchers": Returning to Hollywood

Stevens had written Yvonne in 1944 that back home his "racket" was making "moompitchers." Now it was time to return. Stevens said in 1973 that when he came back to the States he realized the shock of the new;

he had been away for what seemed an eternity and had lived a lifetime in the battles of war. It was a wonder that he or his colleagues could make movies again, after the experiences in Europe. Stevens had seen life almost too real:

> I hadn't seen a fiction or entertainment motion picture . . . for three years . . . except for one time . . . with a lot of people — 2,000, 3,000 — soldiers sitting out in a hollow with these things on the screen. And when I came back, David O. Selznick . . . brought me to the studio, and he's running films of the stars that he had, and I said, "That girl's particularly interesting," and he said, "That's Miss Jennifer Jones, Mrs. Selznick." "Oh yes, I should have seen her films." I'd missed two or three years of catching them . . . and I didn't know them. It occurred to me then . . . that these films that I was seeing then, after the war, in Hollywood, were not made from life, but were made from old films — from other films. You know, it seemed as if the experience that the filmmaker had, he could have been closeted, not with people, but with films over the recent years, or the many years, and then make the same film. . . . Because it seemed to be guided by what he had *seen* in films, rather than what was going on at that time.[13]

The war hit Stevens's fellow directors in different ways. Capra was nervous about finding a studio to take him; Wyler expressed concern that he did not know what the future held. But Stevens never showed what he felt. In fact, as Capra said, Stevens was *silent*. He did not talk about the war very much when he returned:

> The edge had gone off the humor. . . . He had seen too much . . . and I had the same feeling myself, but nothing to what he had because . . . he'd seen the horror and the . . . absolute nonsensical stupidity of war. . . . Burning people up because they were a different religion . . . killing women and children . . . and bombs, these bombs could kill anybody. . . . The whole thing became, for him, a kind of nightmare; a nightmare of the stupidity of man.
>
> It took him quite a while to adjust and to be with us. He became hard to talk with because I don't think he wanted to express his real . . . or maybe he just couldn't . . . express the horror that he'd been through; it just grew on him. But he was a different person. He was not the same George Stevens that left when he got back. None of us were the same after that experience with war, but for him I think it was more visible.[14]

Stevens kept to recording only the mundane in his date book for January 1946, his first weeks back. For January 2, he wrote, "Most of the day spent reading. Picked up Monsieur [Gene] Solo, [who stayed with Stevens for a while] and dropped him off at the dentist. He gave me 'Brighton Rock' to read." For Thursday, January 3, he noted, "Solo, Yonnie, George and I went to the Beachcombers for dinner. Solo's friend, Pat O'Day, gave us a reservation, which is difficult to get." On Friday, January 4 Stevens wrote that he received a script from Charles Feldman, but left out its title, then wrote, "Finished reading 'Written on the Wind,' by Robert Wilder." He also received a call telling him the carpet for the office would not arrive until February 1.[15]

Stevens wrote about setting up an office, but if he was referring to the production company, Liberty Films, he was about to join, he was oblique about it. He was readying properties, though. On Saturday, February 5, he visited Leo Rosten at his house on 602 N. Roxbury in Beverly Hills and read Rosten's story, "Incredible Smith." Stevens wrote, "I told him that this one was not the story of his that I wanted to do. Leo said that he would keep me informed on any new ideas that he developed. I told him that I would call on him if I came upon a good story idea that he and I could develop together.[16]

Liberty Films

Even before Stevens returned from the war, Frank Capra approached him about joining what would become one of the industry's more visible postwar examples of directors going independent: Liberty Films, the production company that became a joint venture between Capra, Wyler, Stevens, and producer Sam Briskin. Feldman had written to Stevens back in 1944 about the new trend toward "independence." Now Stevens would live it firsthand.

When Capra first approached Stevens about Liberty in 1944, Stevens asked him if he could wait before making a decision. Then after the war ended and while he was still in France, Stevens met with Harry Cohn and promised him he would come back to Columbia Pictures when he returned to Hollywood. But the war experience made some Hollywood players think about independence. He reneged on the promise when he realized he no longer wanted to be tied to a studio, incurring a portion of Cohn's wrath in the process. After briefly considering an independent partnership with Leo McCarey, Stevens said yes to Capra and to Liberty Films in January 1946. Capra was just about to begin shooting *It's a Wonderful Life*, which, ironically, would turn out to be Liberty Film's first and only production under its banner.

Capra's biographer, Joseph McBride, argues that Liberty was, in part, the result of Capra's worry, especially after the war (and a good part before it) that he would not be bankable at the studios. Though he did not see combat, Capra had been gone from Hollywood for four years; when Sam Briskin went around to the studios to see how willing they were to take Capra, the prospects did not appear to be in his favor. He even thought about leaving Hollywood and going to work in England. He also considered Briskin's ideas to start his own production company. On January 29, 1945, the two announced their new "post war company." McBride writes "Capra desperately needed the partnership of another important filmmaker to strengthen his bargaining power with distributors."[17] John Huston was approached, but turned them down, worried that he would not have enough say in the partnership. Stevens was another matter. As his date books show for this immediate postwar period, in January 1946, just having returned from Europe, Stevens was unsettled, unclear about his future, and in his usual stoic manner, doing very little about it. He was disturbed by his war experiences and just settling back in slowly. He had enough offers not to be worried. As Yvonne reported, he did not have to worry about money the way Capra did; though he and Yvonne were essentially separated, he moved in with her and stayed. "I think he just knew that he would finally get something . . . and it was the same as when he left Roach. He didn't look for a job at all. He just went out and played golf everyday, for seven months or so. I just couldn't understand it, although I didn't know what he could do to get a job. . . . No, he just took it in his stride. He wouldn't be bothered about anything like that."[18] Stevens was experiencing his own version of shock and awe — not only to be back home after the intensity of filming the most urgent episodes of the war but also remembering the horror of what awaited him at Nordhausen and Dachau.

A contract dated January 1, 1946, was drawn up, and though he makes no mention of the deal whatsoever in his date book, Stevens was now a partner in Liberty Films. The partners — Capra, Wyler, Stevens, and Briskin — set up offices on the RKO lot on Gower Street in Hollywood and held a press conference on February 23 to announce the formation of Liberty Films. Capra, Stevens, and Wyler would each function as if they were independent producer-directors, yet projects had to be approved by all three directors and Briskin. Capra wrote a distinctive account of it in his autobiography:

> Film aficionados may be interested in the modus operandi of Liberty Films. Stock distribution: 32 percent to Capra as president and organizer, 18 percent to Briskin, 25 percent each to Wyler and Stevens. But the voting rights were all equal. It took 3 out of 4 votes to resolve such major company decisions as hiring a star or buying a story. But once bought, the story was assigned to Capra, Wyler, or Stevens who from that point worked autonomously, functioning as producer-director without interference from others. . . . Our deal with RKO called for nine films, three from each producer-director. Wyler, Stevens, and Capra each received three thousand dollars per week from the day the RKO deal was signed. It was assumed (but not obligatory) that each producer-director would make one picture per year.
>
> The financing: RKO advanced the cost of physical facilities — rental fees for offices, studio space, and equipment. Bank loans would cover all other production costs. We put up (proportional to our stock holdings) an initial sum of $150,000 to cover pre-production costs — our salaries and that of writers and office help. We had to pay ourselves three thousand dollars per week (upon which we paid 80 percent income tax) because the Internal Revenue Service had declared it unkosher for film artists to work for less than their going salaries when working for companies in which they were substantial stockholders.[19]

But Liberty, with its cracked bell logo, with its four partners' plans for a new wave of independent producing, lasted not much more than a year. The only film Liberty produced, Capra's *It's a Wonderful Life*, went into production April 1946; when it was completed, the company could not count on any profits from it for a year. As Capra said, "Our original ante of $150,000 had evaporated. Collectively we put up another $150,000. That meant hocking real property. We could not recoup any of this pre-production money until films went into principal photography. But neither George nor Willie was anywhere near principal photography on anything. That meant George, Willie, Sam and I had to keep putting up our own money to pay ourselves $10,000 a week in salaries, of which we netted (after taxes) about 15 percent. On every go-round we lost 85 percent of our own money. . . . It was the fastest and most gentlemanly way of going broke ever invented."[20]

Back in Los Angeles, Stevens had not yet landed or grounded himself emotionally before he joined up with Capra and Wyler. He did not want to go back to a studio, but found himself there just the same:

> I wasn't ready, but because it was Frank and Willy, I went into it. And when I did . . . that meant that I went to the studio. I hadn't been home long enough to go to a studio, I didn't want to see a studio, I wanted to see the town, the beach, the mountains, the old buildings around town, home, you know. And instead I was in a studio. Frank made the first picture, and it was time for me to go to work on a picture. I went to work on a . . . social comedy, which was to star Ingrid Bergman. It wasn't what I felt to do, but I thought that this was the kind of film I should do. And Ingrid was ready to do a comedy. . . . But . . . in the meantime I had been thinking . . . and I thought that perhaps our story was not good enough for this sincere, fine artist. . . . I said [to her] "The truth is that the story just hasn't worked out." . . . I paused for a moment then to reflect upon the value of self-confidence in work such as this. There were many people who had come back from a long period away in the war and couldn't get going again. . . . Obviously something had changed. . . . I decided that I must do a picture that I had a real feeling for, that my present state of mind would allow me to believe in.[21]

Stevens said in many late interviews that after he returned from the war "I don't think I was ever too hilarious again." According to friends William Wyler and Fred Zinnemann, his mood had changed. He returned home "more silent" than before, unable to talk about the atrocities he had seen at the camps. "He wouldn't talk anymore," Frank Capra recalled. Yvonne Stevens later said, "He was out of work, and very bitter about the people who stayed home and made all the movies. But he was a very sensitive man. He just never dreamed, I'm sure, what he was getting into when he enlisted."[22]

By January 1947 Capra wanted to sell Liberty Films — at just about the same time that they could pay themselves all of one thousand dollars per week. Wyler and Briskin were willing to sell to a major studio but

Stevens was not. He believed strongly in being independent—he had behaved that way from the beginning—and wanted to make a go of Liberty. But eventually he gave in, and in a deal negotiated by Jules Stein, the head of MCA, they sold the company to Paramount. As part of the buyout, which was made on April 14, 1947, Stevens, Wyler, and Capra became contract directors at Paramount, and as a way to settle Liberty's obligations to RKO, Stevens was also loaned out to that studio to direct *I Remember Mama*. Liberty would get 25 percent of the film's gross, which it would give to Paramount as part of its assets, along with its interests in Capra's *It's a Wonderful Life* and *The State of the Union* (which he had yet to direct). In the end Stevens agreed to direct five pictures for Paramount at $3000 dollars per week (as it turned out, he was paid $1000). Stevens in truth wanted nothing to do with the Paramount deal but eventually went along with Capra and Wyler. His extensive troubles with Paramount came quickly thereafter.

"Irene Dunne and Fenimore Kipling": *I Remember Mama*

Liberty Films loaned Stevens to RKO for one year from March 17, 1947, through March 16, 1948, to direct *I Remember Mama*. In return RKO agreed to pay Liberty $6000 per week for twenty-six weeks beginning March 27. RKO originally bought Kathryn Forbes's novel *Mama's Bank Account* in 1942 but did nothing with it for five years. In the meantime, Rogers and Hammerstein produced the play on Broadway as *I Remember Mama* written by John Van Druten, probably the version Stevens saw in New York on his way back from Europe.

Screenwriter Dewitt Bodeen, who was under contract at RKO, came onto the project long before Stevens. Bodeen was hired to write a script from the book. He produced two versions before going to New York to see the play, after which he wrote a third. On loan to the studio, Stevens served as executive producer on *I Remember Mama*. Bodeen later recalled that when producer Harriet Parsons, columnist Louella Parsons's daughter, approached Irene Dunne to play Mama (Garbo had already turned it down), she gave her a copy of the book. Dunne read it with her daughter and told Parsons that she would agree to play Mama if the studio let her give them a list of the five directors she wanted to work with on the film. Stevens was on the list and she chose him.

Stevens kept Bodeen on salary and on the set after he had finished what he thought was a final completed script. To Stevens a script was a continually changing, always-evolving entity and this one was no exception. Bodeen recalled Stevens telling him the story changes he wanted, and writing them down himself. "It was a long, long production," Bodeen said, "almost double the budget on a number of shooting days because George wanted it right. . . . Dore Schary, head of the studio, would come down to the set and George would see him come in and he'd just go over to his chair and sit down and wouldn't do anything until Dore left. He knew he was over budget and off schedule. He didn't have to be told that it was a Liberty production . . . he was reminded of the fact that he was cutting down on his own money, but he said, 'I don't care.' . . . So he went ahead."[23]

Stevens first attempted to update the story to contemporary times, but realized early on that it would not work. When the production went up to San Francisco for location shooting, it was noticeable how much faster Stevens worked. "He was really in his element," Bodeen said. The studio sent out notices to the locals that they could be extras in the film if they could come up with a 1910 costume. "People would go to their attics and get things out" and the production was filled with extras.

Much time was spent lightening the dialogue. The actress Ellen Corby, who played the shy Aunt Trina, had a line telling Mama that if the other sisters laughed at her when she told them she was going to marry an undertaker, she would kill herself. But she was not getting it right. Stevens came up to Bodeen, whispering "I can't get her to say it lightly . . . so there's no threat to it . . . she says it as if it were in an Ibsen tragedy."[24] They changed the line to "If they laugh at me, I'll go 'yomp' [jump] in the Bay," and preview audiences laughed just when they should have.

Jessica Tandy had initially been assigned to play Aunt Trina, but early on her agent went to Stevens and asked if she could be released so she could star opposite Charles Boyer in Universal's *A Woman's Vengeance*. Stevens said no because he believed she was right for the character. The story goes that Tandy herself then came in and wept, after which Stevens told Harriet Parsons that perhaps they should let Tandy go because "the circumstance being what they are, she couldn't play the part." Tandy asked Stevens if he could find someone to replace her. "The script girl can do it," he replied. So script girl Ellen Corby inherited the part.[25] Ivan Moffat recalled the way Stevens worked with his actors: "He didn't want the actors to be responding to where they thought the camera was going to be. . . . I remember him moving the furniture around as he was making *Mama* and sort of putting pieces in the way of people so that they couldn't move too easily in a scene where he wanted them to appear awkward . . . he didn't like actors to rely upon dialogue. He said that actors used dialogue like crossing stones across a river to step on . . . to make it easier . . . like a sort of crutch . . . to prevent them from acting and from moving about."[26]

Toward the end of the six-month shoot, Stevens was far enough behind that Dunne, whose contract stipulated that she be paid a good amount for overtime, made more money on her overtime "than she did on her flat deal," Bodeen said. By the time Stevens finished shooting, the editors said "they could have cut *I Remember Mama* six different ways without ever repeating a set-up." Bodeen also remembered, "There were things underneath the supposedly happy surface in George. . . . I remember once he almost threw a worker off the set because this worker said something about the Nazis and the gas houses . . . the way they treated the Jewish people and all of the prisoners . . . this worker said that most of it was a fiction, and George said, 'Are you out of your mind?' He lectured this worker for almost ten minutes. He said to him, 'I was one of the first. . . . I saw. . . . I know what went on!'"[27]

I Remember Mama was itself a crossing stone for Stevens, a safe place to revisit after Europe. It performed a special function for him, now that he was just back from the war, unable to settle in, and looking for a story with good emotional bones. When he turned down the scheduled project with Bergman, he said it was because he wanted a story he could believe in. After the war, filmmaking became very personal. There was no other reaction he could have had after the war. He would have made a comedy if it had *meaning* for him.

In a certain way *I Remember Mama* is a manifestation of the silence Capra spoke of when he remarked that immediately after Stevens's return to the States, "He just wouldn't talk!" *I Remember Mama*, in all of its safety for Stevens, was a means of not talking about the devastation of what he saw in Dachau. It was for him the artistic equivalent of a return to the safety and nostalgia of San Francisco, the city of his childhood, and a fall back into the arms of a loving mother, an all-forgiving, all-nurturing, all-protecting mother. Unlike his own mother, Georgie Cooper Stevens, who traveled as an actor, he needed one who stayed in one place and held the household together, who was learning to speak the language, just as he was. Returning to his past, as he would do in an even more lyrical way in *Shane,* was a way to recall his selfhood, a way of gathering from a specific place in the past an artistic and emotional strength. Though *A Place in the Sun* would articulate how truly serious Stevens was as a filmmaker thinking about America, after the experience of war, *I Remember Mama* was the moment he needed to remember how to be a fictional filmmaker again.

I Remember Mama begins and ends with a camera looking from the outside into the warm room of the family home. Windows always served Stevens well, from *Alice Adams,* where the camera looks in on Alice crying after the dance, to Jean Arthur's rooms in the prewar comedies, and to *I Remember Mama* and to *Shane,* where the camera again locates the heart of the family home. Now, just after the war, there is both an incongruity and a logic to Stevens and the spectator peeking into the heart of a family, especially a family in America's past. Stevens returned from the war as shaken as other soldiers — and returned to a society equally shaken. At some unconscious register, the experience of being an immigrant, being a stranger to a new society and having to learn its codes, could not have been far from Stevens's experience as he returned to the United States and to filmmaking. But the emotional strength of the story's main character, Mama (bolstered by the strength of Dunne herself, who received an Academy Award nomination for the role), had to be the strongest draw. The warmth of matriarchy could hardly have been more of an emotional opiate to a country. And this maternalism was especially useful to Stevens the artist who was now back from the war, living through the breakup of his marriage and through the instability of Liberty Films. Stevens wanted to stay out of a studio but was heading there nevertheless, looking carefully for a property to direct, as the date book suggests, and even looking for an emotional place to land, no matter how temporary that might be. The minutiae of family life that occupies the characters — and the spectators — throughout the story provides continuous solace to ease every conflict: Dagmar's male cat being named Elizabeth; cousin Trina's worry over her sisters laughing at her engagement to an undertaker; the weekly family meetings centered on whether or not they will have to "go to the bank," a euphemism for their constant worry about money. Stevens approaches each of these small catastrophes by giving them the weight of the world. Their resolution — and each crisis has one — pushes the story forward in a slow, deliberate pace and eases the pains of a nation back from the war.

I Remember Mama initiated Stevens's postwar cycle of serious, contemplative, and increasingly personal films. It is a measured return to a past that no longer exists, though it by no means is a light endeavor for Stevens. Looking backward, as he would do in *Shane,* serves the purpose of self-renewal, of gathering strength from the country's, and therefore the self's, past. *I Remember Mama* indicates Stevens's serious intention to mend broken psychological sites for the artist and for the country.

The film opened in March 1948 at the Music Hall to enthusiastic reviews. *Daily Variety* said that it "capitalizes heavily on nostalgia and warm human interest, but does it honestly and sincerely without lapsing into hokum." The *Hollywood Reporter* praised its emotional balance and Stevens's "gift" for "blending a tear and a laugh."[28] The public accepted *I Remember Mama* as a story about family. But another story emerges, too: that of its daughter Katrin's apprenticeship as an artist who learns the important lesson of choosing her subjects wisely, finally choosing those close to her heart. Now, after the war, Stevens had to be listening.

The Stevens family on the vaudeville circuit in Seattle: George Stevens (center), age 9, flanked by parents Landers and Georgie Cooper Stevens, brother Jack (far left), and some troupe members, circa 1914. Reproduced courtesy of the Academy of Motion Pictures Arts and Sciences.

Photo taken by George Stevens, age 9, in Seattle, Washington. Stevens's mother, Georgie, gave him the Brownie camera for his birthday. Stevens already shows his gift for visual composition; similar lines will show up in *Shane* and *The Diary of Anne Frank*. Reproduced courtesy of the Academy of Motion Pictures Arts and Sciences.

On location with George and Rex the Wonder Horse, circa 1926. Reproduced courtesy of the Academy of Motion Pictures Arts and Sciences.

Stevens (second row, far right, hand in pants pocket) during the days at the Hal Roach Studios. Stevens's life-long friend and collaborator, Fred Guiol, sits on table in center. Reproduced courtesy of the Academy of Motion Pictures Arts and Sciences.

Katharine Hepburn and Fred MacMurray find love in *Alice Adams* (1935). Stevens and Hepburn wanted Tarkington's realistic ending with Alice losing her man, but Pandro Berman and RKO prevailed with a happy one.

Fred Astaire and Stevens playing it up during production on *Swing Time* (1936). Stevens looked shy but knew what he wanted in a scene. Reproduced courtesy of the Academy of Motion Pictures Arts and Sciences.

Stevens with recent RKO arrival Barbara Stanwyck on the set of *Annie Oakley* (1935).
Reproduced courtesy of the Academy of Motion Pictures Arts and Sciences.

Stevens took *Gunga Din* (1939) outside on location near Lone Pine, California, and gave it an exuberance that all the critics noticed. Reproduced courtesy of the Academy of Motion Pictures Arts and Sciences.

Cary Grant, Irene Dunne, and Stevens looking serious on the set of the classic weepy, *Penny Serenade* (1941). Reproduced courtesy of the Academy of Motion Pictures Arts and Sciences.

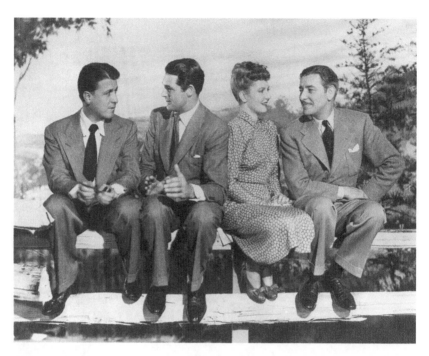

Stevens, Cary Grant, Jean Arthur, and Ronald Colman sitting on the fence during production on *The Talk of the Town* (1942). Reproduced courtesy of the Academy of Motion Pictures Arts and Sciences.

Ivan Moffat, Col. Stevens, and Jack Muth (l. to r.) on the road to Dachau in June 1945. Reproduced courtesy of the Academy of Motion Pictures Arts and Sciences.

Ivan Moffat back in civilian clothing just at the end of World War II. Reproduced courtesy of the Academy of Motion Pictures Arts and Sciences.

PART II

The Postwar Films

5

I See America Kissing
A Place in the Sun

> I was more seriously engaged in films after I'd
> had three years of an unnatural experience, which
> was the war in Europe. And that changed my life
> and my thinking so seriously that it changed my
> professional instincts; I knew I wanted to do very
> different things than I'd done before.
> — George Stevens, USA Film Festival

> The essential American soul is hard, isolate, and
> a killer. It has never yet melted.
> — D. H. Lawrence, *Studies in Classic American Literature*

I Remember Mama gave little indication of how deeply the war affected
Stevens. That would be the province of his very next film. *A Place in the
Sun,* based on Theodore Drieser's novel, *An American Tragedy,* is the first
of Stevens's postwar films to reflect the personal transformation he
underwent during World War II. It is his darkest, most personal and
most intellectually far-reaching film, expressing not only a darkening of
the spirit that came over him in Europe but also the somber turn his art
took after his return.

Drieser's opus, *An American Tragedy,* held profound meaning for
Stevens, before and especially after the war. He had always searched for
his great "tragedy," the drama that would elevate his work above the

"women's films" he had directed before the war — and with Dreiser and his tragic hero, Clyde Griffiths, both spokesmen for the disenfranchised, he found it. *A Place in the Sun* would be the pinnacle of Stevens's career, the result of a convergence of Dreiser's great material and the serious mood Stevens carried home from Europe. Later, even as his films became more ambitious in scope, more deliberate in execution, he would never achieve the poetry — that graceful blend of intimacy and breadth — that he achieved with *A Place in the Sun.*

Returning from Europe, Stevens felt that he had been part of the fabric of a truly great tragedy and though he may not have known precisely why, Dreiser's book figured prominently in his ability to resolve, at least artistically, the anxieties he brought back from the trauma of war. The story of how *A Place in the Sun* came to be made — how tragedy and optimism do battle in the production and in the final poetry of this film — is also the story of how Stevens's aesthetic was permanently altered at this moment in his career, allowing him to reach a new seriousness in his storytelling. His artistic and social canvas might not have expanded as much as it did after the war had Stevens not found Dreiser just after the war. Stevens wanted to make *An American Tragedy* into an audience pleaser, a love story with tragic dimensions. What he actually produced was something far more complicated and troubled than that. Always a man of his times, Stevens made a film that told American audiences, no less than himself, just how unreliable and unstable individual and cultural identity was and would remain after the experience of war. The tragic hero of *A Place in the Sun,* whom Stevens renamed George after himself, is one of American cinema's first postwar misfits, an icon of social uncertainty. The fact that Stevens battled Paramount so extensively to get this film made is evidence that now he was ready to undertake projects that were personal, and even urgent.

Stevens was barely out of his teens when he first read Dreiser's novel in 1925, the year it was published. He read it again in 1945, just after the war, then noting in the book's margins his ideas for visual dissolves and dialogue he planned to use. He later said that he first thought seriously of filming it in 1947. After the war, Dreiser's deterministic view of America — rooted in the story of an idealistic yet misguided young social climber who ascends to the tragic side of the American dream — was especially meaningful to Stevens. He had returned to the States to find himself at an emotional and professional crossroads, questioning his and his country's values, and bearing a decidedly darker view of human nature than before he and his unit saw the horrors of the Dachau concentration camp. Stevens was determined enough to film Dreiser's book to stake his entire reputation on persuading Paramount to back him. Knowing that the book's rights belonged to the studio helped to convince him to go along with William Wyler and Frank Capra to sell Liberty Films to Paramount, a move he initially opposed. "I knew that Paramount owned the rights to the book," he said in 1967. "I had it in my mind that if we sold Liberty to Paramount, I might be able to get a hold of *An American Tragedy*."[1]

Now under contract to Paramount, Stevens campaigned the studio to approve the novel as his first picture for them. But the studio was apprehensive, having already made the film in 1931 and released it to poor reviews. There were also potential censorship problems: *An American Tragedy* was the story of an unmarried pregnant woman murdered by her boyfriend after he falls in love with a wealthy socialite — a delicate matter for audiences at the time. Furthermore, given the anti-Communist mood of postwar America, a story by Dreiser, an alleged member of the Communist party, would not be a particularly popular draw with audiences. Stevens and Paramount disagreed until ties were strained. Stevens finally threatened the studio with a lawsuit and was one step short of going to court when production on *A Place in the Sun* was finally green lighted early in 1949.

Theodore Dreiser based *An American Tragedy* on a 1909 murder trial that the critic F. O. Matthiessen described as "the favorite drama of the American people" at the turn of the twentieth century, a story that "everybody was reading in the newspapers."[2] All of America followed the fate of a man named Chester Gillette who drowned a girl named Grace Brown in Moose Lake, Herkimer County, New York on March 20, 1906; Gillette was electrocuted for the crime on March 20, 1908: "In 1906, Chester Gillette, a poor-relation straw boss in his wealthy uncle's skirt factory became enamored of the daughter of a wealthy Corlandian, who encouraged his suit and his dream of rising through marriage to the town's upper set. The pregnant Grace now represented a menace to his social ascent. So Chester escorted Grace to Big Moose Lake in the

Adirondacks, pretending that he would marry her. Instead, he took her boating, stunned her with a tennis racket, overturned the boat and swam to shore while she drowned."[3] What interested Dreiser, who himself sat in on Gillette's trial, was not the crime itself but, as Matthiessen points out, its detection; Dreiser saw the murder and execution as good source material for a documentary novel he had in the planning stages that would be a contemplation of American capitalistic society. Dreiser had been looking for a man such as Chester Gillette, someone he imagined to be "insanely eager for all the pleasures which he imagined he saw swirling around him. . . . His 'none-too-discerning' mind could so easily be convinced that the chief end of life was having and spending money."[4] What better drama, what greater tragedy, than the fall of a man who will even kill to embrace a dream of money and social position that slips through his fingers even as he dreams it?

An American Tragedy appeared in 1925 to generally glowing reviews and made Dreiser a literary sensation, this after years of struggle that led to a nervous breakdown following the critical beating he took with the 1900 publication of *Sister Carrie*. Critics still view *An American Tragedy* to be the crowning achievement of Dreiser's career. In telling the rise and fall of Clyde Griffiths, who dabbles in petty crime before heading for the city to work in his uncle's factory, Dreiser gave American readers a stinging yet passionate view of the fabric of American factory life, as well as social and economic systems that wear people down, and according to Dreiser, leave them emotionally impoverished. Within this bleak landscape he tells the personal tale of Clyde Griffiths, the quintessential American dreamer whose life is stifled by poverty and eventually snuffed out after he allegedly murders his pregnant girlfriend, fellow factory worker Roberta Alden. Clyde has fallen in love with the wealthy and beautiful socialite, Sondra Finchley, a woman who lies beyond his reach, but he plans to murder Roberta thinking she stands in the way of his life with Sondra. Clyde's inability to distinguish reality from illusion paints a bleak picture of American society and the false values that someone such as Clyde would embrace at the turn of the twentieth century.

The novel's success and commercial potential were not lost on Paramount Pictures, and the studio secured the film rights in 1925 for a then astronomical $150,000. Paramount boss Jesse Lasky offered it to several directors, including D. W. Griffith and Ernst Lubitsch. Both considered the subject matter and turned it down. Eventually Lasky offered it to Russian director Sergei Eisenstein, a good candidate since he had even entertained the politically like-minded Dreiser in his Moscow apartment in 1927. The script Eisenstein eventually produced — appropriately critical of American capitalism — pleased Dreiser but displeased Paramount general manger B. P. Schulberg (Budd Schulberg's father) who, along with production chief David O. Selznick, read it and knew immediately that it would not go over with American audiences. Selznick thought it moving but "positively torturing. . . . When I had finished reading it," he said, "I was so depressed that I wanted to reach for the bourbon bottle. As entertainment, I don't think it has one chance in a hundred." He told Schulberg it would be brave to make the script "purely for the advancement of art," but "braver still and kinder to the stockholders not to."[5]

Eisenstein was ousted from the project and *An American Tragedy* went to German director Joseph von Sternberg, who co-wrote a new script with Samuel Hoffenstein. Selznick was still not pleased, thinking Sternberg the wrong man for Dreiser's "moral realism." "I don't think he has the basic honesty of approach this subject absolutely requires," he said, "or . . . the sympathy, the tolerance, the understanding that the story cries for"[6] For while Eisenstein's script had retained Dreiser's political underpinnings and his critique of American social and economic institutions, Sternberg's screenplay excised nearly all of the novel's political context, paring it down, in the opinion of many critics, to a melodramatic potboiler.

Paramount went ahead with the production, starring Sylvia Sidney, Frances Dee, and Phillips Holmes. Ironically, though Dreiser began writing the novel while living in Hollywood in the late teens, his relationship with the studios was anything but satisfying. He offered to help write a screenplay for the film after Eisenstein left the project but the idea never materialized. When he saw a screening of Sternberg's finished *An American Tragedy* he accused the studio of butchering the plot, not to mention the spirit, of his novel. Despite the large sum of money he made in selling the book's rights — enough to purchase a mansion on the East coast — Dreiser tried unsuccessfully to block the film's release, distributing a four-page pamphlet decrying the producers' "utter misrepresentation of Clyde Griffiths" and their "destruction of the book's theme." In a letter to Paramount on June 26, 1931, Dreiser's attorneys said, "Instead of the picture presenting a universal psychological theme, it tells a specific story of a murder; instead of an indictment of society, the picture is a justification of society and indictment of Clyde. Thus the picture is not only not a fair representation but a complete misrepresentation of [the novel]."[7] Nevertheless, the judge in the case ruled against Dreiser.

Upon general release, the film also took a critical beating. *Variety's* film critic accused von Sternberg of not liking the material of his own film.[8] Alexander Bakshy wrote in the *Nation*, "If there is anything tragic about the film version of *An American Tragedy* it is the pathetic spectacle of its producers trying to crash the gate of the artistic heaven with the yellow ticket of their profligate trade."[9]

Even twenty years later, when Stevens mounted his campaign to win *An American Tragedy* for himself, he disliked Eisenstein's "hopeless" script as much as von Sternberg's dismal adaptation. He later said, "Dreiser is the great observer and he has an ear for verisimilitude, for truth, and he knew the people; . . . the Eisenstein script is something that should have been done by the Bolshoi Ballet in American clothing . . . it was a ridiculous presumption to take a tapestry of life that belongs to a certain milieu and turn it over to Eisenstein's extraordinary technique and say, 'Play "Turkey in the Straw.""'[10]

Bolstered by the failure of his two predecessors to get under the skin of America's great novelist, Dreiser, Stevens was ready to do the job himself. He said in a 1967 interview: "*I Remember Mama* . . . was a nice play, a homely thing that had some charm. . . . I had control of things, and I could move people through houses and down the street. . . . I wanted to do something with some substance. . . . I'm loaded with this war thing, and . . . I tried to think of something for a film that I'd understand and that the public would accept and I'm not sure I understand the contemporary subject matter at that time. I'd been dislocated, I'd been away. So I knew about *An American Tragedy:* I know how one reacts to it. . . . So I decided that's it."[11] In 1948 Stevens ordered books on Dreiser from Paramount's research department: a biography, Dreiser's autobiography, *A Book About Myself,* even books on murder trials such as *Meet the Murderer, Murder Will Out, We Who Are About to Die,* as well as the *Book of Common Prayer.* He said of Clyde Griffiths, "The character [was] something that appealed to me . . .

something I understood. . . . Bill Saroyan told me I made films about the outsider."[12]

Stevens could identify with some of Dreiser's life experiences, much of which became source material for *An American Tragedy*. He read about Dreiser's desolate childhood. Unable to support his family, Dreiser's father moved them from one small town to another and his son grew up with a deep sense of social disapproval. Dreiser grew up poor enough to write and understand what it meant for Clyde Griffiths's family to have been deprived of the comforts and pleasures that many other families took for granted. Reading this, Stevens no doubt remembered his own impoverished youth and relived his ambivalent feelings about his own father, Landers, who insisted that Stevens drop out of high school, get a job, and chauffeur him around Hollywood as he sought out acting jobs.

Stevens underlined meaningful passages about Clyde Griffiths in his copy of *An American Tragedy*, especially where Clyde is "always thinking of how he might better himself, if he had a chance; places to which he might go, things he might see, how differently he might live." Another underlined passage read, "he [Clyde] had nothing. And he never had . . . and yet the world was so full of so many things to do — so many people were so happy and so successful. What was he to do?"[13] He was moved by the dramatic possibilities in Dreiser's "thrashing, hopeless men and women" who look for a way to overcome the smallness of their lives. In as deterministic a mood as he would ever be, Stevens read Dreiser's portrait of Clyde and committed emotionally to this character, seeing in him a vast skepticism and a self-deluding desire to rise in a society that offers no positive view of human potential. Clyde was a reminder of the "tragedy of human waste," the enormous sadness of lost potential Stevens witnessed in Europe; he saw in Clyde the profound sadness he tried to make sense of and held inside since the war. No one felt sadder, more sickened, than he did when he went into Dachau, and no one could project that sadness onto the tragic Clyde the way he could.

Stevens read about Clyde during a time when his mood coincided with society's: when there was great concern for social and psychological upheaval, shared anxieties over the potential chaos of the atomic bomb, and confusion experienced by returning vets struggling to fit in. If Stevens returned feeling none "too hilarious" after the war, he returned to his professional life as a filmmaker in a Hollywood struggling to adjust to a changed America in a truly tumultuous time. As a response to the assault of McCarthyism, the Hollywood community was also about to weather its own professional and moral cannibalism, a Blacklist that ran amok in Stevens's own professional backyard. Even as a vet, Stevens was again in his element.

During the war, American movies in good part reflected the government's effort to pump up a show of widespread patriotism. Betty Grable's legs might have been pinned up in overseas lockers, but at home the image of Claudette Colbert and her two daughters banding together in a domestic show of enthusiasm for the war effort in *Since You Went Away* was a pervasive reminder of the industry's — and the country's — patriotic wish fulfillment. Wives, mothers, and daughters waited at home for their men, bonded in a tolerant, united, and hopeful front. They even went to work to help grease the war machine. But once the war ended, the jubilation that came from victory in Europe and the Pacific was short-lived, and American movies reflected the confusion that grew in its place.

I Remember Mama was a late contribution to a fictive nostalgia that actually broke up earlier, for example with Wyler's *The Best Years of Our Lives* released in 1946, which depicts an America that cannot remain whole after the war. The soldiers who return home are disillusioned, psychologically disoriented, and even physically broken. They are not always welcomed by wives and employers and are far too cynical now to slip back easily into the innocence of the civilian life they left behind. Resolution comes not so much with renewed idealism but with compromise. Men and women such as Homer, the disabled vet in the film, have no choice but to reinvent their identities to accommodate loss. Psychic disorder is everywhere.

Capra's *It's a Wonderful Life*, released the same year, also incorporates transition and sudden uncertainty in small town America. George Bailey's suicide attempt is the result of his deeply shaken idealism; his traditional set of values suddenly looks hollow. Like those returning vets, George needs to die a certain cultural death in order to reorganize his values and relocate their worth. Despite Capra's conservative brand of the American dream, a certain hollowness has crept into his idealism and small town values.

By 1949, the year *A Place in the Sun* went into production, a wealth of commercial films also reflected the dissipation of once-stable notions of marriage and American domestic life, the very same kinds of notions of stability that carried America through the war and saw George Bailey through his crisis. Fred Zinnemann's *Act of Violence*, for example, has a returning vet played by Van Heflin stalked by a fellow vet played by Robert Ryan. Ryan is a nagging reminder of Heflin's unsavory behavior in a POW camp and intrudes on Heflin's home life and terrifies his wife, played by Janet Leigh. Heflin and Leigh are forced to flee Ryan's menacing presence but are unable to escape completely. Their lives are so disrupted they cannot be mended. Their marriage is ripped apart by an emotional destructiveness left over from the war.

In turn, Joseph Mankiewicz's *A Letter to Three Wives* throws disorder into the comfortable domestic setting of East Coast suburbia. The town flirt has allegedly run away with the husband of one of three close female friends, causing each to reevaluate her marriage and home life. When one husband (Kirk Douglas) reassures his wife (Ann Sothern) that life will be back to normal soon enough — the same as it was before — she quips, as if for the rest of the country, "Well, not *exactly* the same."

When Stevens returned from the war, feeling just as decentered as the country and carrying a profound sense of loss, his first artistic response was to return to the hills of San Francisco to film *I Remember Mama*. *A Place in the Sun* was his second response, contingent now on a full investment of his emotional energies in Dreiser's book. His commitment to it stemmed from his personal response to Dreiser's material and from his belief that the story told through his eyes would appeal to a massive American audience. Now he could truly speak, and feel, for a nation.

The Fight for Dreiser

At one point Billy Wilder and Charles Brackett were also interested in adapting *An American Tragedy* for the screen, but the project eventually went to Stevens, who could neither come in on budget nor on time and whose idea of a reality-driven story was a sanguine domestic comedy in search of an appropriate cliché for the time. "Our business is clichés," he said to his friend, Jim Silke, years later, "and clichés are clichés because they are absolutely true."[14] Stevens was always most comfortable with the already proven, the received idea that worked. Since his days at Hal Roach, he successfully employed clichés to get audiences to come to the movies. Ironically, *A Place in the Sun* would be shaped by a personal and cultural angst — a different kind of poetry for him — and audiences would come just the same.

Stevens's resolve to win Dreiser's novel pitted him against Paramount president Barney Balaban and production chief Henry Ginsberg, initiating what would become several years of animosity between them. It was the kind of struggle to obtain a property that Stevens had never known. As a condition of the Liberty buyout, Stevens was legally bound to deliver four films and to begin principal photography on a fifth by July 31, 1951. Before he knew it, he found himself embroiled in months of story meetings instead of an expected production schedule.

Stevens suspected that getting Dreiser's novel would be an uphill battle so he approached it in a roundabout way by suggesting other material first, from *My Dear Secretary* to *The Hero* and then to an adaptation of his friend, Irwin Shaw's *The Young Lions*. He also proposed Humphrey Cobb's *Paths of Glory* and received the same negative response from Paramount that RKO had given him years earlier.

Accustomed to answering mainly to himself — "There can be only one quarterback on a football team," he liked to say — Stevens now found himself negotiating with men who to his mind had little vision and who behaved badly or at the very least ambiguously. His frustration with the studio began with *A Place in the Sun* and let up only after he finished work on *Shane* in 1951 and left Paramount for good.

Stevens first mentioned *An American Tragedy* in a memo to Ginsberg on December 3, 1948: "The studio does . . . own one property whose greatness is so widely acknowledged that it would seem to provide a most likely and satisfactory basis for immediate agreement between us. I refer to *The American Tragedy*. The renowned qualities of this great story would seem to place it far beyond those which now reach us from day-to-day agency circulation."[15] He later said, "I remember I had . . . a choice at that time of making films I wanted to make, a film of *The Naked and the Dead;* but I also had the opportunity of putting my hands on Theodore Dreiser's *An American Tragedy,* and the studio seemed to be less happy with the idea of making *An American Tragedy* than of making *The Naked and the Dead*. And it's always a challenge to oppose the studios, so I took the story that they seemed to suffer the most in anticipation of."[16]

Paramount refused to commit to the property, claiming possible copyright conflicts with Patrick Kearny, the author of a play also based on Dreiser's novel (eventually, Kearney received title billing under Dreiser's name). A little later on Stevens believed the project was approved, but Sam Briskin cabled him on January 21, 1949 to say that as Liberty's parent company, Paramount "has disapproved of your selection of Theodore Dreiser's *An American Tragedy* as the story for one your pictures." Stevens had proposed various other titles also. Frustrated and concerned that by now the studio was preventing him from earning a living, he sent Ginsberg a ten-page letter on January 22, 1949 "to clarify our relationship," listing each of his story ideas the studio had rejected, including *Madame Butterfly* (Stevens had begun negotiations with David O. Selznick for Jennifer Jones's services); *Mary and the Fairy (The Red-Blooded Animal)* with a proposed starting date of January 1, 1949 with Jean Arthur and either John Lund or Ray Milland set to star; *The Hero; Road to Rome* (with Ingrid Bergman interested); *Ticket to Mohawk; He Ran All the Way; The Young Lions;* and again *An American Tragedy*. In this letter from the production files, Stevens reminded Ginsberg of discussions they had had with the front office about "developing new personalities," and that *An American Tragedy* "properly developed could make a male star." The book was "one of the greatest stories in the American language," which the studio's 1931 version "had not explored at all." "It was agreed that the property would be charged to me at a cost of $1.00" and that Ginsberg had "mentioned the name of Montgomery Clift as being particularly suitable for the role of 'Griffiths' [and] I expressed great interest in Clift and agreed that he would be desirable." "Weeks of my time have been devoted to the solution of the duties in connection with this. . . . I will stake my professional reputation, which I have been called upon to do many times, on my judgment of this property. . . . Do you want me to produce four photoplays and commence principal photography of a fifth photoplay by July 1, 1951? . . . If so, how do you suggest it be accomplished?"

Ginsberg fired back with an eight-page defense on February 3: "With all due respect for your story judgment . . . the company cannot permit you to set yourself up as the sole and final judge of whether or not a picture will be good in quality, can be produced at proper cost, and be successful at the box office. . . . We refuse to admit that your judgment is better than that of our entire production organization, our sales department, and our New York home office executives combined. . . . Let's stop writing notes and get to work on a basis of mutual understanding."

On March 7, Ivan Moffat (who since the war was Stevens's close associate) recorded a meeting he and Stevens had with front office men Ginsberg, Barney Balaban, Russell Holman, and Sam Briskin, now Ginsberg's assistant. Ginsberg told Stevens that Paramount lacked the "necessary number of comedies" it wanted but rejected Stevens's suggestion that he do *My Dear Secretary*. Stevens knew he was on his way to *An American Tragedy* but offered to do Norman Mailer's novel *The Naked and the Dead*, a story he liked very much. Balaban, Holman, and Briskin said no; they needed a comedy. They said no to Fay Kanin's *Goodbye, My Fancy* and Richard Nash's *The Young and the Fair* and asked Stevens if he had any more story ideas. He said, "It would amount to little for him to do so" since the studio had rejected the ones he had already submitted. Moffat wrote:

[Stevens] pointed out that his time was limited, and that he couldn't afford to let more months slip by in covering basically the same ground as before. . . . He did not work on this sort of basis, where a story had to be visible in all dimensions and values to everyone in the New York and studio front offices before it was agreed upon. He said that what constituted a good story to him was something which it was not always possible to communicate in all aspects to a large bureaucracy for jury-style approval, and that in all his experience good motion pictures did not really stem from this kind of procedure at all. He said that the resources of his own personal experience had been fully explored in the titles previously submitted, and that if the point of all of these had been missed he felt there was slight chance of similar things being accepted in the future. . . . He said that time was running out, and that sooner or later someone would have to pick up the check. He didn't wait for a "great" story . . . all he wanted was that someone agree to let him go ahead and make a picture which he, himself, felt would have a reasonable chance of being worthwhile. He wasn't waiting for the luxury of great stories.

But he found a path leading to Dreiser when during the course of the meeting Russell Holman praised Rodgers and Hammerstein's current Broadway musical, *South Pacific,* and then Arthur Miller's *Death of a Salesman.* Stevens asked Holman whether or not, "on the basis of the story alone, the studio would have been interested in this property for a film." Holman said yes, and Stevens said "that the same latent values which made 'Salesman' so popular also lay in the fundamental theme of 'An American Tragedy.' Both properties touched precisely upon the problems of life as the audience knew it, and that what made the one popular could also be seen in the other, provided preconceptions could be discarded." *An American Tragedy* could be as tremendous as *Death of a Salesman* or *The Snake Pit,* especially if he could update it.

Still Paramount would not commit. Frustrated, Stevens decided his only recourse was to sue the studio. He hired James Marlin McGinnis, a tough San Francisco criminal lawyer who had no ties to Hollywood and no divided loyalties or desire to get along with studio bosses. Stevens later said, "I told him my problem. . . . I said, 'I can't operate if they don't approve of a story, so they're withholding to frustrate.' So he went to New York to tell [them] we'd been wronged."[17] McGinnis also went to Paramount's Los Angeles offices where he similarly "bothered them." Stevens served two lawsuits, one as an employee of the Liberty Company who accused Paramount of "frustrating me from working, in violation of the [Liberty] agreement." For that "I asked them to get us out of the contract, and I asked them damages." A second suit was organized on Stevens's behalf as a stockholder against the Paramount management "because they were frivolous — they held twelve stories from Capra and they turned down all of them, they didn't know what they wanted, and they were incompetent." With the threat of two lawsuits hanging in the balance, "they didn't keep from giving me the straw to make the bricks . . . and we got that picture [*A Place in the Sun*] out without too much trouble, and everything worked fine."[18] Moffat, however, remembered a different ending — with Stevens, who was bad "at selling himself," who "thought his reputation should stand for itself," finally showing the front office a bit more enthusiasm, so to speak. Immediately after, Moffat said, Stevens's office phone rang and Ginsberg gave *An American Tragedy* the green light.[19]

Now Stevens had Dreiser's book and a $2.5 million budget, though a question remained. Much of *An American Tragedy*'s power lay with Clyde Griffiths's false dream of American success measured by money and social position in a capitalist society. How would a story so cunning, so thorough in its criticism of American capitalist society, fare in the hands of a director who thrived in that very system to produce entertainment for the masses? To be true to Dreiser, Stevens would need to find his poetry in the most commercial of venues.

Dreiser Redux: The Production

God, I hate this movie. . . . God, I hate this movie. . . . God, I love this movie!

—John Cassevetes

Contrary to the legend that Stevens acquiesced to Paramount's demands to soften a script initially aligned with Dreiser's dark mood, production notes suggest that the film Stevens promised Paramount was the film he himself wanted: a contemporary love story with a wide appeal to a youthful 1950s audience. As he wrote to Montgomery Clift in New York shortly before shooting began, he was encouraged by how easily Dreiser's novel could be "updated to 1950." Although he got closer to Dreiser when he came to know the author's widow, Helen, who lived in Hollywood and applauded the finished film, there was hardly a question in Stevens's mind that the American box office required a film considerably altered from Dreiser's bleak view of America.

The actress Anne Revere, whom Stevens cast to play George Eastman's mother, told a reporter in the early 1970s that she especially disliked the close-up of Clift and Elizabeth Taylor's famous kiss in *A Place in the Sun* because its overblown romanticism was, for her, a "cover-up for the real story," meaning the blacklist that held a chokehold on the industry during the time of the film's production and halted Revere's career considerably. For Stevens, though, the "real story" behind that kiss — and behind *A Place in the Sun*'s production — was his internal conflict with Dreiser, a writer whose dark view of the world was antithetical to Stevens's simpler, more optimistic view of how movies represent the social world.

Revere recalled reading a first version of the script that was close to

Dreiser's novel, which she called superb. She said the plot and the characters made more sense. George Eastman (based on Dreiser's Clyde Griffiths) was more ambitious and Angela Vickers (based on Dreiser's Sondra Finchley) was mean and spoiled. Alice Tripp (based on Dreiser's Roberta Alden) was much more likeable. It is unlikely that Revere saw an earlier script, however, her comments point to the differences between Stevens and the film's screenwriter, Michael Wilson, in developing the story.

Stevens knew Wilson slightly during the war and also knew him as a Liberty contract writer. Moffat suggested Wilson write the script and that he be followed by Harry Brown. Moffat said, "I thought we should take a very unusual step and have in advance two writers following each other . . . though this was unheard of in those days. . . . Michael Wilson from the point of view of (and fidelity to) Dreiser's story and structure . . . and then [Harvard-educated poet] Harry Brown, who had a very good ear for dialogue, for the more frivolous aspects of life, which would help us with the [Griffiths] family." Harry Brown "had a sense of humor, markedly, and let's say Michael Wilson didn't . . . or at least not the same kind of sense of humor."[20] Brown also had some Hollywood experience: his 1944 novel, *A Walk in the Sun,* was adapted for the screen and he had contributed to several screenplays. Stevens knew of Wilson's affinity for Dreiser as well as Wilson's Communist party affiliation, for which he would be blacklisted shortly after *A Place in the Sun.* Stevens would wrestle with Dreiser by way of Brown and Wilson, with Wilson's pro-Dreiser script altered until it became — with Brown's input — Stevens's version of the story.

Wilson gave Stevens a first draft of a treatment in early April 1949 that was too sympathetic to Dreiser. Stevens thought Wilson needed to be more pliable. As Moffat said, Wilson would have to write what *Stevens* wanted him to write. "Michael was delighted with the assignment, but he objected to the arrangement" of being followed on the script by another writer. "I tried to explain it to him as best as I could. He said, 'Well, what if my script is good?' . . . and I said, 'Well, then, we won't touch it.' Of course I knew that no script was perfect. Wilson had a couple of drafts and then Harry came onto the thing."[21]

An early Wilson treatment, still using Dreiser's names, opens with Clyde in jail about to go to trial for the murder of Roberta Alden.

Another treatment puts Clyde Griffiths in an unemployment line, "like other men there, looking for a new departure." Here Clyde "was born too late; drafted just as the war was ending, discharged from the army late; others already got the jobs at home," Wilson wrote. Clyde later tells Sondra's father, "I was born in a skid row mission. I grew up among failures. Maybe that's why I came to fear failure more than anything in the world. Sometimes I got the feeling I'd been born too late. All the frontiers were closed; all the pie was sliced and divided before I got there. I was even too late for the war. Too young to be a hero, so I became a bellboy—and ate my heart out envying the rich. I was just another punk kid—with no talent, no education, no nothing . . . that's my background."

Stevens rightly rejected this treatise because it made Clyde too wordy and too self-pitying and too self-conscious. The character needed the self-delusion Dreiser gave him and the romantic hopefulness Stevens would supply. Rather than reject Wilson's first draft outright, Stevens was circumspect. He took his time reading it, then asked both Wilson and Moffat into his office. Moffat called this maneuver "typical Stevens stuff":

> He took us to the Boulevard [Hollywood Boulevard] in his Lincoln Continental to buy one or two things. He went into some hardware store and never made one mention of the treatment whatsoever, which had Michael on tenterhooks, of course. So then we went back to his office, and George said, "Ivan, would you mind if I have a few words with Michael?" I did mind, actually, but I left. Michael came up to my office about a half an hour later, white in the face, and he said "Stevens said I wasn't within seventy years of being able to write this and that I had no idea of the thing, what it should be like," and went into details. Stevens said his whole concept was wrong. I think the idea was that it was too close a version of Dreiser's *An American Tragedy* rather than Stevens's. The suggestion was that Michael Wilson had to take a different path and that he would do so under George's guidance.[22]

Moffat thought Stevens planned the maneuver to make Wilson more malleable, to "superimpose his own conceptions onto the script." After all, it was for good reason that writer-producer Bernard Smith once said of him, "Stevens . . . was a story man as well as a script man. He "would tell a writer what scene to write next and how to write it."[23]

"Though Stevens's conception of this film was not yet formed in his mind," Moffat said, "he knew what he didn't want . . . a gloomy, depressing translation of Dreiser's work. He didn't want to start it out in the dreariness of the soup kitchens, which [Clyde's] mother ran . . . [in] gloom and depression and squalor. He wanted a brighter version of the thing, of a young man's aspirations and hopes . . . a romanticization. Also, from the filmmaker's point of view [the squalor] would mitigate against the audience's enjoyment of it. If you begin in the lower depths, as it were, that takes a certain amount of time and he had a young audience that had probably already been depressed."[24]

Wilson adjusted as much as he could to Stevens's vision of the script, even though — to no one's surprise — it changed daily. He went on salary in March 1948 at $500 per week and eventually shared screen credit with Harry Brown. On May 2 his salary rose to $750 per week. Brown followed him; on August 12 he signed on for ten weeks and a flat fee of $10,000. Wilson's conception of Dreiser's "unreal capitalistic dream" changed to George Stevens's romantic story of Clyde Griffiths and Sondra Finchley's love affair. "Stevens was showman enough" and romantic enough to shape a major audience-pleaser, not a political treatise, Moffat recalled. According to Moffat, wherever Stevens could, he excised Wilson's bitter commentary, saying that, "The American youth in the late 1940s and early 1950s wouldn't have had any relationship to . . . the Salvation Army soup kitchen." Appropriately, then, the film's opening shot puts Clyde Griffith — now George Eastman — on the American highway, hitching a ride to the city of his dreams.

Stevens now needed his actors to tender what he anticipated would be a commercial hit. What better way to seduce an audience than to merge art and industry in the faces of the most beautiful actors he could find? He found his beautiful lovers in seventeen-year-old Elizabeth Taylor and twenty-eight-year-old Montgomery Clift — as one critic later called them, "the two most beautiful people in the history of movies, she the female version of him and he the male version of her." The more beautiful the lovers, the more powerful the audience identification, therefore the more tragedy when the lovers fall.

Stevens had seen Montgomery Clift in *The Search* and agreed with Henry Ginsberg that *A Place in the Sun* would make him a star. Stevens went to New York to see Clift, who signed to play Clyde Griffiths on March 23, 1949 at $60,000 for ten weeks of work (including no salary for the first two weeks of overtime and $5,000 per week after that). On April 27, Clift wrote Stevens from New York, "At last I have started reading *An American Tragedy*. I am writing you this meager fact — simply because I can hardly believe it myself. . . . At last I can indulge in the luxury of reading what I want with time to myself. . . . I heard Mike Wilson is working on the script — don't know if it's true, but if so — I'm delighted. Don't let the Front Office open its mouth to you." After a letter back from Stevens, telling him Wilson's script "was falling into place nicely," Clift wrote on May 5, "Victory — I am a third of the way through the book and not an interview in sight, so I shall keep reading until I am finished and then call you . . . it seems a very novel sensation to me to be looking forward to a job as much as I am to this one."

Clift lore has it that Stevens could not tolerate the intrusion of Clift's mentor, Mira Rostova, during shooting and eventually had her banned from the set. Stevens remembered later that Clift — not withstanding Rostova — was "perfect" to work with. He gave it his full attention, Stevens would say in publicity bites for the film.

Casting Elizabeth Taylor was Stevens's idea entirely. His concept of Sondra/Angela emerged directly from Dreiser's description of the moment Clyde first sees Sondra Finchley at the Griffiths home: To Clyde's eyes she was the most adorable, feminine thing he had seen in all his days. Indeed her effect on him was electric and thrilling — arousing in him a curiously stinging sense of what it was to want and not to have, to wish to win and yet to feel almost agonizingly that he was destined not even to win a glance from her.[25] Clyde's electric reaction to Sondra forecasts his tragedy: he knows what it is to want and not to have, perhaps not ever to have. Though he already senses his loss, he is so seduced by the illusion of wealth she brings him, he mistakes the illusion for the truth. Stevens's Angela needed the kind of physical beauty that would drive the illusion and therefore the story forward. She would have to appear so breathtaking that, in Stevens's mind at least, when Clyde walks to the electric chair — taking the audience along with him — he would still believe that his fall was worth it.

Years later Stevens told an audience of film students, "I wanted [Elizabeth Taylor] to be sort of the symbolic girl in the Dreiser story. Dreiser didn't explore much about the characteristics of the women. And this girl was the sort of dream girl for the young American boy who was in reach of his hopes and explorations."[26] Which American boy did Stevens have in mind? Clyde, or perhaps himself? He could have been that "American boy" whose dreams seemed to be within reach after the war. Stevens's camera, Stevens himself, loved Taylor's beauty, enough so that his film was organized around the notion of possessing it. He got MGM to loan Taylor out to him and wrote to Paramount executive William Meiklejohn in May 1949, "Of course our most important problem is solved with Monty Clift, but Sondra must be a 'dream girl,' the kind of a girl that a young man could see at first glance, and find his eyes so fixed upon her that his attention will not turn, nor can it be turned elsewhere. She looks and seems to be the personification of a young man's ideal. Her beauty and poise as well as her wealth and background, must give to this young man the impression that she is unattainable, so that when he discovers that this is not so and that he can have her, he is willing to commit murder and does to bring this about. The only one of whom I am aware could create this illusion and is young enough, 18 or 19, is Elizabeth Taylor." If he chose an actress with less physical allure, Stevens would have had to "let Clift and the picture carry the load. . . . It might appear," he wrote, "that Sondra . . . has only the responsibility that any bright, interesting and attractive girl would have in a love story, but in this case it is more — it is much more. It is the fundamental part of the machinery that goes to make this whole story work in relationship to its audience, and to keep the audience in a frame of mind that is sympathetic to all that it portrays." Taylor got the part.

Casting George Eastman's cousin, Earl, brought in young hopefuls that included the nineteen-year-old future producer Robert Evans before Keefe Brasselle was cast. But casting the important part of Roberta Alden/Alice proved trickier. Roberta needed to be strong enough to carry the burden of her pregnancy and still elicit sympathy from the audience, but not so strong that she might overpower Clift's essentially weak character or derail the story from its drive to possess the illusive Sondra/Angela. Cathy O'Donnell was Stevens's first choice to play Roberta, but after talking with Moffat he decided she was "too soft and feminine." Stevens also considered actresses such as Donna Reed and Ruth Roman, and later remembered a conversation he had with Barbara Bel Geddes, who also wanted the part. "I said, 'Barbara, if you play that part — and she had all that kind of thing that's humanly seductive — you play that girl, and when the boat turns over and you go to the bottom of the lake, the film goes with it.'"[27]

Then the idea of casting Shelley Winters came to him; he called it "an inspired afterthought" to O'Donnell (Winters later said that Stevens was down to his last actress when he agreed to see her). She had enough strength of character and could appear sympathetic but not overly so. In the late 1940s, however, Winters projected herself as a blonde bombshell, an image she claimed was hoisted on her by Universal. The effect was strong enough that Moffat felt apprehensive about casting her. He told Stevens that she was too sexy, but Stevens believed the bombshell act was only a cover. Though he himself harbored doubts that she could appear plain enough for the part he decided to meet with her. He set up a meeting at the Hollywood Athletic Club but Winters never arrived. After waiting for what seemed a long time, Stevens made his way to the exit then noticed a mousy-looking woman in drab clothes sitting at a table in the back of the room. It was Winters, who convinced Stevens she could play Roberta Alden. She tested for the role at the end of September 1949 and was signed two days later.

Sondra and Clyde were now renamed Angela Vickers and George Eastman. If their love affair was to be the emotional centerpiece of the film, Roberta — now Alice Tripp — needed a major revision from the way Dreiser wrote her: likeable and attractive, possessing "so much hope and vigor" that she seems "above the average of the girls" in the factory. Winters wanted to play Roberta the way Dreiser wrote her, but Stevens disagreed, which caused some friction between them and frustrated Clift as well, who sided with Winters. But Stevens needed a Roberta who was close to being dour. "There's more to it than poverty that squelches her," he later said, "she lives a very homely life . . . maybe I loaded the dice. Maybe in the Dreiser book she's more acceptable physically . . . [but] if this girl is an attractive girl, when she leaves us, certainly the boy is now accused of murder." Alice became "the kind of a girl a man could be all mixed up with in the dark, and wonder how the hell he got into it in the daylight."[28]

Dreiser: The Road Not Taken

A lot of the film was anti-Dreiser and we had a
lot of conflicts about that. The thing was recut to
that effect. . . . It was shorter and more poignant
and made Clift almost a hero.

—Ivan Moffat

Before shooting began, Stevens had what he thought was a successful revision of Theodore Dreiser to invigorate his audience and give the film,
as Wilson put it, "a soaring quality that marks great tragedy." To this
end, Stevens worked painstakingly to create a love story of immense
emotional and physical proportions. George and Angela's love was elevated and Alice was made unsympathetic, almost an interruption to the
love story. Stevens turned Dreiser's sympathetic factory girl into a visually uninteresting and eventually emotionally threatening woman whose
only visual function is to remind the audience of Angela's great beauty
and social status. Angela, in turn, changed from Dreiser's spoiled, selfish
socialite who considers Clyde as a summer fling girl into a woman who
matures emotionally and truly loves a man far beneath her in social
stature. "Something very important can emerge from the idea that [An-
gela] becomes a mature human being at the climax of the picture," Wilson wrote in a memo to Stevens. "What I have in mind for this scene
would emphasize that [Angela] realizes at the end that both she and
[George], deeply involved in the adult world and its ways, are yet children in matters of experience." Angela would be worth the price George
pays to reach for her, enough so that he would walk to the execution
chamber, call up from memory the image of her face and look heavenward even in his darkest moment.

The view of Angela is so idealized that her pivotal love scene with
George Eastman raises them to mythic stature. In a now-famous 2 A.M.
rewrite, Stevens penned Clift and Taylor's passionate love scene to fill
the entire screen and with it the audience's full consciousness. He shot
the scene completely in close-ups with a six-inch lens and in doing so
practically merges George's and Angela's faces with the spectator's. In
the scene, Angela invites George to a party and once there, panics believing that they are being watched. She pulls him outside onto the veranda, where they profess their love for each other, their faces and their

passion filling up every inch of the screen. "I wanted the words to be rushed," Stevens said. "Monty had to let loose — he was so enormously moved by her. Elizabeth must be compelled to tell him how wonderful and exciting and interesting he is, all in the space of a few seconds . . . it had to be like nothing they had ever said to anyone before."[29]

The scene included new dialogue Stevens wrote and handed to Taylor just before he shot the scene. She had to say to Clift, "Tell Mama. . . . Tell Mama all," and she buckled: "Excuse me, but what the hell is this?" Stevens later recalled that Taylor "thought it was outrageous she had to say that — she was jumping into a sophistication beyond her time."[30] Clift and Taylor rehearsed the scene; then Stevens shot it, this time using three cameras with Stevens going from one side of their faces to another. He wanted them to speak as fast as they could so as to build up the tempo and give their words a sense of breathlessness.

Stevens edited the sequence by setting up two projectors placed side by side. He viewed the reels of Clift and Taylor's close-ups simultaneously on a screen covering an entire wall, "then spliced the film together" to get the effect of the camera rolling "from one face to another, each dissolving into the other." The finished scene gives the effect of the lovers' breathlessness that transcends specific time and place. Stevens called it "a mood that was at once primitive and basic, a kind of preordained meeting."[31]

As the production neared its end, Stevens continued to move painstakingly, shooting each scene from every possible angle. Over the course of shooting, disagreements with Wilson on story structure were not exclusively Dreiser-related. He vetoed Wilson's idea of an intimate jury scene with, in Wilson's words, "a montage of cross cuts between the summary arguments of each attorney and a scene where two jurors hold out stubbornly before they give in." Stevens wanted it briefer. In fact, after Wilson and Brown finished the script and departed the production, Stevens and Moffat trimmed and even altered the scene. It was initially written to be suspenseful, with audiences moved to wonder, "Is he guilty or not guilty?" but after it was cut the dynamics between Clift and Raymond Burr, who played the district attorney, forced another change: "Due to the performances of the actors, it took too long and it occurred to George and myself — the screenwriters were long gone — that Clift's performance under interrogation and the terror was moving in [the direction] that he was vulnerable . . . that he was almost being impaled by the performance of Raymond Burr, and he reacted with such vulnerable action, and [seemed] almost lost in the terror, and we decided that it couldn't be a question of 'is he guilty or not,' but that the created atmosphere was almost that he's a victim. So it's a foregone conclusion: how is he going to react to the verdict of 'guilty,' because it seemed almost to be inevitable."[32] The rewritten scene ensured that George Eastman became a victim, garnering him some of the audience sympathy that might otherwise have even gone to Alice Tripp.

As Moffat saw Stevens diverging from Dreiser he urged him to keep some of Dreiser's prose by using "the subjective voice" through a "voice-over for Clyde." Fearing Wilson and Brown might "slough off" on this, he offered to "go through the original novel, marking every passage which has a value to us that could not be gained in a better way than by use of this voice . . . in many of these passages lie some of Dreiser's best writing, which otherwise will be lost. At least we will be able to save some of this golden material." But voiceovers detract from the power of the visual image and are not a staple of Stevens's cinema: Moffat's suggestion repeatedly went unheeded.

Actual shooting began on October 4, 1949 on the Paramount lot and moved to Lake Tahoe, Nevada for location shooting in January 1950. Stevens played Franz Waxman's score when they were on the set to get the actors in the right mood, and before asking them to rehearse their scenes in silence with looks and gestures. Conflicts arose when Winters tried to keep her character close to Dreiser's concept, but Stevens kept Alice pared down. He argued with Clift, who told others he could never understand Stevens's way of working with actors. He thought Stevens "abrasive and manipulative," and as the death march scene grew closer he often retreated to bouts of silence, as if he were rehearsing for it. Stevens wanted him to imagine some terrifying emotion as he walks to the death chamber; Clift argued that a man on his way to the electric chair has no expression except perhaps a visible numbness. "He labeled George Stevens a craftsman. He was bitterly disappointed in what he felt was his lack of flexibility, his lack of imagination with actors. 'George preconceives everything through a viewfinder,' he said."[33]

Winters recalled a different Stevens, in hindsight one she tended to idealize. She said of the scene where Alice goes seeking an abortion,

"I remember he sort of sprung it on me. . . . It was in the book but it wasn't in the script. And when we came to do it, I said, 'Alright, how do you want me to do this?' He said, 'you decide.' Which was his usual answer. He didn't want you to plan anything you were going to do, he wanted it just to happen . . . he also said, 'If you can do it without words it's much stronger.'" Moffat and Stevens later told another side of the story: Winters wanted to cry in the scene, but Stevens refused to let her. After they bumped heads for a time, Stevens ended the disagreement, saying, "Shelley, I'll keep the cameras rolling until you begin to cry."[34]

Before settling on Lake Arrowhead, Stevens and Moffat visited numerous locations for the lake scenes, with Stevens one time alarming a boat keeper at Arrowhead by remarking [as a joke], "This would be a good, isolated place if you wanted to kill your girlfriend, don't you agree?"[35] For the important drowning scene, Wilson's early drafts included close-ups of George desperately searching for Alice after they fall into the lake. The shots would have left no doubt that George is innocent. Winters remembered that Stevens promised her and Clift that he would use stunt doubles to go into the water but later changed his mind. Winters reminded him that the lake was bottomless and that one of the oars might hit her on the head after she tumbled into the water. Seconds later Stevens jumped into the water fully clothed and after swimming around the raft and climbing on it, jumped out again — to give her an example.

The shooting script contains a less distant, less objective view of the drowning, but in the editing room Stevens cut shots of the oars hitting George and Alice over the head after the boat tips over and they fall into the water. Shots of George trying desperately to save Alice were also cut in favor of a completely objective shot of the tragedy without close-ups. Just when George and Alice fall into the lake, the camera pulls back for a long distance shot, obscuring them, leaving the audience to question what happens. This is just the suspense Stevens wants. During the year-long editing process, he cut the scene even further, from thirty minutes down to a brief four.

George Eastman and Angela Vickers's on-screen passion was even better served by the apparent attraction Clift and Taylor had for each other off screen. Their closeness to each other was apparent to everyone on the set (before he cooled to her) and served not only to cover-up

Clift's homosexuality but also to drive the engine of studio exploitation to find the film a title. Wilson's early treatments used titles such as *A Modern Story* and *An American Story,* and though the studio at one point even created an ad campaign for the title *The Prize,* Paramount publicist Russell Holman found another of Wilson's titles, *The Lovers,* more appealing, not just because it mirrored real life but because it effortlessly merged art and advertising dollars. He cabled a memo to J. H. Karp in October 1949:

> Particularly after seeing at the studio last week footage shot so far on current George Stevens production, I strongly urge setting immediately "The Lovers" as final title of this picture. Title ideally fits picture since both script and footage indicate primary motivating force of whole drama is love between Clift and Taylor. This will also be picture's primary interest for world audience both before and when they see it. . . . Additionally, Clift and Taylor are already being linked together press wise, as witness newspaper and publicity stills from their presence together at "Heiress" preview, page 32 of current Time Magazine, etc. . . . In addition to being provocative particularly in connection [with] Clift and Taylor, "The Lovers" is high quality title as witness use of word "lovers" in literary classics such as D. H. Lawrence's "Sons and Lovers," etc. . . . Such an action will at once have an electrifying effect on entire Paramount international sales and theatre organizations and I believe set picture up with general public as a must-see particularly if we keep linking this title with Clift and Taylor publicity wise. It is such a marvelous natural that it would be a terrible showmanship shame not to use it. It can be difference of $750,000 or more gross on this picture.

The Lovers promised what the studio wanted: literary import and box office gross potential — but no title was satisfactory to Stevens or Paramount at this point. Stevens eventually offered one hundred dollars to anyone who could come up with a title. Then, sitting in his office one day, Moffat had a prophetic dream: he envisioned a statement made by Kaiser Wilhelm in 1911 that Germany demanded its place in the sun. He went to Stevens's office to tell him he had come up with a title, and Stevens asked Moffat to translate it into three different languages before saying "That's it!" Moffat never received the one hundred dollars.

It took Stevens nineteen months to edit over 400,000 feet of film, after which *A Place in the Sun* had seven previews. After the last preview

Moffat suggested changes in Waxman's score, beginning with the opening credit sequence. "Where the main title music clears and Monty's face appears looking at camera," he said of the opening shot, "the music was belligerent to the point where it takes away from our deliberately gentle, calm and urbane opening. It leads one to expect an immediate storm of bullets — not a girl on a poster, and creates an over-anxious mood in the audiences." Waxman's music for the film's opening sequence was eventually replaced by a passage composed by Daniele Amfithatrof. Several other sequences used music composed by Victor Young.

Moffat thought that some of Waxman's score was heavy-handed, even forcing a reaction from the audience. In the scene where Angela learns that George has been accused of murdering Alice Tripp, she walks upstairs to her room and faints to the floor, her fall reflected in a wall of mirrors. Moffat wrote: "The music *anticipates* Angela's collapse, instead of letting it come as a sudden shock. Why should the audience be forewarned of this — its value was shock and suddenness? Only the slightest, gentlest touch of music — and then only after she has fallen. She is a snowflake, not a rhinoceros — when a princess falls, it should not be the Walls of Jericho."

Moffat, an acquaintance of Marion Davies, later recalled how he screened the film in Davies's living room (while William Randolph Hearst lay upstairs dying) thinking she might get it some advance publicity in Hearst's newspapers. Paramount was not happy, wanting no advance word out on it.

A Place in the Sun premiered at the Fine Arts Theatre in Los Angeles on August 14, 1951 and received generally laudatory reviews from critics across the country. More than one reader of the novel breathed a sigh of relief if only because Dreiser's often elephantine prose had at last been tamed. The film critic for the *Hollywood Reporter* was almost grateful to note that Stevens "successfully reduced Dreiser's verbiage and his sprawling narrative style." This was "plainly a task for a patient, painstaking man." He added, "Reducing, actually, is not the word. What Stevens really does in his superb production and direction is to sharpen and refine a great literary work into a great motion picture." *Newsweek*'s critic called *A Place in the Sun* "one of the most brilliant films to come out of Hollywood in years but disliked Stevens's omission of George Eastman's early years. "George Eastman is presented to the audience in full manhood, without his poverty-stricken background as the son of street-singing Evangelist parents, without his contrasting apprenticeship as a bellhop at the Hotel Green-Davidson, and without his naive dream of marrying the boss's daughter and living happily ever after. . . . As a result, both the film and the [story] lose significance. Unlike Griffiths, Eastman is tentative, even weak, and more to be mothered than censured."[36]

Fifteen years later in 1966, Stevens sued the NBC network for what he considered their mutilation of *A Place in the Sun* when they telecast it broken up by commercials. Stevens lost the case when the judge declared that the "power and strength of the film" ultimately was not destroyed.

"Tell Mama All"

Stevens's love story served a purpose. Faithful to his own temperament and artistic responsiveness, Stevens collaborated (unconsciously perhaps) with Paramount and constructed a beautiful fiction aimed at convincing postwar American audiences no less than himself that neither his nor America's soul had darkened. He believed that the process of film going was something entirely estranged from the real world. He believed in the romantic notion that audiences would feel uplifted as they "created"—in the watching—his impassioned story of love and loss. "He knew how awful the world is," his friend, Jim Silke, said. "And yet he stayed the romantic . . . he [had] faith that the romance [would] work, and that somehow or other it was embodied in those films."[37] There could be no greater exhilaration than the knowledge of an audience of spectators bringing Dreiser's great story to life.

Stevens continued to believe that he and his audiences could outdistance the darkness while sitting in that safe movie theatre. Not as rigorous a thinker as Dreiser, he translated his version of the novel for the screen by recasting it into what he wanted to see, and filtered through an imagination formed entirely by the movies. He spoke publicly about Dreiser's book, during production and in the years after, very often interpreting the novel by submerging its politics. He seemed to ignore Dreiser's deep conviction that society fails Clyde Griffiths, and instead saw Clyde as a poor soul who made wrong decisions yet made them on his own. He said, "It seemed to me, we were examining . . . the law, as far as the taking of a life is concerned; He [Eastman] had considered [murder], contemplated it . . . but at the time that the girl lost her life, his intention was not to kill her. And it was an enormous dilemma on his part, and it was an accident. . . . He did consider it, he did create the circumstances that brought the accident about. And so there we are. A thing of that character, I suppose, is not only unsatisfactory for the poor individual that is torn and dragged by his emotions in a situation like this, but also it is a large dilemma for the jury, judge and audience, we who are responsible in a community for law and order."[38]

On some occasions, though, Stevens could embrace Dreiser's determinism, and saw George Eastman as someone who was "dragged by his emotions" rather than in control of them. Still he believed that George Eastman's tragedy was a crisis of "morality" and that the fate of any moral universe rests with the actions of a single man. It was natural that he think this. His film sense told him that audiences see themselves fully in that single face up on the screen and that this identification itself creates an "enormously" positive response in them.

Stevens even told Robert Hughes that George Eastman could be called a fortunate man, "I think a young man that had . . . the extraordinary misfortune of having a mundane ideal presented to him in the most glamorous form — the girl, the money, the success, and what you've never hoped to gain — is an extraordinary experience, even if it's only envisaged, but to envisage it, and then tortured by it, in actuality is, expanding the opportunity for life's awareness to an extraordinary degree."[39]

On one hand, the film experience is exciting in and of itself. On the other hand, Stevens simply did not want to make a depressing motion picture. To this end, he told a reporter from the Los Angeles Times just prior to the release of *A Place in the Sun* that there was "no place for futility" in any of his pictures. "When Eastman goes to the electric chair . . . the audience feels a tremendous desire to live." George Eastman's death "is the same as a happy ending because it is simply another means of charging an audience's vitality."[40]

Yet *A Place in the Sun* belies every bit of optimism Stevens sought for it, emerging instead from the tragedy he saw in Europe, whether or not he knew it. *A Place in the Sun* is Stevens's first elegy (the second would be *Shane*), a story shaped by a certain sadness after the war, an awareness,

conscious or not, that the world has tragic dimensions, and George Eastman is his first ambiguous — and ambivalent — protagonist. Eastman is
a sign of things to come. Beginning with *A Place in the Sun*, Stevens's
men and women are tinted with a deep seriousness and hold a somber
view of the world. Shane rides in and out of the frame a forlorn, world-
weary traveler; Bick Benedict ends up on the floor of Sarge's hamburger
joint in the middle of the salad and dirty dishes, finally a hero in his ac-
knowledgement of racism's disruptiveness in postwar Texas. George
Eastman walks to the electric chair and into an immutable darkness. He
might walk there thinking of the beauty of Angela's kiss, he might even
look heavenward as he goes — just the way Stevens wants him to — but
he walks there nonetheless. He never would have before in a Stevens
film.

With *A Place in the Sun* Stevens is the speaker in a poem who is ambivalent about accepting his own sense of darkness and disorder. Both he and
the film — personified in George Eastman — want the one thing that can
fight off that darkness, but it is the very thing neither can fully possess in
this fragmented time: the false dream of wholeness that Angela Vickers
promises. Angela is the fantasy that dangles before George's (and our)
eyes, and the closer he gets to her the more his dream and his life dissi-
pate. He tries but never reaches the heights of the flickering neon that
flashes the name "Vickers" above his boardinghouse room.

When George Eastman appears on the highway in *A Place in the
Sun*'s opening scene, hitching a ride to the city of Carthage — the mythical city of destruction that Dreiser calls Lycurges — he is no longer
Dreiser's Clyde Griffiths. Stevens and his writers have essentially lopped
off the first half of Dreiser's novel to focus only on the love triangle between George, Angela, and Alice. Doing this, Stevens cuts off George's
entire past. Standing on the highway in his leather jacket — Stevens
called him a vet — he is bereft of his own history and comes from
nowhere specific. Putting George on that highway, Stevens seems to be
reaching back to America's literary past. George arrives an archetypal
figure from our collective imagination: an American Adam, a Natty
Bumpo, an innocent — a character the critic R. W. Lewis described as
"an individual emancipated from history, happily bereft of ancestry,
standing alone, self-propelling, self-reliant, his moral position prior to

experience, his future before him." He has nowhere to go but into his future and nothing to prevent him from going there," Lewis says. "He signals the innocence and the exuberance of a nation Emerson called "forward-leaning."[41]

But George Eastman arrives on that highway in *postwar* America, a place of shifting identities; he is American cinema's symbol of ambiguity. Arriving on the landscape with no identifiable history, George is a tenuous, uncertain hero in an uncertain time. As he stands with his back to the camera and then turns around to face us during the film's opening credits, George Eastman is as unclear to us as he is to himself. He will come to life only when he meets Angela Vickers, and even after that he is inarticulate, confused and emotionally under drawn. A Clift biographer later wrote, "George Eastman is a definitive Clift creation, and Stevens must take credit for coaxing it out of him. As one writer put it, Monty 'was born to play doomed men,' and the callow, cringing bumpkin who arrives in the city is almost visibly doomed. Here is an anti-hero *par excellence,* not because he is evil or scheming but because he is so uncertain, so flustered, so, at moments, *blank.*"[42] George is no longer Dreiser's misguided, scheming opportunist but Stevens's sad, doomed, beautiful, and entirely sympathetic loner.

George is the unstable end of the Eastman family, whose name appears everywhere in the film's earliest shots: atop his uncle's factory, on his uncle's business card (in a close-up), and on the door to his uncle's office. When George goes to find his uncle, another "Eastman" configuration appears. George's cousin, Earl, steps off the Eastman building elevator just as George steps on, the camera framing them and catching their physical likeness — collapsing their identities as if to point out their differences: though Earl Eastman is almost George's physical double, their futures lie worlds apart. George will never reach the position Earl was born into and takes for granted.

But the camera has already identified George in the film's very first scene. Standing on the highway George looks up and sees a billboard, on it a woman in a bathing suit. Above her, the advertisement reads, "It's an Eastman." It is simple: the moment George looks at the billboard, he sees (and is owned by) the film's central image: a woman who holds the world of the story within her. George looks at billboard and a wave of pleasure crosses his face, indicating a partial coming-into-identity that will be completed a few moments later when he first sees Angela Vickers at his uncle's house. For now, though, three symbols collapse together on the highway: the slogan "It's an Eastman," the woman in a bathing suit, and George's face in close-up becoming one to form a single identity and meaning. George is an "Eastman," but in this shot an Eastman is also a woman wearing a bathing suit. The image of the woman is the only agency of value through which George can find identity (what little he *does* find) so he can enter into society. With this image taking hold of him in the film's very first scene, George's life is determined by the will the female represented by Angela Vickers and Alice Tripp. Since he is ambiguous, incomplete, his life hangs in the balance of their desire and actions. After all, both Angela and Alice are given a musical theme in *A Place in the Sun* while George is not. He cannot make the journey alone; he comes into being only through identification with Angela and Alice. He either desires Angela or aches to be rid of Alice when she threatens his place in the sun.

Stevens had already expressed the desire to return to a mother figure with *I Remember Mama*. After Americans returned from Europe, the image of the mother held a promise of nurturing and healing for a nation. But her figure is so heavily idealized in *A Place in the Sun*, she can be more easily *imagined* than truly found. "I think he idolized women," Jim Silke said of Stevens. "They are the anchors of experience" for him and for the films. . . . Women make men get interested in the moment itself . . . the intimacy of the moment. . . . [Stevens] just loved the idea of women ruling. . . . George and I used to talk about that."[43]

The motive that drives *A Place in the Sun* forward is George Eastman's *and* the camera's desire to possess one female, Angela, personified in Elizabeth Taylor's beauty — a perfectly formed, seemingly nurturing but entirely idealized configuration of womanhood that seems to hold the promise of wholeness and acceptance. Silent, inarticulate, already debilitated, George falls into her arms not so much from his own free will but from the lack of any context of his own to contain him.

George, a son in search of a mother and nurturer, drifts without real direction until the moment he first sees Angela at his uncle's house. Invited there to meet his extended family, George suffers the Eastmans' disdain (though he hardly seems aware of it). Stevens's long and medium shots suggest the emotional distance between George and his family.

Then, the moment his aunt asks him about his mother and her religious work, Angela bursts through the front door and into the foyer, bringing with her the lilting, romantic theme Waxman wrote for her character. She interrupts the conversation and installs herself in George's "mother's" place, usurping her authority. In the scene's only close-up George is born the moment he stares at her in wonderment. He finds his purpose in the film: to regard Angela as the possible source of a dream — his emotional and social nourishment and sense of well-being. Angela walks through the door and the world begins.

Stevens's camera does not sexualize Angela as much as it *idealizes* her. She is breathlessly soft-spoken yet powerful to George. Stevens puts them in her car repeatedly: she holds George in her arms, he looks up at her beside him, his head rests on her shoulder or breast. She interrupts him on the phone to his mother at the Eastmans' party, chiding, "It's me, Mama." Together at Loon Lake, Angela sits with her back to the camera, her arms outstretched the length of the frame. She tells George it is her lake, and visually she possesses it fully. She owns the world George wants: it is made of money, power, and nourishment. In their important love scene on the veranda, their faces in extreme close-up, Angela beckons to George, "Tell Mama. Tell Mama all."

George has already seen Angela when he meets Alice Tripp at the factory. Alice traverses the storyline going from lonely, to annoying, to threatening. George and Alice's romance is tentative, born of loneliness. Most of their scenes together occur in Alice's bedroom around her bed, which is often the centerpiece of the frame. Stevens and Paramount spoke of the film's intended "sex angle" to bring in the younger audiences, but sexual feelings between George and both women seem impossible to manage, especially for someone with George's unstable identity. Angela is too idealized, Alice too cloying. Having sex with Alice *almost* seems George's fatal mistake; Alice's pregnancy destroys even further his tentative grasp of Angela's world. Angela is desirable; Alice is unremarkable. The film prefers *desire* as its subject and must be rid of Alice, who interrupts George's desire of Angela. So the story sets out to punish Alice, extracting energy from her and eventually killing her. She often looks at the ground when she speaks, and her scenes often look dreary. The film pushes her toward her watery demise from the start as Waxman's theme for her is immediately linked to the sound of a heartbeat that anticipates her death. From her first scenes with George, she is linked to boat and water imagery, as if she has no other purpose than to drown in Loon Lake. On the walk back to her room after they meet at the movies, Alice and George both begin using boat imagery. Alice tells George, "If you're an Eastman, you're not in the same boat with *anyone*." Later, when George tells her he has not seen his family since their initial invitation, she tells him, "It's better not to be with the Eastmans; you're in the same boat as the rest of us." During the same walk, she tells George she cannot swim and is deathly afraid of water.

In expending so much energy in pursuit of Angela Vickers, the film impoverishes Alice, visually and emotionally. Her room is suffocatingly small and she frequently voices her disapproval of money. "It gets you into trouble," she tells George. Later on, when they later drift on the lake, she tries to convince him that they can be happy without money. "It's the little things that count," she says. Alice is a forbidding reminder of the dissipation that stalks George Eastman. Though Dreiser, and later Ivan Moffat, invested her with a youthful exuberance, Stevens changes her into a force that is first static, then menacing, and ultimately deadly.

By the time George takes Alice out into the boat, as they symbolically drift from daylight into darkness, her threat overwhelms him. In the boat, the close-up distorts Alice's face; she appears hideously large. In the boat together, Alice dwarfs George with a deadening kind of oppression — the opposite of a dream. The pain on his face is enough that in Stevens's camera the face dissolves into a shot of the dark trees and the lake; George almost wishes to disappear. To his horror, Alice tells him they are like "the only two people in the world" and that they are "not going anywhere. . . . We can just drift," she says. Her menace so overpowers George (and Stevens) that the frame cannot relinquish her. The close-up of Alice in the boat undermines the close-up of George and Angela kissing on the veranda earlier. When she stands up to go to George, the boat overturns and she and George fall into the water. The shot implies, whether meaning to or not, that she causes her own death. Immediately after the fall, Stevens pulls the camera back to a long distance shot of the lake and the surrounding trees, offering no evidence to the audience to implicate George in Alice's death. It does not matter; George has really been damaged, deadened, from the start.

With Alice's death George's hopes for a life with social position are dashed and Angela is lost to him. His life is all but over. Before he leaves Angela and runs into the forest they stand before her parents' house, holding onto each other. He holds her as if for his very life and buries his face in her shoulder. He knows his dream is over and he sobs into her body as if to acknowledge the huge proportions of his loss. Though the moment is an intimate one for George and Angela, it also carries broad public signification. Moffat wrote Stevens notes for the scene, echoing the mood Stevens creates: "[George] is now clutching the last and greatest symbol of a life he knows is doomed. It is . . . the knowledge of the ending of life that feeds this passion. . . . This is the moment when the audience gets its reward — the reward it must be given in full. . . . We can see not only how perfect it would have been, but that they were both young and both good for each other in every sense."

In this important scene Stevens maintains his uneasy relationship with Dreiser. He has changed Dreiser's Sondra into Angela, a girl in love with George rather than a girl dangling him as a summer fling. Stevens has made his love story. Still, when George sobs with the knowledge of a tragedy bearing down on him he embraces Dreiser's fundamental subject: the love of illusion and the tragedy of its loss.

After the war Stevens understood first-hand the heartbreak and failure of George Eastman's life. But he nevertheless believed that audiences needed cinema's power to invigorate and to romanticize — no matter the story told. The promise held out by Angela Vickers/Elizabeth Taylor's allure was a large part of that power to invigorate. Believing this, he took Dreiser's novel and fashioned it for a mass audience, for a nation. Now a piece of popular entertainment, Dreiser's novel will be known to the massive movie going public through Stevens's eyes — broad and romantic until the film's very last shot. "You'll find a better world than this one, George," a fellow inmate tells George Eastman as he walks to the death chamber. He has already found that better world as the camera replays *A Place in the Sun*'s great love scene: the moment George and Angela kiss out on the veranda. Their kiss is so huge it fills the screen and we cannot help but be implicated in it; yet it is so intimate we think we trespass. It is a kiss, a moment even, that Whitman might have dreamed up: an instance when two lovers kiss and with that act create a poem, therefore a culture with that poem. When George and Angela kiss, all America is kissing.

In a Dark Place

George Stevens came down to DeMille's chair
and he said, "By the way, C. B., when I was up to
my ass in mud at Bastogne, how were the capital
gains doing back home?"
           —Elia Kazan, *A Life*

While still in production on *A Place in the Sun,* Stevens accepted without hesitation two stories Paramount offered him; they would help him fulfill his obligation and loosen his ties to the studio. One story was Jack Schafer's novel, *Shane.* The other was a darker drama, *Something to Live For,* scripted by Dwight Taylor and supposedly based on the life of his mother, the actress Laurette Taylor, and her battle with alcohol. Stevens began shooting *Something to Live For* with Joan Fontaine and Ray Milland in May 1950, but after an August 1951 preview Paramount held up its release until March 1952 when it was met with poor reviews and a meager box office reception.

In the midst of work on all three films, Stevens became involved in another kind of story — a real-life Hollywood drama that erupted in the Directors Guild, on whose board of directors Stevens sat. The Guild faced dark hours in October 1950 when, in the spirit of anti-communist zealousness sweeping the industry, a conservative faction of its members, led by Cecil B. DeMille, attempted to oust its president, Joseph Mankiewicz, who was a Jew and a liberal. In Mankiewicz's absence, De-Mille and his cohorts had passed the "Mandatory Loyalty Oath" (in essence, a second oath to the one all directors legally had to sign). Upon his return Mankiewicz wanted to call a membership meeting to discuss it, whereupon DeMille sprang into action to oust Mankiewicz, implying that he was a fellow traveler and a pinko. A meeting was held on October 20 during which Stevens denounced DeMille's behavior and resigned from the board of directors. He told Kevin Brownlow, "It was a goddamned conspiracy . . . it was the most thrilling experience. . . .

I drove 50 miles up the road to Ventura and back, I was so exhilirated by a victory [that] had been won over the McCarthy thing."[44]

There were enemies to be slain in this dark time. The war had been won in Europe but a certain kind of menace had followed the boys home. Small victories were won against some kinds of villains here at home, the kind Stevens and his fellow members such as John Ford and John Huston had waged in the Directors Guild that October night. But it was still a precarious time.

Menacing images show up as well in *Something to Live For*, a film Stevens may not have had his heart in as much as *A Place in the Sun* and *Shane*, but which nevertheless displays a lyricism (no doubt aided by Franz Waxman's lilting score) that raises it out of the ashes, the place to which many critics at the time relegated the film. As the alcoholic actress Jenny Carey, Joan Fontaine conveys a wistful quality, a softness that is clearly touching to Stevens. The married man with whom she falls in love, Alan Miller (Ray Milland) is a prototype for Stevens, for men returning home after the war who set out to do the right thing and re-enter society. Alan sets out to help the alcoholic Jenny through her crisis and onto a new, fulfilling life. When the two fall in love, it is the film's central moral crisis. The menace is all around: the liquor bottles and glasses that take up much of Stevens's frame; the sometimes off-kilter images of rooms and the people in them. In the end, Alan and Jenny part, both committed to upholding the social rules already set in place. In spite of the temptation all around them, the villainous imagery and the emotions that almost seduce them, now in the early 1950s Stevens knows which path — albeit sad — to take.

6

The Art of Gun Slinging

Shane

The poet's particular relation to his culture — his
self-imposed obligation to make the best possible use of the language he is given — is such as
to put him at the center of the web of communications which gives his culture its characteristic
style and spirit.

— Roy Harvey Pearce, *The Continuity of American Poetry*

The war is all over this conversation — and all
over *Shane.*

— George Stevens, Ohio State University, 1973

Stevens's troubles with Paramount were by no means limited to getting
A Place in the Sun green lighted. As he edited that picture and began
preparing *Something to Live For* (originally titled *Mr. and Mrs. Anonymous*), he could still not get the studio to commit to projects he suggested
or start dates he proposed on projects they did okay; this tension went on
for months and followed him to *Shane*'s production. He wrote to Henry
Ginsberg on April 20, 1950, that he expected the studio to "fulfill completely" all of its obligations to him so that he would not be prevented
"from beginning principal photography of my fifth picture under that
contract by July 31, 1951."[1]

While still editing *A Place in the Sun* and about to go into production on *Something to Live For* Stevens received a memo from Ginsberg telling him about a vehicle Paramount planned for Alan Ladd called *Shane:* "Herewith story and treatment entitled *Shane,* which we would like you to consider for one of your two remaining pictures after Mr. and Mrs. Anonymous. This property is now being supervised by one of our studio producers, but no serious problem would be involved in re-assigning it to you, and we are prepared to do so if you like it."[2] The studio wanted Ladd in the picture, Ginsberg said, "after he first makes *This Is Dynamite* and *Detective Story.*" But there was no special loyalty to him. "If you like the story but prefer not to wait for Mr. Ladd and the picture could be cast with another star comparable or nearly comparable to him and still remain within reasonable budget," Ginsberg wrote, "that would be satisfactory to us."

Stevens asked for the assignment, not only because a story about the Western frontier appealed to him personally but also because taking *Shane* put him one step closer to being out the door at Paramount. In a letter back to the studio Stevens accepted "regardless" of the studio's past "omissions" that it would "perform all of the terms and conditions of the contract." In the midst of his continuing disagreements with the front office Stevens could not, at some level, have missed the irony here, since *Shane* was the story of a family of homesteaders battling villainous cattle ranchers so that the homesteaders could keep what little property was theirs. In a larger sense still, *Shane* could very well have been a metaphor for the machinations of the postwar studio system as it began to disintegrate and had to cope with producers, directors, writers, and actors who wanted to go independent (though, as Liberty Films proved, going independent did not necessarily mean *staying* independent). As one historian explains the real facts behind the story of Jack Schaefer's novel *Shane:* "As the open range became less open, the cattle kings attempted to protect their empires by preventing the small rancher, the homesteader, even their own foremen and cowboys from competing with them. Men like Fletcher were willing to let men like Starrett work for them, but they could not tolerate them if they competed independently."[3]

The independent Stevens was a thorn in the side of Paramount bosses from the beginning. By the time he took cast and crew to Jackson Hole, Wyoming, in the summer of 1951 for location shooting on *Shane,* arguments with Paramount had still not subsided. It was perhaps no co-incidence, then, that with *A Place in the Sun* and now *Shane* Stevens pro-duced his two most expressive and personal films, and his saddest, under conditions Shane himself would have recognized: while in the midst of a good fight. The effects of this antagonism on *Shane,* the film by which Stevens is best remembered, can only be surmised.

In interviews and retrospectives late in his career Stevens was asked about *Shane* more than any of his other films and was only too glad to offer the story about why he wanted to make it. Even before he returned to the United States after the war, he often said, he was disturbed to see groups of children in Germany playing with guns, emulating American cowboys, the mythic heroes who reminded them of the American sol-diers who had defeated Hitler. Stevens said in 1971: "At the time we made this picture, there was a great vogue of kids with cowboy hats and cap pistols — even in Germany I ran into it. All the little boys, remnants from World War II, were shooting one another with American cap pis-tols." When he got back to the States, he said, American children watched Gene Autry and Roy Rogers on television, believing that these singing cowboys were also heroic gunslingers: "Guitars were just replac-ing .45s and, very interestingly, .45s were becoming as harmless as guitars in the American film. I kind of felt it was an outrage. I wanted to show that a .45, if you pull directly in a man's direction, you destroy an upright figure. I wanted to make that one point. Because all the kids are going bang, bang, bang in the streets with one another. . . . And we wanted to . . . set the scene properly, as far as costumes were concerned, and indi-cate the violence of the West for what it was."[4] Stevens developed a sce-nario with which to talk about *Shane* in the years to come. When a man is shot, he liked to tell interviewers and film student audiences, he does not simply get up and walk away, as it happens in cowboys and Indians stories. "A living being," he said, "is not able to get up and when a man is shot a life is over." As Shane tells Joey, "You can never go back from a killing." Stevens wanted to get guns "out of the valley," evoking Shane's words to the boy. Before he rides back into the Tetons, he tells Joey to let Marion know that "there are no more guns in the valley." Stevens wanted to find holes in the gunslinger myth and to demystify it once and for all. The wish was intensified as Stevens returned to Hollywood and saw his contemporaries direct war pictures after their experiences in the service. Stevens said, "As time went on, however [after he directed *I Remember Mama*], I kept feeling I should do a picture about the war — all the other guys had done or were doing pictures about their war experiences, [John] Ford, [John] Huston, Wyler, and so on. And here I was avoiding the subject. Until I found *Shane* — it was a Western, but it was really my war picture. The cattlemen against the ranchers, the gunfighter, the wide-eyed little boy, it was pretty clear to *me* what it was about."[5] In an interview with Joe Hyams for the *New York Herald Tribune* during shooting of the film, Stevens even talked about *Shane* using battle metaphors: "There's a present-day moral in 'Shane.' . . . It takes great provocation to push people into the business of battle. But if they're pushed far enough they'd better get in and fight. . . . In some sense Shane is a boy called to go into the Marine Corps because he's the strongest and best qualified to carry out his country's point of view. When you ask a man to fight and to take a life, you not only ask him to risk his own life but you ask him to make a great sacrifice of his moral ideals."[6]

Yet the war's aftermath cut a deeper cloth than simply this conscious plan to make a war film and to try to defuse a powerful American legend. For Stevens *Shane* emerged also from a different kind of response to the war, perhaps best summed up in the film's final shooting sequence played out in Grafton's saloon where two adept killers — the golden-haired Shane, dressed in buckskin, and Wilson, evil incarnate in black hat and gloves — meet for their final showdown. The men are not simply gunslingers, nor animated players in a legend or mythic story; Shane and Wilson are artful poets who know their craft and dress it up with ritual. When Wilson slips his hand into his glove one finger at a time just before he kills Stonewall Torrey, when Shane twirls his gun back into his holster not once but twice after shooting Wilson and taking up Stevens's entire frame to do so, both are consummate artists who can count on their skill and daring to do a job when the time calls for it.

Shane and Wilson, good and evil, are mythic, artful, often solitary (Stevens called them "melancholy") figures. As they are conceived on-screen in 1953, they emanate from a world that has long passed away and that can be recaptured, recreated, only through artfulness. They belong to a fictional, perfectly realized netherworld, and their precision is played out in an artfully constructed fiction stemming from Stevens's emotional response to Schaefer's material. *Shane* the novel offered Stevens, and therefore American filmgoers, the chance to retreat into the past, to find a purer self, and a purer world within which to experience self-renewal — a chance to go home again to the idealized past to relocate the self that got tangled up in war and its aftermath. In one sense it was the adventure of pure myth. As Stevens told Joe Hyams, "We carefully reappraised [the Western legend], which is incidentally much the same legend of British knighthood, in which a single horseman rides to do battle against tremendous odds. Shane as played by Alan Ladd is the White Knight and Wilson, the hired killer played by Jack Palance, is the top of violence."[7]

Also, Schaefer's novel had a specifically *American* meaning for Stevens. It presented the opportunity for self-renewal, to go home again to the landscape of *his* fundamental self: the West. His psyche always lay with the Western frontier — ever since his days growing up on the West Coast and then his days as a cameraman shooting footage of Rex the Wonder Horse in Wyoming and Montana. For Stevens the West was the place of endless romance where men and women were tested during a time when there was a purer American selfhood. Stevens created a world that consciously demystified the gunslinger but also deeply embraced the mythologized West because it was an idealized, safe past. Stevens would be conflicted about these two wishes, and conflict would come to characterize *Shane*. But it would be conflict that also is the property of art.

The prose in Schaefer's novel appeals to the part of our national character that desires to return to more innocent times, the frontier of the late nineteenth century. Schaefer reveres childhood by writing from the point of view of a young boy, Bob (who would become Joey in Stevens's film). This reverence of childhood is something both the narrator and the country share. The young boy remembers Shane in Schaefer's romantic style: "I would think of him in each of the moments that revealed him to me. I would think of him most vividly in that single flashing instant when he whirled to shoot Fletcher [who would become Ryker in the film] on the balcony at Grafton's saloon. I would see again the power and grace of a coordinate force beautiful beyond comprehension. I would see the man and the weapon wedded in the one indivisible deadliness. I would see the man and the tool, a good man and a good tool, doing what had to be done." *Shane* exemplifies America's romance of its own past as told through a child's point of view. It was a time when collective identity was still forming. Art forms that return to this past see it through archetypal characters and events. Going back, Stevens also creates a new version of the mythic past. As Richard Slotkin has said, "myth-making is articulated by individual artists and has its effect on the mind of each individual participant . . . its function is to reconcile and unite these individualities to a collective identity."[8]

A few years before his death, Stevens watched the ending of *Shane* in an auditorium full of students and as he described the film, shot by shot, his narrative of *Shane* seemed almost to be an artful dream as he constructed it one more time. He talked about individual shots as they connected with the film's emotional meanings:

> I notice in taking it apart [that] there's very little unity to the film as shot; because there are so many different pieces. They're inside the saloon with a variety of shots around the room, and the reverse angle shot, and the boy's face coming under the door — all shot in the studio; then, outside there is the shot where Shane is sitting on a horse and the boy is talking to him — shot on location, so he can leave the front of the saloon. There, again, is the camera around from Shane's point of view into the boy's face, taken in the studio at another time — sometime after the work that was done in Jackson Hole, Wyoming. There there's the shot, shooting up at Shane on the horse, seated in the saddle in front of the saloon. And then a strange "Ring-around-the-rosy" business in which Shane leaves the front of the saloon and heads toward the back of the saloon from another angle, then back to the front of the saloon when the boy comes around the end of the saloon, heading toward the Teton Peaks, the grand Teton in the background there, at the right time, when the cloud happened to be with us, with a long focal-length lens to give the mountains some structure and some height — because it's a grand thing, with the horse moving into the distance. Then the boy coming around the building — a wide angle shot; then a reverse angle with the boy in the foreground and the horse in the middle distance going away toward the Tetons; and then around for what became the major aspect of the scene — the boy's face . . . as he sees he's not convincing Shane. Further shots with the camera now moved away from the saloon, following the horse and rider — it's the horse and rider and the mountain. The same shot on the boy, back into his face, and, eventually Joey weakens — having the first experience in his

life when something really doesn't work his way—when he realizes Shane is not coming back. And his spirit dims a little bit and he grows up a lot . . . and then in the far distance, Shane going away . . . then back into Joey's life with him looking rather bewildered and somewhat wiser. And then we're way up in the mountain looking back as Shane comes toward us, going into his never-never-world, whatever that might be. And there's a distant landscape below, where the farmers were, where we spent the hours of our adventure with them, and so to fadeout.

As he continued, Stevens talked about his editing process: "As we can see, it breaks up into quite a bit of work as far as shooting is concerned. It has to do with a variety of the aspects of the view that [gives it] an immediacy and a kind of continuity. And also, hopefully, in editing, a graceful relationship of scenes, so that the relationship of one shot isn't repetitious with the following shot, but a great difference of relationship of size of figure. The size of the figure in one shot being small and diminutive with the horse going away; then the face of the boy being immediate and close, which gives a kind of charge to the editing of the film."[9] The way he spoke, Stevens translated the shooting and editing process into a personal narrative whose dream-like properties carry the rhythms and internal conflicts of poems. "*Shane* is sort of a fine piece of poetry," Woody Allen once said about his favorite American film. "For whatever reason, probably because Stevens himself had some of the poet in him."[10]

A Good Man and a Good Tool: The Production

> If I was ever . . . qualified for anything, it would
> have had to do with making Westerns.
> —George Stevens at the Dallas Film Festival, 1971

Stevens shaped *Shane* into a personal kind of poetry, a work some have said contains the classic rhetoric of the Western, while others have called it a self-conscious display of a culture's mythology and symbolism. Despite the critical terminology handed down over the past fifty years, *Shane* is the work of a director whose *self* is very much present in every frame.

Five days after Ginsberg sent him the treatment for *Shane*, Stevens asked Stanley Garvey in Paramount's story department for reviews and information about Schaefer's book. "This is a first novel by a Connecticut newspaperman," Garvey wrote in a memo. The book appeared first as a serial called *Rider from Nowhere* in *Argosy* magazine in 1946 and was published in book form by Houghton Mifflin in October 1949. Paramount bought *Shane* in December 1949, six months before offering it to Stevens. "Being a Western," Garvey reminded Stevens, "it was not generally reviewed," meaning that it was overlooked by the critics and not taken very seriously. Still, there were some who wrote an obligatory review. The reviewer for the *New York Herald Tribune* called the book an "idyll" and a "first novel of horizon and depth," while the *Chicago Sunday Tribune* noted that while it was not "another VIRGINIAN, it has the same quality, dignity, and appeal which made Owen Wister's famous novel read by people who scoffed at 'westerns.'" Reviewers were kind but did not take the novel too seriously, a fact that Edmund Fuller summed up nicely in the *Saturday Review of Literature:* "For those who like this kind of book, this short special Western is just the kind of book they will like."[11] He suggested also that "Mr. Schaefer would have done better not to spin the tale so completely in the familiar clichés and bromides of the genre." But this would not be the first time, or the last, that Stevens took a cliché and turned it around. In a few years he would do the same with Edna Ferber's *Giant*.

Stevens asked Frank Cleaver, also in Paramount's story department, if any work had yet been done on a script. Cleaver said that Michael Wilson had already written "an excellent treatment," and sent it to him, adding though, that he would "be glad to talk about any other writers at your convenience." The studio had Wilson on salary and working on *Shane* from the beginning of February to the end of April 1950. He gave them a seventeen-page step outline of the book on March 15 and revised it on April 7; in his introductory note he suggested using what he called "a memory piece" in which a man would narrate and comment on remembered events. "There are structural advantages in telling the story from the boy's point of view" since "the heart of the story is the developing relationship between Shane and the boy." Also, Wilson said, "a key factor in the story is the gap between the boy's limited awareness of the conflicts at home *at the time they occurred* and his full awareness when viewing the events in retrospect. The narrator can make the contrast clear." Wilson was concerned about providing "a swifter and more economical means of projecting necessary exposition." By the time Stevens took on the project Wilson was out of the picture.

But Stevens again turned to Fred Guiol before anyone else. When he wrote to Cleaver on June 22, 1950, about getting a writer to "start the preliminary screen treatment," he sent Guiol the novel the same day, saying, "I would like you to read it at your earliest convenience as I would like to have your views in regard to the shape this might take as a movie."

However, recriminations between Stevens and Paramount still flew. Now that he had finally gained approval for two new pictures (along with *Shane*, the subsequently dropped *About Mrs. Leslie*), Stevens found that the front office would not be pinned down to setting starting dates In a June 28 letter he said, "I am therefore setting December 21, 1950 as the starting date for picture #4 on contract, and May 31, 1951 as the starting date of picture #5." Neither Stevens nor Paramount had a set idea of exactly what numbers four and five would be, and it turned out that Stevens would end his obligations to Paramount after only three films. A July 1 memo from Stevens requested that the studio "initiate" immediate action to "do SHANE in Technicolor." Still having gotten no response from Ginsberg about which picture he should shoot first, he added: "I do not propose to inject continuing recriminations into our necessary exchanges in completing my responsibilities here, but I cannot pass this subject now without calling to your attention, as I have often done in the past, to the failure in not planning ahead, as so many of the 'springs and summers,' one of which you now request be the time for the filming of SHANE, have passed as I watched the seasons come and go waiting for your green light while I could have been making this 'outdoor picture' and others, but adieu to recrimination short, of course, of a final accounting. Sincerely yours."

Ginsberg replied on July 10 that *Shane* absolutely had to be shot after *About Mrs. Leslie*, then made slight adjustments to Stevens's proposed dates and asked again if Stevens wanted to use Alan Ladd in the picture, which at the time seemed uncertain. In answer to his request to use Technicolor, Ginsberg offered a vague, rather circumlocutory response: "The thought that we should do *Shane* in Technicolor has been considered. There is, however, no action that need be initiated now to make Technicolor possible for this picture. We can assure you that if, at the time a budget for this picture can be realistically computed, the additional expense which Technicolor would represent can be justified, we will be in accord with the idea of doing this picture in Technicolor." Still, in the midst of ongoing "recriminations," Stevens prepared *Shane* even as he finished editing *A Place in the Sun* and worked on *Something to Live For.*

Before looking for a screenwriter, Stevens made notes to set the characters in place. He wrote of Starrett, "Father is an older man, big and strong," then, "but does not know the fighting ways. Big enough to carry Shane." He briefly noted that "Mother dresses Shane's wounds," and also wrote, "writer must be able to write talk for kid and Shane." Thinking of casting Montgomery Clift as Shane, Stevens noted, "Shane — Clift — much to do, much riding — so as to become one with horse, . . . Shane's first test [in the story] might be an Indian fight. . . . Starrett might be a weaker man — just a family man and Shane supplies the fighting." Stevens always went for the more elaborate idea first, only to trim it later on. He wrote, "Put in a Rodeo scene and let Shane do some horse bustin' — just when everyone thinks he's just a farmer. . . . The night that Shane goes in for the fight (the farmers are having a meeting and they are telling Starrett that they haven't confidence in his leadership) — Shane is yellow. Starrett fails . . . to hear it but he believes Shane is yellow and might be a bad example for the boy. . . . The boy is the only one in on the secret that Shane is a killer and carries a gun. We see Shane (first) returning from the west now lead[ing] a civilized life."

In a July 12 letter, literary agent H. N. Swanson (whose clients included F. Scott Fitzgerald and Raymond Chandler) suggested Stevens consider either W. R. Burnett or William Wister Haines to write the screenplay for *Shane.* "Burnett and Haines know the material and are available to talk about it," he said. At the beginning of October, Ivan Moffat again assumed the role of Stevens's associate producer and sent him a list of possible writers, including Richard Llewellyn (*How Green Was My Valley*), William Saroyan, Charles M. Warren, Harry Brown, Jack Sher (who would get screen credit for writing additional dialogue), and later the English writer Christopher Isherwood, a close friend of poet W. H. Auden who had moved to Los Angeles. There is no mention of Michael Wilson at this later time. Eventually Stevens took Moffat's literary lead and on January 11, 1951, writer and professor A. B. (Bud) Guthrie, who had won the Pulitzer Prize for his novel *The Big Sky*, signed on to write the script. Stevens later said that Guthrie was a good friend of his but was very reluctant to come to Los Angeles because he would have to leave his family and his teaching post at the University of Kentucky. But Stevens had absolute confidence in him. "In fact they were doing *The Big Sky* across the street at RKO, and they had tried to get Bud to do the screenplay. I had read of couple of Bud's novels; he was the only damn Western writer that could get Westerners to be as voluble as GIs were in bull sessions. He wrote GI dialogue. It wasn't just a parody of other Western writers, who seem to put a limitation on how much a man should say. I'm not sure those Westerners were so much silent as their authors were ungifted."[12] Guthrie's change of heart came after Stevens's offer of $1,500 per week for the first four weeks and a weekly salary thereafter. This later included reemployment at the same salary on May 1, 1951.

Guthrie worked quickly, finishing his script in April 1951, after which, under Stevens's direction and prior to Jack Sher's work, Ivan Moffat and Fred Guiol added additional dialogue. Guthrie did not stay around long. In June, Moffat wrote to him after his return to Kentucky, asking him to do "an additional stint on the story. . . . I think it would be a great shame for you to have to share screenplay credit with another writer, and as you know [Writers] Guild regulations do not leave us any option in the matter. I think it would be a good thing, too, from the point of view of your name here if your solo could be kept as is." Stevens later said that Guthrie gave him "about two-thirds of the script" before leaving. "He rushed through some sort of a conclusion, and let it ride. I never really got through the whole script before we started. After we straightened out the chronology, the night before or sometimes during the day, we were still doing some scenes to finish it. But by then I knew the actors, and it's very easy to write to the actuality of a situation."[13]

As always, though, Stevens took complete charge of the script, annotating the structure, character, and dialogue in his hardbound copy of Schaefer's book. On the book's inside front cover he had a little fun, making a casting note to himself to get the "Los Angeles Rams or [maybe some] Egyptians for Fletcher's [Ryker's] men." Just coming off the production of *A Place in the Sun* he noted, "Monty must train to show mucsels [*sic*]." Stevens could not have failed to notice Schaefer's first description of Shane's beauty as he climbs down off his horse, evoking the kind of precision and artistry Stevens later assigned to Alan Ladd when Shane at last kills Wilson and Ryker in Grafton's saloon: "Father and I watched him dismount in a single flowing tilt of his body and lead the horse over to the trough." Schaefer's Shane is adroit and graceful: "He took off his hat and slapped the dust out of it and hung it on a corner of the trough. With his hands he brushed the dust from his clothes. With a piece of rag pulled from his saddle-roll he carefully wiped his boots. He untied the handkerchief from around his neck and rolled his sleeves and dipped his arms in the trough, rubbing thoroughly and splashing water over his face. He shook his hands dry and used the handkerchief to remove the last drops from his face. Taking a comb from his shirt pocket, he smoothed back his long dark hair. All his movements were deft and sure, and with a quick precision he flipped down his sleeves, reknotted the handkerchief, and picked up his hat."[14]

While beautiful, Shane is also a comforting figure, a symbol of self-certainty, which probably appealed to Stevens in the same way it appealed to other Americans in postwar America. Though it resembled a dime novel — some have called *Shane* pulp fiction — its 1949 publication date places it among a tradition of postwar fiction seeking to make sense of cultural disruption and psychological chaos. Schaefer's prose is sentimental and always self-conscious in the way it creates a heroic male whose mythic stature has roots in hundreds of years of American frontier writing. In the book's first pages Shane tells Bob (Joey in the movie) "a man who watches things going on around him will no doubt make his mark someday." The comment more than likely appealed to Stevens and might even have described him. When asked by film critic Kenneth Tynan in the early 1960s if he had any hobbies, Stevens replied, "I sure do, Ken, I sure do . . . just lookin' around, Ken, just lookin' around."[15]

Stevens looked to identify relationships between Schaefer's characters. He noted Marion Starrett's attraction to Shane and wrote "Romantic girl" and "love" next to passages describing her behavior around him. Schaefer has Starrett tell his son not to get too attached to Shane, but Stevens changed it for the film, giving the line to Marion to suggest her own growing attachment to him, which in the film is far subtler than in the novel. Stevens also noted Bob's (Joey's) growing identification with Shane. "I wanted to be more and more like Shane," Schaefer wrote, "like the man I imagined he was in the past fenced off so securely. I had to imagine most of it. He would never speak of it, not in any way at all. Even his name remained mysterious. Just Shane." Stevens underlined the last two words and next to the full passage wrote "The theme [of film]," suggesting how central Shane's mysteriousness is to the film. Also, in the book young Bob is mesmerized by Shane's shooting ability, exclaiming "Gosh agorry!" at seeing him shoot. Stevens wrote in the margin, "Put this in Shane's gun technique," meaning he would pump up the final shoot out with Shane's fancy gun twirling to impress not only Joey but the audience too.

Stevens also inserted "The show starts" at the beginning of chapter 6 when Shane goes into town for the first time and is harassed by Chris Calloway (played by Ben Johnson in the film). In the subsequent fight scene, for visual emphasis Stevens wrote "Make Chris' face up [unreadable] between cuts; he goes behind the table and comes up with a bloody face." In the film Chris rises up into the close-up with a bloody nose, making it one of the most effective shots in the film. Then, when Starrett says, "Ernie always did believe in telling the truth," Stevens underlined "the truth" and inserted in the margin, "Use. The best thing in picture. Wait this out with big C. U.s back and forth." Stevens also planned to use specific passages for the film's beginning and end. At the beginning of the final chapter Stevens wrote, "Use this for opening" next to the first and second paragraphs: "I guess that is all there is to tell. The folks in town and the kids at school like to talk about Shane, to spin tales and to speculate about him. . . . But . . . he belonged to me, to father and mother and me, and nothing could ever spoil that. . . . For Mother was right. He was there. He was there in our place and in us. Whenever I needed him, he was there."[16] However, the framing device never made it to the final script. In addition, in the scene just before Shane rides off saying, "Bobby boy, this is no time for you to be out. Skip along home and help your mother," Stevens inserted the line, "And tell her everything is all right now." On the same page, Shane tells Bobby, "A man is what he is, Bob, and there's no breaking the mold. I tried that." Here Stevens inserted the line, "and it didn't work for me." He also wrote in the margin, "Ending" next to the line where Shane says, "It's a lovely land, Bob. A good place to be a boy and grow straight inside as a man should be."

Schaefer's prose is often sentimental, especially in describing young Bob's attachment to Shane, a fact that no doubt inspired Stevens's view of Shane as Ladd would play him: as with Elizabeth Taylor, Stevens's camera adores Ladd, often focusing on his physical beauty (aided in large measure by the hair pieces Ladd, and Van Heflin, wore). In an early script Shane wears black as he does in the book; Stevens changed this, giving Shane buckskin and blue shirts to wear as a way to soften his persona for the camera and the audience; he also changed the precise year of the events from 1879 to an unspecific time, thereby heightening the story's romantic quality. An early script dated July 10, 1951, ends the story with Starrett and Marion hugging and Starrett reaching for a towel to wipe his face. "He might be drying tears," it reads. Joey's calls to Shane as he rides off into the Tetons was a later addition. Also, Stevens made additional changes to Guthrie's script, making it more visual by jotting down notes such as "This line just won't do" and "This kind of talk just won't go" where the story relied too heavily on description written into the script.

To ensure *Shane*'s authenticity, Stevens hired a technical advisor, an authority on Western history, Joe DeYong, a man who was deaf and mute and communicated by long written narratives describing western life also through elaborate drawings. He looked at Guthrie's script and told Stevens, first off, that the homesteaders would never say "someone," but "somebody" instead; this accounts for numerous dialogue changes Stevens made.

DeYong instructed Stevens that "A man killed at the first shot is said to fall forward," but in the film, when Torrey (played by Elisha Cook Jr.) is killed by Wilson, he falls backward with a sudden jolt given by the rope Stevens had strapped around his waist to convey the violence. He wanted the same kind of violence associated with gunshots throughout the film. He told Joe Hyams when *Shane* was released, "There's no shooting in 'Shane' except to define a gun shot, which for our purposes is a holocaust. It's not a gesture of bravado, it's death."[17] For this reason, when Shane teaches Joey how to shoot and fires that awesome shot that makes Joey's eyes open wide, Stevens effected the sound by shooting a cannon into a barrel.

Stevens made several changes in the final white script, dated July 18, 1951. Stevens wanted the scenes when Shane rides into the frame at the beginning of the story and when he exits on horseback at the end to "Be bold, and to play 'Riders in the Sky'" as background music. For the final shootout scene he added Shane's lines, "You're dealing with *me* Ryker," and Ryker's reply: "You can walk out now, Shane, and no hard feelings." He also gave Shane the line, "Wilson, you know what I heard — that you're a low down lying Yankee," added Joey's warning, "Lookout, Shane," and replaced Shane's words, "You've lived too long. The home-steaders are sticking. The range days are over" to "You've lived too long. Your kind of times are over." After Joey and Shane exit the saloon, Guthrie wrote: "Joey and Shane meet on the porch and begin descending the steps. It is only now, in the hint of uncertainty, of extra care in Shane's walk, that we begin to suspect that something is wrong with him." Stevens's change put Shane on his horse ready to ride off. Though Shane reassures Joey that he is all right, his wound, and his future, remain as ambiguous as he is.

On June 6, 1950, Moffat sent Stevens a memo with casting suggestions. "I think the difference between the two main male characters in this story has much to do with the attractiveness of the piece," he wrote. He noted that Shane is "slight of build, but with lightning-quick, almost feline-smooth movements — a man who was born alert. . . . Joe Starrett . . . is big and ordinarily slow-moving, but with an air of great underlying power and strength." One character is dependent on the other, assistant to the producer Howie Horwitz said: "The ideal combination would be Monty Clift as Shane, with Broderick Crawford as Joe, or Alan Ladd or Gregory Peck as Shane and Brod Crawford, Paul Douglas or Burt Lancaster as Joe." Eventually Stevens had it narrowed down to Monty Clift playing Shane and William Holden playing Joe Starrett. But Holden pulled out of the project because he was exhausted from doing back-to-back films. George Stevens Jr. recalled that his father eventually made the casting choice an easy one. After Clift and Holden dropped out, Paramount head Y. Frank Freeman (whom Stevens liked to call Why Frank Freeman?) didn't want to commit to going forward until a cast was in place. Stevens walked into Freeman's office, asked to see the list of Paramount contract players and pulled his three stars — Ladd, Heflin, and Arthur — from that, adding that Arthur had always done good work for him and would not let him down.[18] Jean Arthur was a first choice as Marion and Brandon de Wilde was the only choice for Joey. *Shane* was the first film Arthur had done in a long time and was the last she made before retiring and moving to the East Coast to teach. She recalled the difference in Stevens after the war. "He was very serious, no jokes. It was like I never knew him before. He wanted me to look tired and worn. If I got a funny tilt to my voice we'd have to reshoot. I had to be very careful. I felt kind of sorry for him. . . . It was very sad. I felt like I was doing nothing."[19]

Stevens had always wanted to shoot the film in Wyoming. After he found the location near Jackson Hole, with the Teton Mountains looming overhead, he searched until he found the spot he wanted to shoot, but only after he was able to visualize specific points of the sets to be built. By July 25, 1951, he had sets built and cast and crew installed. Production got underway despite continuing pressure from the studio when production lagged, and despite pain from a chronic ulcer (George Stevens Jr. recalls that when others saw Stevens loosen his belt to accommodate his swollen stomach caused by the ulcer, it was understood that he would be in for a rough afternoon).[20] As they shot, the weather was not congenial, but when the scene of Wilson murdering Torrey was shot, an unexpected thunderstorm and cloudiness nevertheless helped the foreboding atmosphere Stevens wanted. Elisha Cook Jr. recalled details about the scene: "[Stevens] walked the streets of Jackson that night [before] and . . . he came up with what you saw." He and Fred Guiol used a Laurel and Hardy gag and said, "Let's put him on a wire! So, under that curious outfit I had on, they had me wired [with a harness], and when [Wilson's] gun went off it pulled me six feet through the air and into the mud. . . . Stevens came up to me afterwards," Cook remembered, "he said, 'You dumb son of a bitch! That's what happens to you when you stand up for a principle.'" Cook recalled also the method Stevens used with him. "He wanted me terrified and not terrified." After seeing if riding a horse would frighten Cook, a New Yorker, Stevens tried something else. "He called me aside. He said, 'Come here.' Now, he hadn't told me what I'm gonna do. He said, 'You know, I've got you eight weeks on the picture, and I'm stuck with you. You're the worst actor I ever saw in my life bar none.' What are you gonna say? . . . You don't say anything. What are you gonna do? . . . So he shot it. Then when he saw the rushes, he came up to me, he said, 'Greatest piece of film I ever shot in my life!'"[21]

Filming ended on October 19, after the crew and cast had moved back to Hollywood to shoot interior scenes, including the Fourth of July celebration, which was shot on a sound stage. When he finished shooting, Stevens then took fifteen months to edit the footage; editing credit went to William Hornbeck and Tom McAdoo though Stevens made the decisions. George Stevens Jr. remembered his father's preferred technique was to use a small theatre instead of a cutting or editing room: "He'd have the controls on two projectors so he could run the film back and forth on the screen, [and] could really see it in the size it was going to be shown, rather than a small image on a moviola machine; and running the scene of [Jack] Palance getting off the horse *backwards* [a process Stevens learned with Laurel and Hardy and later repeated with the cat moving a utensil on the sink in a burglary scene in *The Diary of Anne Frank*]—which was Palance getting *on* the horse—he saw how much more graceful a person is when you run the film backward . . . so they reversed the film . . . and [Palance] gets on like a ballet dancer."[22]

Shane was previewed four times between July and October of 1952 and released almost seven months later in April 1953. It was Pauline Kael who noticed the obvious: that Paramount had lopped off the bottom and the top of *Shane* to fit the screen. The film won critical praise across the country and of all of Stevens's films it continues to make appearances in academic film books. Frank McConnell writes in *The Spoken Seen*, for example, that Ladd's character "exhibits a kind of existential ennui with the role itself, a disgust with the necessity of being a private bearer of justice." *Shane* "remains one of the most singularly weary Westerns of all time: perhaps more tellingly than *High Noon*, it reflects the shattering pressure of politics upon the most political of American popular daydreams."[23]

Into the West

> In the back of my mind there's always a Western
> film I'm going to make, and I'll see it later on in
> a place where I have gone.
> —George Stevens to Eduardo Escorel

In a 1969 interview with Stevens, Brazilian journalist Eduardo Escorel called Shane a sad, lonely figure. Stevens concurred.

There's a good reason for that beyond any aim in the storytelling. . . . It has to do with a lone . . . country. All the great wilderness is sad. The great open plains under the mountains are sad, the wind blows sadly. When you hear it, it's the melancholy. And so all the cowboy songs that you learn when they're sitting around at night on a horse trying to keep the cattle from moving are sad songs . . . that's the wind, you know, and that's the feeling of a man alone in the awesome landscape.

[At night] something that helps you is that the sky is dark and the shadows are dark. And in the building there are two yellow lights in the window . . . they're lights of a yellow reflector that's caught the sun and brightens up both those windows . . . but I think it's the warmth of that cold, forbidding interior, the warmth of those lights that gives us the feeling of loneliness. It should be the shelter, you know, to go in that building, but it's not . . . the melancholy has to do with the loneliness of the open country. One man in a landscape, thirty miles and no one else. That's the melancholy time. It's a lonesome time.[24]

The lonesome, melancholy self was the essential Stevens. Belonging to a singular, lonesome time, he was the solitary self who made movies, the artist who holed up for long periods cutting a picture or even contemplating a scene. This is the Stevens who artistically, emotionally, trusted very few colleagues in his life — perhaps Fred Guiol, perhaps Ivan Moffat for a time, perhaps his cameraman William Mellor — and who was open to advice, never shunning it, yet never completely trusting it unless it paralleled his own inner sense of organization.

The melancholy figure is not so much lonesome as he is alone, in a pure state of thinking, creating, planning. Often a man of few words, Stevens could wax poetically about the loneliness and the melancholy of the frontier in a way that he would about nothing else — as if he were speaking of himself. He could easily appreciate Shane as Jack Schaefer wrote him. When young Bob first sees Shane, Schaefer writes of him, "The stranger took it all in, sitting there easily in the saddle . . . his voice was gentle and he spoke like a man schooled to patience." Then, at the end of the story, Shane has at last killed Fletcher. "I gave him his chance," Shane murmured "out of the depths of a great sadness."[25] More than sadness, it is a deep understanding of humanity and a sure sense of what needs to get done.

Shane is Stevens's personal ride. He understood the West and had his roots in it. Before his parents ran a vaudeville theatre in San Francisco, his grandmother, Georgia Woodthorp, was a popular actress during the California Gold Rush. When he landed a job as an assistant cameraman for Hal Roach Studios and found himself shooting footage of Rex the Wonder Horse in Wyoming, Montana, and Utah, it was already like being home. Now, after nearly two decades directing sophisticated light comedies in urbane settings, and after the sobering effects of seeing the war in Europe, finding *Shane* was like going home again, at last. Now Stevens would shoot outdoors whenever he could, in Jackson Hole, Wyoming, for *Shane*, soon in Marfa, Texas, for *Giant*, and later in Arizona for *The Greatest Story Ever Told*.

Locating the melancholy, singular self means finding the expression and the poetry in that self so that the sadness and aloneness is nourishing, not depleting. For Stevens *Shane* is a psychological place from which the poetry comes. Stevens knew Shane — not only the deadliness in his gun fighting but even more so the poetry in his movements. In response, *Shane* works and looks as if it were a visual poem. From the start, from the opening credits, with letters resembling hay, from the moment Shane rides down from the Tetons left to right in the frame, the film announces itself as poetry because it announces that its first subject is its own beauty, as if the film will be a *contemplation* of beauty. This accounts for what film historian Andrew Sarris (often disparagingly) called Stevens's "classicism," his heavy use of symbolism in the moment when Shane rides into the frame from the left, he and his horse framed by the antlers of a deer that young Joey is trying to shoot with his unloaded gun. Looking as if the shot were too conscious, too heavy-handed, it is, instead, a telling moment indicating Stevens's fluency with the poet's tools — the western imagery at his disposal — in order to create a poem, an ode, to the West.

Stevens sets up a strong rhythm to *Shane*, with recurring accents and motifs to which the camera regularly returns: high angle shots that place Shane or Joe or even Ryker's face against the mountains behind them or to the sky; shots where the camera returns to the fundamental contradiction between the grandeur of the Tetons and the smallness of the characters below. The camera consistently returns also to shots of characters seen through windows (such as Marion walking and singing inside the house at the beginning; or shots of Shane standing outside the window while Marion or Joey talk to him from inside the house). These kinds of shots repeat throughout the story to set up a pattern of expectancy. They rhythmically repeat, fulfilling one of poetry's fundamental characteristics: variety in uniformity. Each time the shot reoccurs it does so in a slightly different way — either by changing the character or the location but nevertheless repeating the same visual set up.

From its opening shots *Shane* is a contemplation of beauty. The three-strip Technicolor process (three rolls of film going through the camera and later combined) creates a world drenched in yellow or blue, both colors identifiable with Shane. This is coupled with the ever-present expansiveness of the landscape, which Stevens considered one of the film's characters. He used 75mm and 100mm telephoto lenses that essentially pulled the background up to make the mountains look taller, more grandiose. Cinematographer Loyal Griggs won an Academy Award for his work on *Shane*.

But as much as the camera loves the beauty of the landscape, it loves Shane more. From the first close-up of Shane on his horse bending over just a touch to speak to Joey, Stevens's camera transforms Schaefer's somewhat menacing, certainly mysterious Shane into a blond god, a knight on horseback, an object of beauty whose effect on Marion and Joey can hardly compare to Ladd's effect on the spectator. Shane is a soft-spoken, often childlike, always gentle creature whose effect on the characters is less important than his effect on the audience.

As a piece of poetry the story is full of internal conflict and paradox that add tension to each stanza-scene. Stevens overloads scenes with simultaneous actions of different characters (this could be said to be another form of Stevens's use of the dissolve: the intention to couple two shots together to show their difference *and* simultaneity). In an early scene, when Shane first sits down to dinner at the Starrett's home and he and Joe Starrett are talking, Shane is also aware of another action taking place: Joey is sneaking up on Shane's holster and gun, trying to get a good look. Later, in the fight sequence in Grafton's saloon, the set is broken into two parts: one side representing the domestic scene, with women looking at goods and fabrics, and the other side the bar where men drink and are fighting. They create more havoc, as the fight spills over from one to the other through the swinging doors that only tenuously divide the two spaces. Even later on, when the Starretts and Shane return from the Fourth of July celebration and are stopped at their gate by the Ryker gang, the scene is a complex blend of different dramas: Ryker speaks to Starrett while at the same time Shane and Wilson eye each other. Another kind of tension exists in Joey's looking back and forth between the action. Then Joey is caught in the action when Ryker walks up to him in the wagon ands asks him to join his side. All of this occurs, of course, within the context of a larger paradox: the presence of Stevens's majestic, almost religiously symbolic Tetons contrasted to the chaos of all fighting taking place on the landscape below. Even in fight sequences Stevens adds visual complexity by shooting some of the scenes from within diagonal beams in the saloon and store or from beneath staircases; when Joe Starrett and Shane finally fight each other to see who will go to town to meet Ryker, Stevens shoots from angles between the horses legs as they move to get out of the way of the action. The tension extends also to its central villain, Ryker. His recurrent plea to Starrett to "be reasonable," his tendency to appear contemplative and emotionally complex, moved Darryl Zanuck to write to producer Sol Siegel during production of Twentieth Century Fox's *Broken Lance* in August 1953: "I think we have got to do with the three brothers what. . . . Stevens did so well in *Shane* with [the] old villain. You hated him. But suddenly halfway through the picture, they gave him a big speech in which he justifies his position and his villainy. His position was wrong, nevertheless he was no longer just a villain. He had understandable motivations that anyone could accept, even though you knew his view point was wrong."[26]

Contrary to Stevens's plan to demystify the gunslinger legend, he only half succeeds, displaying instead an intense ambivalence about Shane and the mythic world this gunslinger so beautifully represents. Neither Stevens nor the camera (nor, by extension, Joey or the spectator) is able to dislike Shane, or his counterpart, Wilson, for that matter. Stevens creates them as artisans as much as killers; they are revered as much as they are feared. Each is pure myth, needing to be revered as much as demystified. Stevens's point of view, especially his view of Shane, makes it appear as if he chips away at something he also idealizes: the mythic past in which this gunslinger lives. As evidence of this contradiction, Shane's physical beauty is as outstanding as the threat of violence of his gun. He is as much the property of the hero-myth and of childhood dreams as he is the gunslinger.

Stevens's camera so adores Shane that it pays *homage* to Shane while it simultaneously wants to disapprove of his "violent" legacy. In his physical beauty Shane is a constant contradiction, as much unreal as he is real, as much a child as he is a man. His first contact with the family is Joey, who, when he gazes at Shane from a distance takes ownership of Shane's image. They share not only an emotional identity but a physical one as well. Both are light-skinned, blonde, and as feminine as much as they are masculine. The only difference between them is that Shane has a loaded gun (that Joey wants always to peek at) and Joey has an empty one. The camera consistently places them in identical profile, most of the time looking to the right, the same direction Shane took when he emerged from the Tetons. At the dinner table or sitting riding in the wagon, Shane is positioned to be the second son, sitting between Marion and Joe. The sexual feelings between Shane and Marion are of course squelched since he is her child as much as Joey is. The only significant break in that pattern comes when Shane replaces Joe Starrett as her dancing partner at the Fourth of July celebration. She wears her wedding dress to help restage her marriage vows but Joe Starrett is "fenced out" when Shane takes her as his dance partner. Yet just minutes before, as Joe and Marion stand underneath the wedding canopy, young Joey and Shane stand behind them to complete the family portrait. It is no wonder, then, that in his first trip into town to buy family supplies and his first set of "store-bought clothes," Shane walks into the saloon and asks for a bottle of soda pop — a phallic yet childlike configuration that is mimicked by Joey's stick lollipop in the subsequent bar brawl when Shane actually initiates the violence.

Shane's constant repositioning as adult, child, son, or substitute husband confuses the family structure so crucial to endurance in the frontier. In some instances when Shane is aligned with Joey's childlike qualities he appears almost to be Marion's son. At other times Shane is Joe Starrett's rival and therefore a threat to the family: Joey has asked his father to teach him to shoot (a rite of passage), yet ultimately it is Shane who gives the boy a lesson in the ritual of wearing a holster correctly and firing a gun. It is no coincidence that at that very moment of the lesson Marion walks out in her wedding dress to talk to Shane about keeping Joey away from guns. The doubling between Joey and Shane comes first from Schaefer's book, as does the sexual threat Shane poses to Joe Starrett. Yet Stevens deemphasizes the threat and plays up the confusion between Joey and Shane's physical (and psychological) resemblance. Shane and Joe Starrett behave as adolescents might during the fight scene at Grafton's; in the midst of punching out their opponents, they take a second to look over and smile at each other. The scene is reminiscent of the rousing fight scenes in *Gunga Din,* a film Stevens later said was a Western every bit as much as *Shane.*

Stevens's ambivalence about Shane marks his ambivalence about Western myths and the violence embedded in their narratives — as if the pleasure of returning home again to one's now-romanticized childhood were compromised by having to confront the violence contained within that childhood and yet not for long. Stevens adores the myth more than he wants to debunk it. His tendency to see it in its purest, most symbolic terms — an impulse that leads him to framing Shane on horseback within the deer's antlers, or to have Shane emerge from and return to the Tetons to begin with — confounds his conscious agenda to demystify the gunslinger myth. Repositioning in frame after frame Shane's goodness and Wilson's evil confounds the possibility of seeing its flaws.

The secreting away of guns amounts to a concealment, or even a fear of masculinity itself, certainly a recurring motif in *Shane* that begs Freudian interpretation: the soda pop bottle; Ladd's short stature and feminized looks (not to mention Joey's); Shane's threat to Joey's otherwise established family romance. Joey admits to Shane one morning that he uncovered Shane's weapon and quickly covered it back up with the blankets on top of it. He tells Shane, "I saw your gun in there one day — are you mad? Could I see it again?" But from Stevens's postwar point of view, masculinity easily figured as weaponry and destruction. In this sense, a gun, even with its sexual overtones as a phallic weapon, is every bit the threat it is believed to be.

Yet the wish-fulfillment dream that *Shane* ultimately achieves is Stevens's response to what one critic of Schaefer's book called the writer's "symbolic hyperbole," the impulse to romanticize the past to find self-regeneration in the present. While Schaefer demonstrates a rather pessimistic view of the West, this view coexists with a sadness because the frontier is gone. At heart *Shane* is a nostalgic return to a purer time in the country's past. But the prominent theme in Schaefer's book is young Bob's strong identification with Shane, a figure whose identity is mysterious yet who nevertheless affords the boy an attachment he would not otherwise have had.

Stevens further romanticizes Joey's experience of growing up and moving from childhood to manhood (which signals a country growing up too). George Stevens Jr. remembered calling to his father's attention that after the final shootout when Shane kills Wilson, the full-frame shot of his elaborate gun-twirling might seem a bit too corny. Stevens told him that it was fine; the fancy, overdone twirl would be just the kind of maneuver a child who is watching (meaning Joey) would understand.[27] Art and childhood collapse in that shot. Joey's romance with Shane, which is just about to end, and in another sense is just about to begin as a life- and myth-narrative, hinges on experience that is as pure as that moment of an elaborate piece of handiwork. The film is a flight into fancy, just as Stevens remembered and reconstructed it with an audience of students some twenty years later — a collection of shots that make little sense until they are put together in some fashion that the director dreamed up. Stevens controls these pieces of film with a wish to return to his own past and to take audiences with him. When Shane rides off into the Tetons, perhaps hurt, perhaps dying, Joey calls after him with the growing recognition that Shane is never coming back. His childhood ends in that melancholy moment. But the melancholy is different for Stevens, who finds in it a poetic energy that converges in contradiction and purity. Stevens insisted during the film's production that Shane must appear to be going somewhere else when he first rides down from the Tetons. But he rides in seeming just as melancholy as he does riding away. Stevens wants to return to the past, and manages to do so — and how glorious to be able to escape from the studio's front office and into the West. But he — and the rest of us — have seen too much by 1951, the year of *Shane*'s production. Earlier in the story Stevens gives Torrey a funeral in a cemetery on a hill overlooking the town. After the war Stevens especially understood that death is a part of living. His look back at America's — and his own — childhood in the West has become a beautiful elegy. Joey doesn't notice, yet the spectator does, that just before Shane heads back into the mountains he rides right into a graveyard.

7

Our Town

Giant

We know that Mr. Stevens is very meticulous
and will demand perfection in selecting props,
wardrobe, cast, etc.... causing expenditures
that are impossible to foretell (I mention as an
example that he interviewed 1,500 horses before
selecting Alan Ladd's horse in *Shane*).
—Memo from Eric Stacey to Jack L. Warner

In *Shane* Stevens reached back to America's past to express a social conscience that could only have been the result of reevaluating his war experiences and their impact on him as an artist. For the first time he began
to think of America as an *idea,* as a canvas expansive enough to contain
art *and* intellect expressed through archetype and myth. In revisiting
America's mythological past he painted the American landscape as a
moral universe where men and women fail as much as succeed, where
they are conflicted as much as certain. Released at the height of the postwar boom in American myth criticism when writers and critics promoted the idea that America indeed *had* a usable past and an identifiable
tradition, *Shane* enabled Stevens to participate in an ongoing dialogue

about America that major artists and writers had been conducting for hundreds of years. He evoked James Fenimore Cooper in viewing the western landscape as a collision between social forces and individual ideology; and when Shane rides back into the Tetons and away from the family, Stevens articulated what the critic Roy Harvey Pearce would come to call the American male's impulse "to say no to culture before ultimately saying yes," that is, the impulse to remain self-reliantly singular before (if ever) joining a community of others.[1]

In 1952, though *Shane* had yet to be released, reports of its casting and production in the trades and in consumer magazines and newspapers made Stevens more recognizable to American audiences than ever before. For the rest of his career he would receive large amounts of fan mail from moviegoers around the world inquiring about upcoming projects, casting him as an arbiter of America's cinematic language whose movies deeply impacted their lives. If he was adept at expressing American social sentiment and picturing shared cultural situations before the war, now he was able to dream his country's mythic dreams and even help to invent them. Soon the success of *Shane* would assure him of that.

But as Stevens's postwar reputation grew, the commercial and personal stakes also grew higher for each film he directed and produced. Each of his pictures took longer to prepare, longer to shoot, longer to edit. *Shane*'s Grand Tetons stood imposing and unreachable for good reason; they forecasted the ambitious direction Stevens was headed. He had seen, as he put it, the best of men and the worst of men in the war. This kind of hyperbole left an impression and held meaning; each of his films grew larger and took on more personal import. In February 1952 he had locked in his independence by forming George Stevens Productions to produce, sell, and distribute films and television. Stevens was now free of Paramount — and in *Giant* his exuberance began to show.

Bolstered by the expansive vistas ushered in by *Shane*, Stevens now found another story, Edna Ferber's *Giant*, that easily accommodated his attraction to large ideas. Those huge proportions that crept into his aesthetic in the 1950s matched the mood of an industry that had just invented CinemaScope and the mood of a country feeling the surge of economic growth. A week before *Giant* opened, Stevens promoted his movie when he wrote a piece in the November 19, 1956, anniversary issue of *The Hollywood Reporter* supporting "big" films. "I cannot help but feel that the future of the industry will be based on the big, expensive carefully-prepared films that appeal to audiences solely in terms of new and unique experience," he wrote. "For this reason, I feel that the present trend toward the 'Big' impressive film is perhaps the healthiest and happiest development in the entire history of the industry. It is by no means new. In 1914, D. W. Griffith proved very conclusively that the 'big' film, if it is a unique and worthwhile experience, would attract both vast audiences and vaster revenues. . . . For many years I have been an outspoken supporter of 'big screen' presentation of films. I believe in simple terms, in filling the audience's entire range of vision with the entertainment to which their attention is directed."[2] Stevens paved the way for his own expanding vision.

Edna Ferber's novel *Giant* was big in many ways. The story of three generations of a Texas family, it embraced pressing social and racial issues that attend a growing economy, relating the expansion of the Texas landscape from the 1920s to post-World War II. For Stevens, expansion in Texas reflected postwar America's exuberance with the idea of change, and especially with the idea of *size*. At this particular time Americans expressed that exuberance by becoming almost euphoric consumers, buying things that were shiny and large: appliances, automobiles, houses. Whether or not he knew it, Stevens shaped his movie, *Giant,* into a luscious, colorful, exuberant kind of national epic, a commodity that Americans would be helpless to resist.

The Euphoria of Size

Stevens's mood to direct a movie that could be larger-than-life and still embrace the intimate details of a family's life reflected the mood of America in the fifties. As the postwar economy and its concomitant consumerism flourished during the decade, American audiences who went to see *Shane* also relived another popular and mythic American experience at the same time, the move westward. Freed from the uncertainty and disruptiveness of the war and the years immediately following, American GIs brought their families west in droves to find once again that new frontier, a landscape that promised reinvention and prosperity. As one veteran put it, "after the war, going back to Chicago seemed crowded, closed-in; we went to California because there was space, there was room to grow and they were building everywhere."[3] Borders changed both physically and culturally as American families swept into, as Alan Nadel notes, the expansive economic and technological growth of America in the 1950s: "From 1949 to 1960, for example, the American economy showed a rise in *real* gross national product of 51 percent, and one-fourth of all the housing in America as of 1960 had been built during the preceding decade. In the ten years from 1946 to 1955, automobile production increased 400 percent, to eight million a year, and the 1956 National Defense Highway Act authorized constructing over forty thousand miles of new limited access roads."[4] David Halberstam also notes the way families moved not only west but also up the social and economic ladder. In the early and mid-1950s all manner of American growth became the story of the moment: "It was all part of a vast national phenomenon. The number of families moving into the middle class — that is, families with more than five thousand dollars in annual earnings after taxes — was increasing at the rate of 1.1 million a year, *Fortune* noted. By the end of 1956 there were 16.6 million such families in the country, and by 1959, in the rather cautious projections of *Fortune*'s editors, there would be 20 million such families — virtually half the families in America. *Fortune* hailed 'an economy of abundance' never seen before in any country in the world. It reflected a world of 'optimistic philoprogenitive high spending, debt-happy, bargain-conscious, upgrading American consumers.'"[5] To Americans it was the story of you and me, the story of your family and mine.

The upswing translated into a new enthusiasm for spending and owning. Consumerism itself triggered a new kind of postwar mass market and with it a new definition of the consumer. What changed was not only who was *buying*, but what size and color was selling. As Shelley Nickles writes:

> Manufacturers understood this new postwar "mass market" as the low and low middle-income classes of our national market. [They] wondered whether they could connect with this new mass market without losing their former [upper-middle class] clientele. Designers perceived that consumers had diverse tastes, and social class became the most useful way to categorize these tastes for national markets. As opposed to designers' own upper-middle class preference for elegant simplicity, con-

sumer research revealed that the working-class masses generally believed worth was expressed through three design features. One was "bulk and size": if "it looks bigger, it must be worth more." Bulk signified solidity. Another was "embellishment and visual flash." The third was color. Although surveys indicated that men generally held the purse strings, manufacturers conceptualized the consumer as female and more specifically attributed the desire for styling to the influence of women. As one study argued, "whether she has a job outside the home or not, the wage earner wife decides most family purchases or investments." This reflected a dichotomy that engendered function and production as masculine and ornamentation and consumption as female.[6]

It was in this context of social change — of the woman's increased power in the social sphere where big was better and where women had influential buying power in a large, "streamlined" mindset — that Americans were reading Edna Ferber's *Giant,* first serialized in *Ladies' Home Journal* before Doubleday published it in the fall of 1952. The book captured the imagination of masses of readers, given its wide appeal: a love story set within the context of racial tensions and recounting the lives of three generations of a Texas dynasty. Ferber herself had a long and fruitful history with Hollywood, as no fewer than ten of her books had been adapted for the screen, including *Tulsa, So Big,* and *Showboat.* In fact, *Showboat* saw two screen translations, one in 1936 starring a singing Irene Dunne, and the glossier 1951 remake featuring Howard Keel and Kathryn Grayson. It was only natural, then, that Ferber expected a rousing response from Hollywood to her latest and very popular, if controversial effort. In this vein a rather crafty announcement appeared in the May 20, 1952, edition of *Daily Variety* telling industry readers that Ferber refused to let Hollywood studios get an advance look at her new novel. For a short time this reverse psychology worked: the "hands off" sign made the book seem a forbidden fruit that studios would have to fight each other for in order to win, and *Giant* briefly shot to the top of studios' must-have lists as story editors were sent spinning to find out the real details of Ferber's latest book.

The book created outrage on the part of some Texans who believed that Ferber painted them in a bad light: as racists and, worse yet, as nouveau riche social climbers. The story included nothing less than an interracial marriage within the book's family of protagonists, the Benedicts, after the family treats their Mexican hands as poorly as does the rest of their community. There was outrage that Ferber, "not a Texan," would draw such a shameful portrait of Texans, especially Texas millionaires.

The heightened interest in *Giant* proved short-lived and eventually Ferber found herself unable to get a taker for the property. But the controversy surrounding the book's publication interested Stevens at the same time that it caught the eye of Henry Ginsberg, Stevens's former nemesis at Paramount. After *A Place in the Sun* and a brief consideration to film some Ambrose Bierce short stories, Stevens and Ginsberg parted company. But *Giant* brought them back together. Stevens liked the controversy surrounding Ferber's book and believed it would lend itself quite nicely to public interest in the project. He was also predictably interested in the book's love story. "In one sense . . . it's simply the story of what happens ever after," he said. "So many of our romantic pictures just lead up to the altar and leave you with a general assumption of inevitable happiness. But this is a story about the hazards of the marriage relationship."[7] To Stevens, *Giant,* with its large landscape, was also a kind of Western. The decade saw its share of big scale Westerns, most notably Wyler's *The Big Country* (1958), or even his Civil War drama based on Jessamyn West's *Friendly Persuasion* (1956), or earlier, Hawks's *The Big Sky* (1952), even Anthony Mann's more quirky *The Far Country* (1955). While these Westerns looked backward to America's past, *Giant* looked enthusiastically to the future.

Giant Inc.

Stevens and Ginsberg did not dislike each other enough to let a business disagreement over *A Place in the Sun* interfere with what might become a lucrative film property. Ginsberg already knew Ferber and knew how to broker deals. To get hold of Ferber's book he and Stevens formed an independent production company and in December 1952 made Ferber an offer for the screen rights to *Giant.* Then Ginsberg came up with the idea that the three form a production company for the purpose of "producing, distributing, exploiting motion pictures beginning with *Giant* and also photoplays based on other literary properties of Edna Ferber."[8] Ferber would write, Ginsberg would produce, and Stevens would direct — each for no compensation. Giant Productions was formed on May 4, 1953, and on November 16 the company formally acquired the film and its allied rights for ten years.

Finding a studio to back Giant Productions, however, was not easy. Despite Stevens's popularity with the movie-going public, *Shane*'s financial and critical success was still untested and uncertain. Then-Fox producer David Brown later recalled meeting Stevens at this time: "The first time I met George . . . he and Henry Ginsberg and Edna Ferber were putting together *Giant*. They evidently had trouble getting backing for it. Ginsberg was a friend of mine. Miss Ferber couldn't sell the book so they sort of became a partnership. . . . I had presented the subject to Darryl F. Zanuck, who was very interested in the idea of Stevens directing *Giant*, with Mr. Ginsberg producing. But George at that time had an unreleased film called *Shane*, and the word was that the film was in difficulties. Nobody seemed to think it was going to be very commercial and as things go in this town, George was at that time perhaps not, in the parlance of the film community, 'bankable'; . . . eventually . . . Jack Warner took a chance and again made one of the early deals in which the director and producer and author work as substantial profit participants."[9] But Paramount released *Shane* in the summer of 1953 after a plan to sell it to Howard Hughes fell through. It became a hit with moviegoers and critics, helping to pave the way for Warners to take on *Giant*. A contract between Warner Bros. and Giant Productions signed on December 14, 1953, stipulated that the studio would completely finance the picture as well as handle its distribution and advertising (giving Giant Productions a large say in how the film would be advertised). The studio would also add an overhead of 25 percent of the total cost to make the film, which was estimated at that date to be $1.5 million — this in return for use of the studio's facilities. Neither Ferber, Stevens, nor Ginsberg would take a salary but would share fifty percent of the profits after the studio recouped its costs and took 30 percent of the worldwide box office gross as a distribution fee. Any expenditures over the budget had to be approved by Jack Warner. Stevens had to deliver a final script thirty days before shooting began and a finished film four months after principal photography was completed.

The Production

Even before signing with Warner Bros. Stevens went out selling *Giant*. In *The Hollywood Reporter* he told readers about both *Shane* and *Giant*.

"I've always been sold on the idea of the picture-maker standing squarely behind his product," he said. "I've taken advantage of every opportunity afforded to go out on the road and help sell the picture I have made — to the press, public, exhibitor and anyone else who might be interested." He said that he had traveled "some 30,000 miles of 'Shane' touring" and looked forward to "double that mileage both before and after completing 'Giant,' which with Henry Ginsberg and Edna Ferber as partners, is next on the production list . . . we are both highly in accord with the idea of taking the film under the arm and going along with it."[10]

"Actually our picture is not just a story of Texas," Stevens said later from the set, "It is a saga of America. We are presenting a tale in which the leading characters are depicted honestly with their weaknesses as well as their virtues. Though the film chronicles the rise of a great Texas cattle and oil dynasty and its relationship to the rest of the community, it could be the story of any section of the United States, confronted with parallel problems. It is Americana."[11] Before anything, *Giant* would be *big*, and if spectators had been watching carefully, they would have seen that coming in Stevens's movies. In A *Place in the Sun* Stevens tackled the biggest of American writers and one of the longest of American novels. In *Shane* the physical landscape got wider and more expansive and Stevens's social conscience swooped back to the time-tested strength of American mythology itself. Issues important to him mattered now, and the larger the size the greater the expression, and the greater the voice. In one sense, then, there was nothing big enough to contain *what* he had seen in the war. The closest he could get to expressing it would be to find stories that had personal, and hopefully, social meaning. He liked *Giant* because it was big and wide, incorporating contemporary issues such as consumers moving westward, women earning emotional independence, and racial conflicts beginning to surface in America's social fabric. All these issues emerge in his first — and last — exuberant postwar film.

He was already thinking in larger-than-life proportions when he read the first page of Ferber's novel. In his copy, when he read her description of "the vast and brassy sky . . . spangled with the silver glint of airplanes" and "glittered with celestial traffic," he conceived of a sight even larger than that, writing in the margin, "tornado beginning and tornado at the end. The drought. The dust." He added anxiety, even catastrophe, to Ferber's descriptions. "They worry about the twisters coming like the

Californians worry about the possible earthquake. The accumulated anxiety if harnessed, could strain more masonry and bend more boards than the occasional earth tremor does and the occasional cyclonic updraft as it passes by," he wrote. Natural disasters and their consequences are imagined in extraordinary terms, epic in scale. At the end of chapter 1, Ferber writes that Reata Ranch is a "kingdom" — also an appropriate descriptor of what would be Stevens's finished film.

Again Stevens hired Ivan Moffat and Fred Guiol as "story consultants" and, after several treatments, the three eventually finished a final script together. As Moffat later put it, Stevens's contribution was pivotal. Referring to screenwriter credit, Moffat said, that one could easily replace Fred Guiol's and Ivan Moffat's names with Stevens's. Each draft treatment sent Warners research department reader Carl Milliken looking for potential legal hazards. He found many since Ferber patterned her characters after actual — and worse, living — Texans. Milliken issued a long memo to Ginsberg on December 14, 1954, listing the most obvious problems: that the Benedict family was based on a family named Kleberg and their King Ranch, and that, among other obvious borrowings, Jett Rink very closely resembled a Texas millionaire named Glenn McCarthy. "Edna Ferber's GIANT is a specially worrisome property because it has been accepted, to a large extent, in the public mind as a true document about not only life in Texas but also specifically of the lives of the Kleberg family, which owns and operates the King Ranch, and of Glenn McCarthy, the much publicized Texas oil millionaire." Characters, the sizes of the ranches, even events in the characters' lives too closely resembled these actual Texans for Milliken to feel comfortable. He also said, for emphasis, that "the individuals with whom we are . . . involved are very wealthy and well able to sustain any lawsuits they embark upon." Stevens commissioned a long report that detailed the comparisons between the film and the real-life prototypes. He promised the managers of the King Ranch that his characters would be kept separate from the Klebergs and the rest. Yet to those who know the comparisons, they seem less than distant cousins.

The treatments evolved. Production notes show the first one setting up a flashback where a middle-aged Leslie and Bick sit on their sofa wondering whether or not the Benedict family is a failure after twenty-five years. The camera focuses on their two grandchildren, "a boy and a girl, each about eighteen months old. The girl is a redhead, the boy a brunette, showing a definite Latin strain [a Stevens addition, as is the fight in Sarge's diner]. One on the side of the playpen is a baby calf. Bick points to the playpen, saying, 'Look at that—my own Grandchild, Jordy Benedict IV—looks like a real cho . . .' Leslie: 'Don't talk like that.'" Then a flashback occurs; the older Bick dissolves into, and looks at, a young Bick: "Old Bick's eyes watch young Bick drive out [of] the gate of Reata. [Bick says]: 'Yes sir. I went to Virginia to get some of that fine blood stock we needed here. . . .' His voice trails off." We see a somewhat misty image of a traditional old Virginia mansion. A carriage is drawn up at the steps, a coachman standing alongside of it. The camera pans to the girl. She is winding roses on the trellis the same way she was doing in the scene we just left. She smiles at the figure seated beneath her. The camera pulls back and it is young Benedict, smiling back at her and pleading. "Leslie, I want you to understand I'm not going back to Texas without you."

The flashback was scrapped by the next treatment, which included Stevens's addition of the early scene when Leslie and Bick realize they love each other. After breakfast in the Lynnton dining room, the group disperses outside so that Dr. Lynnton can drive Bick to the train station. But emotional fireworks have flown during the meal. Stevens writes, "[Leslie] walks to the fence—War Winds comes galloping to her. Bick comes up and we fade out on B shot. Man, Woman and Horse Nuzzling." Additions and alterations finally led to a finished script. Stevens later said, "We had a terribly long script on *Giant*— Fred Guiol and I and Ivan Moffat. . . . When we finished the script, it was 370 pages. . . . I had talked with Edna and I took the script back to New York and had her read it. She was an exceptionally effective novelist and she liked the script very much. She said, 'You know I want to write this book once again. I wrote it twice and I want to write it the third time and fill it out.' She said, 'I think you've done it with the screenplay,' which is a surprise assessment to get from a lady whose novel you're massacring possibly." After that Stevens and Guiol sat down and cut the script down to 240 pages; he said, "We did everything we could to accordion [it]." Stevens also asked friend Fred Zinnemann to look at the treatment. Zinnemann suggested cutting several scenes that had Leslie and Bick out on the range—one in a car, the other on horseback—that Stevens then eliminated.

More to the fact, Ferber found the first draft (and subsequent drafts) to have numerous faults, "for the most part in dialogue, characterization and (in very few cases) scenes such as the tea-drinking bit," she wrote Stevens, referring to the scene when Jett serves Leslie tea at his shack on Little Reata. "Curiously enough — or perhaps not so curiously — it is the LESLIE dialogue scenes that are faulty. The male characters are almost always right, except occasionally in the case of DR. LYNNTON. The LESLIES and the DR. LYNNTONS seem to lie outside the ken or the liking of the writers of the script." She also objected to the name War Winds for Leslie's horse. Stevens wrote a reminder to change the name, but the name nonetheless stayed in the picture. Nor did Ferber like the moonlight scene between Leslie and Bick on the Lynnton's veranda, especially Leslie's line, "It would be too touching." She also disliked Leslie's line, "Elsewhere being gracious is acceptable," when she and Bick have their first fight on the porch at Reata. Ferber called it "pure Bronx. . . . It is Arthur Kober's Bella Gross. Leslie doesn't talk like that. I took it out once, but there it is, back again. I suggest leaving out the sick-making word *gracious*." Both lines stayed.

Ferber found further fault with the script, especially disliking Leslie's line in the film's last scene. Sitting next to Bick on the sofa, she tells him that, finally, "The Benedict family is a real big success." For Ferber, the word, "big" was (emphatically) *not* the speech of a woman of taste. Finally, Ferber was moved to write to Stevens: "I want only to say this: I know nothing about the making of motion pictures. I know about writing. I know dialogue, characterization, situation. I know how powerful words are to convey the meaning of a situation. The people who wrote this script know how to cut and shape a scene; transpose; visualize effects picture-wise; sense the impact of a scene or character. . . . As a writer, I find some of these GIANT speeches wooden, unvital, and uncharacteristic. A writer of proven talent and experience could not have written them. Also I am sorry to say, some of them are ungrammatical. I say this not with a desire to offend or to be rude. This picture is a huge business venture. We cannot afford to use dialogue which is inept. I can't bear to read it, much less hear it."

Eventually Ferber wanted to try her own hand at writing the script and volunteered to spend three weeks in Los Angeles. She wrote to Stevens and Ginsberg on May 4, 1954, "I want to work as an unsalaried

writer," she said, adding that her expenses should come out of "the kitty."
She closed with a list of her needs: "A reasonably quiet comfortable place
in which to work; A standard size Remington Noiseless typewriter; A
right-height desk or table or stand for the t.v. . . . No publicity, please,"
she insisted, also saying, "Just let me work with someone who knows
GIANT and likes its basic idea. I'm hoping it will be you, George."

Ferber flew to Los Angeles on June 20, 1954, and worked a six-day-
a-week schedule with Stevens, Moffat, and Guiol, although the bulk of
the script was her doing. On August 8, she gave Stevens a finished
screenplay not much longer than a treatment that Stevens thought to be
visually impoverished to say the least. She had a knack for dialogue, but
not for the cinema's visual grammar. In the shot where Jordy Benedict
(Dennis Hopper) tries on his father's Christmas present to him, for example, a hat much too large for his head, Ferber has Jordy say, "They
never did fit me, did they dad?" Stevens wrote in the margins, "Let the
picture say this — Do all our jokes need explaining?" In Jett's closing
scene, when he is, according to the script, so drunk he can hardly get up,
Ferber gives him the self-conscious lines, "Stand up. . . . Ought to stand
up." Stevens wrote over the line, "NO! (The art is to tell what he is thinking — without having the actor leave his part and explain changes for the
author — Bad as the Chinese stage hand that comes on and hands the
dagger)." Stevens, Moffat, and Guiol then went ahead with their own
script.

Ferber was not the only person keeping an eye on *Giant*'s production.
Volumes of letters from around the country reached Stevens's office. An
animal rights groups asked him not to use a real animal in branding scene
(he did not); representatives of local Hispanic groups such as the League
for Spanish Speaking People, asked Stevens to be mindful not "to mis-
lead people to believe there are such things as a Mexican race, English
race, German race, etc., because they are Caucasians" and "not to bring
derision, ridicule or criticism to the eight million Americans of Mexican
ancestry."

Again, the screenplay was Stevens's all the way. Despite Stevens's liberal politics and humanistic values, *Giant*'s depiction of racial tensions —
and what critics like to call Leslie's feminist views — have more to do
with their contribution to the story's dramatic tensions than anything
else. After all, Stevens was initially attracted to the controversy sur-

rounding Ferber's novel. Telling a good story mattered; invigorating the audience mattered. To this end he told Ginsberg that the Benedict daughter Judy really had one purpose in the story: "She participates only for the purpose of making it possible for *two* grandchildren to be in the playpen at the finish: a blond and a brunette. In contrast: one of pronounced Latin strain and one of the more Nordic, or if you please, 'pure Aryan strain' as I recollect a description of not so long ago." Stevens especially wanted these two grandchildren in the playpen in the story's last shot to "make what we hope to be [an] important comment on Leslie and Bick's appraisal of the success or failure that their life has resulted in." He also asked Ferber at one point "to consider the possible value of the two children in the playpen — in their innocence or wisdom, as you please — contemplating the past and prophesying the future. This could be the most significant thematic illustration we have in the film if we pull it off effectively."

The Road to Marfa

> Miss Taylor called Mr. Stevens at 7:20 this morning saying that she was ill and not feeling well, had a very bad headache and did she have to come in so early? . . . It may be suggested that we ask Miss Taylor if she would care to move on the lot until the picture is finished.
> —Warner Bros. Interoffice Memo
> from Tom Andre to Eric Stacey

Giant made headlines as Hollywood columnists picked up press releases about its casting almost immediately. For Stevens, finding the three principals had to be somewhat like being a kid in a candy shop with so many A-list actors vying for parts. Early on he thought of reteaming Billy Wilder's *Sabrina* stars Audrey Hepburn and William Holden, but eventually both turned him down. The road to casting the three main characters then took twists and turns that kept Stevens occupied from late in 1953 to the middle of filming halfway through 1955.

Ferber's novel detailed the excitement of social and economic change in Texas before and after World War II. But Stevens wanted to give the story more realism than Ferber's prose could muster. Also, her characters lacked a certain depth. Stevens asked the more literary-minded Ivan Moffat to construct psychological profiles of the three principals. Moffat supplied Bick, Leslie, and Jett with the interiority that Ferber had left lacking. He wrote that Bick "saw through a good deal of the gaff and nonsense of professional Texasism"; he said that Leslie "romanticized truth without necessarily understanding it"; and he wrote that Jett was "discontented, cheated out of his birthright, and feeling deeply the inequality of his position." Stevens pinned these profiles to his office walls, sent them out to agents and used them as a guide to cast these principal roles. But as it turned out, Moffat's descriptions held more depth of character than spectators ever saw on the screen. As his friend Jim Silke said of Stevens, "He was a storyteller. He's not digging that deeply into character; he's digging into the *world* they're in. There are the hills, the village, the people, the mountains; the relationship *between* them is the story. He's a cameraman and a visual movie director; he's telling you a story in a visual manner."[12] A show of emotions between characters is a visual part of the frame, but not the questioning and conflict behind it.

Clark Gable was one of the first actors to go after the part of Bick Benedict. But Stevens wanted a younger actor, one who could age throughout the story. He also considered actors such as Charlton Heston, Henry Fonda, Sterling Hayden, Gregory Peck, Burt Lancaster (whom Ferber wanted), Kirk Douglas, James Stewart, and Tyrone Power. Then a Warner Bros. press release on November 6, 1954, whipped up the desired Hollywood frenzy with news that Rock Hudson had been loaned out by Universal and was cast to play Bick Benedict. It has been said that Hudson had caught the eye of Joan McTavish, who worked in Universal's talent department and was at the time Stevens's girlfriend and later his second wife. McTavish apparently noticed that Hudson aged twenty-five years in the film *The Lawless Breed*, although rumor also had it that Stevens was impressed when he saw Hudson age in Douglas Sirk's soaper *Magnificent Obsession*. Nevertheless, a Warner Bros. press release soon appeared: "The prize acting plum of the year, and one which has often been reported in the grasp of a number of Hollywood's top male stars, goes to a dark horse who has never once been mentioned in the spirited competition. ROCK HUDSON has been selected by George Stevens out of all of Hollywood's great as the best to play Bick Benedict, the towering Texan." Hudson cabled Stevens from out of town November 4, 1954, "Just heard the wonderful news. Am walking in clouds [and] will arrive in Los Angeles Monday. Will call you if I may." "Didn't I tell you last week Rock Hudson would get 'Giant?'" Louella Parsons wrote in her November 6 column in the *Los Angeles Examiner*. "At first Universal-International was reluctant to loan out their boy wonder that clicked so big in 'Magnificent Obsession.' But Rock begged so hard he finally won."[13]

Elizabeth Taylor was far from Stevens's first choice to play the pivotal role of Leslie Lynnton. In fact he thought her too young at age twenty-three to play a woman who ages twenty-five years as the story's unwavering matriarch. Again he turned to Audrey Hepburn before anyone else and traveled to New York with Moffat's profile in hand to discuss the part. After she said no, agents all around town called Stevens offering their clients, actresses including Irene Dunne and Anne Baxter. Stevens briefly considered Grace Kelly, Jane Wyman, Jennifer Jones, Jean Simmons, Rita Hayworth, and Olivia de Havilland, among many others. Stevens especially wanted Kelly because she was, in his words, the "most important female star" of the time. As much as Kelly let it be known that she wanted the part of Leslie Lynnton, MGM refused to loan her to Stevens. Taylor persevered. She was due to have a baby but promised to be ready to work soon after. Eventually Stevens hired her, saying that he liked her too much and had too much respect for her "possibilities" to turn her down.

For Jett, Stevens reconsidered some of the actors he originally thought of for Bick, such as William Holden and Robert Mitchum, the latter whom Stevens made serious attempts to get. But when conflicting production dates with another project put Mitchum out of the running, Stevens also considered, among many, Anthony Quinn, Rod Steiger, Nick Adams, Van Heflin, Montgomery Clift, and even Richard Burton, who after giving the part some thought wrote to Stevens from Spain on March 18, 1955, "I have worked at the 'Texas' material, but to no avail. I just don't seem to drawl in the right places and my 'You-alls' don't quite come off. There are quite a few Texans staying at this hotel — Castellana Hilton — and my efforts totally fail to impress them."

Stevens later recalled how James Dean came onto the scene. Dean was at work on *Rebel Without a Cause* for Warner Bros. and especially became friends with Fred Guiol. "When we were finishing the script . . . this boy used to go by [Stevens's office]. . . . Jimmy Dean. He had to come in the back door because the girl in our office wouldn't let him in. She said, 'There's this fellow out here; I don't know who he is, he's got a rope and he's making tricks with it out there.' He used to come in the back and visit with Freddie Guiol and me. . . . Jimmy was not the man to play this part . . . it should have been . . . a physically larger man and bigger boned. [But] this guy was fascinating. He wasn't looking for a part in the film, but Freddie and I said, 'What would happen if he played this part? He's such a brilliant chap.' And so we engaged him."[14]

Filming got off to a precarious start. On January 20, 1955, six months before cast and crew went to Virginia to begin shooting, Warner Bros. executive Eric Stacey sent Jack Warner a confidential memo spelling out his less-than-optimistic budget predictions for a Stevens film:

> The preliminary estimate for *Giant* has come out at $3,367,750, based on a 72-day schedule. I do not believe this picture can be made for this figure. . . . Mr. Stevens has never made a picture in less than 72 days. His daily average on *Shane* and *A Place in the Sun* comes out at 1 3/4 pages per week. *Giant* is bigger and more complicated than any he has made . . . and should *not* be compared to *Shane,* which had only a few sets and people. . . . I believe that once the green light is given to go ahead with this picture it will be next to impossible to control the costs, due to Mr. Stevens's methods of shooting. . . .
>
> I consider it extremely dangerous to start a picture of this magnitude and know expense before (a) the script is in better and shorter condition, and (b) all locations and sets have been ok'd by Mr. Stevens and time allowed to estimate them properly in accordance with his views. I feel that cast commitments previously made should not force us to start before we are ready and have had a chance to give you a more realistic budget.[15]

Jack Warner was not yet moved and Stevens began shooting on May 19, 1955, with an allotted seventy-seven-day schedule. But it was clear soon enough that the initial estimated $1.5 million budget was not going to work. A revised $2.5 million budget did not look much better, nor did Stevens's shooting schedule, which production manager Mel Dellar thought to be about thirty-five days short. Eric Stacey predicted that *Giant* would eventually cost about $5 million dollars. Jack Warner wanted Stevens to keep the picture under two hours, but Stevens had no intention of doing that. Nor did he agree to film *Giant* in CinemaScope (he once quipped that it was the perfect process if you were a boa constrictor), despite Warner's constant urging him to do so. Finally the studio settled for Stevens's choice: 1.66 to 1, which, not being as wide as CinemaScope, made the characters seem especially tall.

After working in Los Angeles on interior scenes such as the Lynnton dinner party, on May 30 cast and crew went to Virginia to shoot exterior scenes at Keswick, seven miles east of Charlottesville. By June 4 the company arrived in Marfa, Texas, where they remained for a long — and very hot — part of the shoot. Stevens knew enough about public relations to include the townspeople in on the production, hiring locals as extras, janitors, and guards. He extended the gesture further by getting Texas millionaires to appear in the large party scenes. It was not long before Marfa became too hot and boring for many cast members and crew. In her autobiography, Mercedes McCambridge, who plays Bick's sister, Luz Benedict, described the Marfa locale for the most part "the ugliest landscape on the face of the earth. Sheer nothing! No hills, no water, no trees, no grass, just vast acres of creepy-crawlies and dive-bombing bugs and biddy towns thousands of miles apart."[16] Jane Withers, who played the Benedicts' neighbor, Vashti Synthe, recalled setting up her own brand of the USO, flying in deli food for the cast and crew each night. She remembered also that card games helped pass the time; Hudson especially liked to play bridge.[17] Dialogue coach Bob Hinkle — who also pinch-hit on some dialogue, coming up with Jett's line to Leslie, "You look might good enough to eat" — also remembered spending time with Dean hunting jackrabbits, for which local cattle ranchers were grateful and paid Dean and Hinkle since the rabbits dined heartily on precious grazing land.[18] Earl Holliman recalled that for the most part James Dean stayed a loner and did not especially extend himself to get to know the crew. Holliman remembered also that three of the younger actresses, Carroll Baker (who played young Luz Benedict), Jane Withers, and Fran Bennett (Judy Benedict) shared a house during the shoot and that he, Dennis Hopper and other cast members would spend evenings there listening to records.[19]

While still in Marfa, Stevens received a letter from agent and producer Leland Hayward in New York asking him to think seriously about directing Peter Viertel's script for Hemingway's *The Old Man and the Sea*. But Stevens could not give it much thought. Back at Warner Bros., the front office was worried. On June 6, 1955, Steve Trilling sent a memo to Jack Warner telling him that as of that date the company was already behind by eight days and would be $200,000 over budget by the end of June. The notion of epic scale seemed to go in different directions. Trilling estimated that the scheduled finish date of August 22 would never be met; shooting would probably wrap in the first or second week in October. By the beginning of August, after almost seventy days of shooting, Warner executives again worried. Stevens's habit of overshooting, aggravated by Elizabeth Taylor's all too-frequent illnesses, added up to serious production delays. To Jack Warner they shaped up to financial woes: Stevens looked to be perpetually just one step behind defaulting on his agreement with the studio. While Warner vacationed in France during much of the production's stay in Marfa and for some postproduction, he kept a running dialogue of letters and cables with Steve Trilling on the film's errant progress. The two men were poised from the start to stage a coup and take film away from Stevens. In that same June 6, 1955 letter Trilling told Warner that the "approved budget [of] $2,500,000 must be exceeded by 10% or $250,000 additional before WB can take control . . . they spend roughly $10,000 to $12,000 daily, therefore within one week they will have exceeded the $25,000 margin or where WB can assume production control." But if they elected to take over the picture they would have to finance completion and retain all of the film's employees "so long as they are not personally in default." Still, they could "exercise any and all economies." Trilling continued: "We could then demand that Stevens follow our request for the reduction of coverage, setups, eliminating pages, sequences, and etc. and if Stevens refused our directives then we could take the position that he had breached his contract and replace him as director. I'm reciting all these facts so that if we have any phone calls or cables regarding the matter you have a complete bird's eye view of the situation as it stands. Possibly Gordon Douglas or somebody in that category could take over if it becomes necessary." He added Elizabeth Taylor to his list of complaints, since the actress had been holding up production, especially in Los Angeles, with various illnesses. Trilling said, "Elizabeth

Taylor has been ill the past week with a blood infection — I believe a small clot in her leg, which probably is the aftermath of her recent childbirth. The company has been able to work without her since Monday but was forced to close down today, Saturday. . . . The dailies have been excellent; still all in daily form so there has been no way of seeing any assembled footage. As you know, Stevens waits until the picture is completed before he starts assembling and cutting and it's a very long-length procedure."

On August 11 Warner cabled Trilling, "Stevens now has two hours forty minutes / Have you explained [to him that] first cut will be upwards five hours, can't use more [than] two and a half hours. He must not squander dollars / certainly make eliminations now / is he using more [than] one camera? / They have now exceeded ten percent maybe can frighten Stevens / We may take legal position protect our investment." The tides of disapproval turned temporarily when, several cables later, Trilling told Warner that "any delays last few days [were] attributable to Elizabeth Taylor illness as Stevens was going faster." On August 19 Trilling told Warner that "after lengthy conference [with] Ginsberg [and] Stevens, George promised less coverage and footage, enable cut finishing date from Sept 23 to Sept 16, etc. . . . both Ginsberg Stevens alarmed figures / particularly appreciate overage practically / negates possibility their participation / Stevens claims feels badly / not lack faith his part but unfortunate illness / Taylor and other circumstances created delays." Warner responded: "Talk over major seriousness [with] Giant [Inc.]. Try insist finished 16th Sept / does Giant need carry expensive second unit don't see why / have we established properly Giant's breach contract, if not do so, may wait take over picture to expedite cutting as Stevens will take year or more we cannot tie up tremendous cash while Stevens takes year cut." Trilling told Warner that Stevens "insistent second unit saving time coverage," but that Roy Obringer [general council for Warner Bros.] was studying Warner's contract with Giant Productions to determine "advisability" of "now sending written notice" to them. He advised Warner to do nothing at the present time, since taking any action might precipitate "bad feelings" on Stevens's side. Trilling later wrote: "Contract provides Giant required within four months after completion principal photography delivered to Warners the negative and a final cut positive print including the sound track fully cut, titled, edited and scored. If fails to do Warners must notify then Giant has ten days to cure failure after which they in default and we can take over."

By July 10 much of the cast and crew — with the exception of Fred Guiol's second unit work with Dean on his oil rig — returned by train to Los Angeles. By the end of August, however, after more of Taylor's illnesses and Dean's routine lateness to the set, Stevens was further behind schedule. Hudson and Taylor, along with other cast members, would have to be paid additional money. Shooting was finally completed the second week in October 1955.

In contrast to schedule trouble at Warner Bros., newspapers around the country were spreading cheerier, gossipy news of *Giant* to the millions of Americans awaiting its release. *Giant* was simply, and continuously, big news. Fans learned that Stevens had interviewed over 150 babies for the film; that James Dean liked to listen to opera, especially to Renata Tebaldi, before going to the set at Warner Bros.; and that Stevens had a sixty-foot swimming pool constructed on stage 7 of the lot for the short scene when Leslie walks into another political discussion about tax cuts late in the film. It was also said that 250 extras were hired for the banquet scene at the Jett Rink Airport. Especially newsworthy was the fact that production designer Boris Leven had the Reata mansion built in Los Angeles, then shipped, in pieces, to Marfa where it was later assembled. The most colorful bit of news to emerge from the set appeared in Sidney Skolsky's syndicated column on July 7, 1955: "One day while he was directing a mob scene on the vast Texas prairie location of *Giant*, with more than 200 visitors watching the action, George Stevens was interrupted by the blaring P. A. system on the set. 'Mr. Stevens, your office in Hollywood wants to know where you left the keys to your garage. The termite inspector is there and can't get in.' Unfortunately Mr. Stevens had them in his pants pocket and they had to be flown back to Hollywood with the day's rushes. P.S. The termite inspector got in the next day."

Stevens now had to edit 875,000 feet of developed film to what would become a 180-minute film. This precipitated yet more angst for Warner Bros. Jack Warner plotted yet another takeover of the film in late summer 1956. Again in France, Warner cabled Steve Trilling on August 19: "Worried *Giant* only five reels scored." On August 20 Trilling told him the film would be completed on September 26 and then sent word, on August 27, that nine reels had been scored. Jack Warner telegrammed Trilling from Antibes on August 30: "Did you correctly legally record Stevens 26th will take over positively?" After several more missives back and forth Warner wired Trilling on September 4: "Will positively 26th take over *Giant;* fed up [with] this genius remove all from Giant other payrolls [as] soon [as] possible."

But a takeover never occurred, nor could it have, and Trilling had better news by September 10. Soon after, Warner wrote from New York after a preview, "*Giant* reviews here unanimous one hundred percent great. Audience loved picture. Confidentially picture needs two or three good cuts down at end. Going over this thoroughly with Stevens this afternoon."

Stevens spent close to a year editing. He told Bruce Petri in 1973 that he catalogued the film in fourteen editing books: each take was given a number and description so that it could be easily referred to when it came time to put the film together. By including frames from each take, he could quickly recall how the take had gone and decide if he wanted to use it. Later editor William Hornbeck told Richard Dyer McCann, "and sometimes after we have worked on a scene till it has become substantially different, we go back to the book and pick out a take that we had rejected before, because now it fits better with what we've got."[20] In an interview with Philip K. Scheuer of the *Los Angeles Times* Stevens explained his editing process:

> I want height and I want to be able to edit freely. Height because the movie is a world of upright things and tall men. Freedom to edit because, in the case of *Giant,* I am telling a story that goes through three generations and it has to roll right along . . . I've never seen anyone who can cut Cinemascope yet . . . why not? because it's too inclusive: the wide picture is just all there. It doesn't put the demand on the filmmaker or editor for selectivity and it makes it difficult for him to eliminate things — things that he could save for the next shot. When you eliminate your opportunity for cutting you eliminate the possibility of creating the varying rhythms that give film its form — slow rhythms, fast rhythms. The process just doesn't allow for the variety I like in cinema. Taking cross-cutting out of photography is like taking the net out of tennis: there's no longer any reason for going back and forth.[21]

The matter of height was just as important. After seeing *Shane* cut off at the top and bottom by projectionists, in *Giant* he masked the top and bottom of his camera as a way to force projectionists to align their equipment with the newly proportioned image. Stevens later said:

> [*Giant*] was made for a road show with an intermission. They hadn't had any of those shows for a long time. There was an end of the first act when Jett Rink's oil well came in and he confronted his rich friends on the porch, saluted Bick Benedict's wife, got punched in the chin for his trouble and then hit Bick. He came in with his old battered truck; that was the ending. That was a very good act ending, strong, with promise because things were difficult. The next act started with the oil wells coming in. We had this whole oil well development, a good start to the second act. While I was cutting the picture my partner [Ginsberg] went back to New York to get a theater to open it as a road show. By the time I got to New York with the picture, C. B. DeMille had come in with *The Ten Commandments* and Mike Todd had come in with *Around the World in Eighty Days* and there was not a road show theatre. . . . Now I had contractual control, but it's like you have control of your fate at sea but you're afloat with a life preserver. I had organized it for a very big theatre. The film ran about three hours and nineteen minutes. I didn't see how we could keep an audience sitting three hours and nineteen minutes without an intermission. We had previewed it with an intermission. We had also worked to cut to move it along as fast as possible. So we went into the theatre where people were going to sit for three hours and nineteen minutes. Hopefully we could get by. Well, somehow or other the pace of the picture let the audience get along without an intermission . . . the picture went straight through and it has always been run that way.[22]

When Stevens finished editing, and after a powerful Texas film exhibitor attempted, with no luck, to convince him to cut the scene where Bick and his friends mention their twenty-seven-and-a-half oil depletion tax, *Giant* went through six previews around California. Warner Bros. premiered the film first at New York City's Roxy Theatre on October 11, 1956, at Hollywood's Chinese Theatre the next night, and then one night later in Texas theatres. One year later Edna Ferber sold her share of *Giant* stock back Warner Bros. for $650,000 and in 1958 Jack Warner declared *Giant* and *Sayonara* to be the two top grossing films in the studio's history.

The Mother of Us All

> The character development herein is the story of
> the change of Texas. Leslie is the agent of this.
>
> —George Stevens

Stevens's takeover of Ferber's book put Leslie center stage and sent her into a happy, mesmerizing wilderness that filmgoers would love. When Ferber's novel opens, Leslie Benedict is a middle-aged woman and has been married to Bick Benedict for twenty-five years. We first see her planning one of her famous weekends: the Benedict family, along with close friends and neighbors, politicians, and perhaps a Hollywood starlet or two, are about to fly to Hermoso for the opening of the Jett Rink Airport and Hotel. Leslie and Bick are old hands at lavish weekends. By now they have cast a wide social net of friends and neighbors extending from Reata outward. Their grown children, and their children's children, are an integral part of the structure.

The most important change Stevens made to Ferber's novel was to rearrange this opening and restructure the entire narrative. His film opens twenty-five or so years earlier. Bick Bendict, a Texas cattle baron, travels to Maryland (changed from Ferber's Virginia) to buy a beautiful horse called War Winds owned by Dr. Horace Lynnton. While there Bick falls in love with the beautiful Leslie Lynnton, the doctor's daughter, and after a whirlwind courtship marries Leslie and brings her back to his ranch, Reata, one of the largest in the state of Texas. There they settle into a rocky but lasting marriage.

Stevens rearranged the narrative because his story sense told him that audiences needed a great adventure—of course, a *big* adventure. He changed his focus to Leslie and made her the story's centerpiece. According to Stevens's cinema, whatever she experiences the spectator should also experience. As Stevens said repeatedly in press releases and interviews during the production of *Giant*, "The character development herein is the story of the change of Texas. Leslie is the agent of this."

Stevens opens *Giant* with Leslie Lynnton marrying Bick Benedict and then going west with him to Texas. When she arrives there, Leslie finds a Texas that is desolate: the closest neighbors are miles away and unsophisticated at that. Whatever Leslie finds, Stevens decided, the spectator must also find. Her disappointment is ours as well. She is shocked and bewildered by the life — or lack of it — she finds in Texas; she is sickened by the condition of the Mexicans who work for her husband and live on his land; and she is outraged at the misogyny all around her. "You gentlemen date back one hundred years," she tells Bick and his friends at one point. Leslie is now (as we are) bereft of family, lush, romantic surroundings, and the cosmopolitan lifestyle she has come to know (as we also have, briefly). As she apprehends the isolation she gathers up her resolve to make a life for herself and to take possession of Reata as its mistress. She is temporarily halted in her efforts by Bick's unmarried sister and family matriarch, Luz, but this sister is soon ousted from the picture. When the story ends over three-and-a-half hours later, the Benedicts are two generations larger, Bick is an oil baron as well as a cattle baron, and because he was "raised" under the influence of Leslie's absolute lack of racism, their son, Jordy, has married a Mexican woman, Juana, in the midst of all the anti-Mexican sentiment in Texas. Of all things, Bick Benedict eventually comes to terms with this marriage. Reata, and by extension, much of Texas itself is a different landscape under Leslie's hand.

While Leslie is central to the changes at Reata during the course of the story, she is absolutely *essential* to Stevens's voice and vision as the director of *Giant*. Given her powerful position *within* the story she is, in fact, a displacement for the director's creativity and his voice, powerful enough not only to change culture, as Leslie does, but also to *make* culture, as Stevens does with each of his postwar films. Leslie is the benevolent creator — the "agency," as Stevens himself said — of change and therefore of the narrative movement in *Giant*. She can turn feminist criticism on its head and even challenge Oedipus's ownership of a story.

As Stevens saw himself become a spokesperson for the masses back in America during the war, his ability to use his camera to create a record of the war put him at the center of a web of communications that reached out to all Americans. When he returned to Hollywood to make movies he understood the influence of his voice as he connected powerfully once more with American film audiences who enthusiastically embraced *A Place in the Sun* and *Shane*. This connection only intensified during *Giant*'s production as the media kept vigil and created an open line of communication between Stevens and waiting moviegoers. *Giant* was to be a huge, influential cultural document the public awaited, a populist text that Americans waited to consume even before it arrived. *Giant* turned Stevens into everyone's director, America's essential, democratic storyteller. His frame got higher and wider, his subjects became more serious, more personal, as they now swept up central issues of the decade: racism, corporate greed, familial relationships — all for the sake of telling us a story. The cinematic vista widened to accommodate Stevens's large voice and growing vision.

When Leslie Lynnton Benedict comes to the West she is an evocation of the Pilgrims coming to an uncharted American wilderness in the seventeenth century, imposing order onto a physical and psychological space where a familiar culture has yet to exist. She is also Stephen Crane's nineteenth-century heroine in "The Bride Comes to Yellow Sky," the newly married young woman who travels with her sheriff husband to his Texas hometown. On the train he tells her, as Bick similarly tells Leslie, "'It's a thousand miles from one end of Texas to the other; and this train runs right across it, and stops but four times.' He had the pride of an owner."[23] When the bride comes to Yellow Sky, she tames the land on which she sets foot simply because she is female and creates order wherever she goes. Leslie's organizing, nurturing presence tames Reata, makes it a more "tolerable" place, ushering in a new sense of emotional satisfaction, the kind George Eastman could have imagined but never truly grasped. She makes women spectators feel just as powerful. Leslie's predecessors are large in historic and mythical import, just as Stevens's stories are.

Giant opens with just this largeness, with credits that reach skyward, evoking Stevens's almost stratospheric response to the first page of Ferber's novel. His camera captures the same large vista as it perches high up above Leslie and Bick when they first drive through Reata's gates. The large sense of space creates an almost giddy atmosphere, a certain euphoria of possibility. *Giant* is Stevens's only happy postwar film, and Leslie is his postwar heroine who affects the film's psychological landscape in a positive, nurturing, *enduring* way. Where *A Place in the Sun* and *Shane* are films about longing, the impossibility of fulfillment and self-definition, unfulfilled desire, sadness, even tragedy and loneliness, *Giant* is a film that is giddy with the idea of large spaces, the sensual nature of consuming, and the fulfillment of wishes and desires. The way it enjoys its own sense of space, its emotional tenor is the cinematic version of

Lucy, Ricky, Fred, and Ethel singing happily, childlike, on the ride west from New York to Los Angeles. *Giant* is especially about *things*, material things. It is about ownership, about the going after, the getting, and the having. It is about the achievement and the aesthetic of wealth and material goods—about money, accessibility, profit, and excess. "Of course it's a story about Texas," Stevens reiterated to the press during production. "But only because Texas, right now, represents the American dream in a special way—as the place where there is perhaps the most dramatic realization of material possibilities."[24] But it is not so far removed from the real to acknowledge the down side of money and power. The two, in the case of Jett Rink, do not signify the equality of one dreamer to another.

In its shiny coating and glossy sensibility, *Giant* is a pop fantasy story, a text upon which we see our fantasies, where we imagine our collective dream of comfort and happy endings in a time when, after the war, it first became possible to wish, fantasize, and desire again. *Giant* is so big there is no *end* to desire.

Still, Leslie is not the prewar Stevens heroine, the sexually playful Jean Arthur in a two-piece bathing suit and platform heels in *The More the Merrier*; she is not Katharine Hepburn the kittenish flirt who meets Spencer Tracy in *Woman of the Year*. Leslie is a maternal figure who helps to keep the affluent dream afloat and teaches tolerance. She is a figure of postwar domesticity: a married woman who nurtures, and unlike Angela Vickers and Marion Starrett, she does not merely represent the *possibility* of wholeness that is forbidden to the loner male who cannot possess her. Leslie Lynnton Benedict can actually be possessed; she can create family. When you create family you also create and *sustain* culture.

But to be that nurturing presence, to make the landscape tolerant, Leslie cannot be maternal and sexual at the same time. She needs to exchange one for the other. The sexuality that led her to Bick in the first place, the signal of her sexuality, War Winds, must be sacrificed. Bick first saw Leslie riding War Winds in Maryland; he looked at them both, locked together as they were, and called her "a beautiful animal." Leslie is the one to tell Bick all of War Winds's "bad habits." She and the horse are interlocked in their beauty, power, and wildness.

But the necessary transference from sexualized female to mother occurs in an early scene. Leslie rides out on War Winds to be with Bick at

Reata. Jealous that Leslie can handle this obviously dangerous animal, Luz drives out with Jett Rink in a jeep and tells Bick to send Leslie back home. Bick complies: Leslie is sent home in Jett's jeep and Luz climbs onto War Winds. But rather than go right home, Jett Rink takes Leslie through Vientecito, the vicinity where Reata's poor Mexican workers live. In a simultaneous action that Stevens achieves through cross-cutting, Leslie discovers the horrid conditions of Vientecito's population while Luz attempts to ride War Winds. As Leslie sees the terrible conditions in the village — women lay sick with the children and have no milk to give them — she becomes motherly (the first time in the film), wanting to help and protect these people. At the same time, Luz digs her spurs into War Winds's sides and the horse eventually throws her. When Leslie returns to Reata she finds War Winds hurt and tied up outside the front of the house. As she goes into the house she and War Winds (with a close-up on the horse's face) exchange glances — almost predicting his impending death. Luz dies from a concussion just as Leslie tells the doctor to visit Vientecito before he leaves the vicinity. With Luz now gone, Leslie has become mistress of the house. But at the same time, Bick has War Winds destroyed, and along with it, it is suggested, any last traces of Leslie's sexual behavior and appeal. Whereas her sexuality drew Bick to her — and to War Winds — that sexuality has no place in the domestic life Leslie now takes on.

In soothing and civilizing the Texas landscape Leslie makes it receptive to the tolerance she has brought from the East. But she is not the radical feminist. This is the 1950s and Leslie blends in and accommodates as much as she teaches. Stevens's large vistas likewise accommodate and even smooth Leslie's rough edges along with the rough edges of the racism Stevens inserts into the story. The house at Reata is huge, the swimming pool Bick later builds is enormous, Jett Rink's airport is so big we must first see it in a small-scale model. Even Bick's fight with Sarge at the diner — a Stevens addition to the story because Bick must demonstrate his transformation — is big stuff, played out to the song on the juke-box that became the Texas state anthem, "The Yellow Rose of Texas." The surroundings are so lush, so large and shiny, that the uncomfortable subject of racism slips in without seeming a threat to the audience.

But the threat is there nonetheless. Leslie and Bick's son, Jordy (Dennis Hopper), marries Juana and produces a grandchild who, as Bick later laments, "looks like a little wetback." Bick is a long time coming around to accept his biracial family. Earlier, when he offers Reata first to Jordy and then to Bob Dace and is unable to get a taker, the camera speaks for Bick. Stevens wrote in the script, "When Bick offers Bob Dace the job and Bob turns it down, have Angel ask for the job. Although Bick is very fond of him, and proud of his ability as a cowboy, he can't, of course, give him the position because he is a Mexican. This will build for finish with grandson." As each "son" turns down his offer the camera finds Angel Obregon (Sal Mineo), the son of Reata's foreman, sitting back in the foyer, listening to the offers. Later, when Angel is killed in the war, Stevens illustrates the irony of the event. The train rolls into Reata and stops. Only after it pulls away does the camera catch Angel's coffin lying in the space the train left behind. The life-death cycle touches a Mexican family no differently than it would one of Reata's white Anglo sons.

But when Jordy marries the Mexican Juana, integration is still not easy in the land Leslie has tamed. When Juana is snubbed at the beauty salon at Jett Rink's hotel, Jordy confronts Jett in front of hundreds of banquet guests. Jett knocks Jordy down and Bick is ready to attack Jett in return. But he realizes Jett is "all through" and reneges. Nevertheless, as Jordy later reminds his father, Bick felt humiliated to see his son punched by Jett in such a public display. Jordy (the product of Leslie's racial tolerance) shames Bick into realizing this fact. Later, when Sarge insults Juana, and by extension the entire Benedict family, Bick springs into action in a fist fight to add dramatic import to Bick's newfound beliefs. He loses the fight but wins the battle to accept his now biracial family. This acceptance paves the way for *Giant*'s final shot and what must have been a jolt to the complacency of the film's undoubtedly predominantly white audience: with a full frame of Bick's grandson, the half-Mexican Jordan Benedict III. Though Stevens thought that a director's politics had no place in the film frame, the shot is bold dramatic move, and an *unconscious* political one at that.

Jett Rink, on the other hand, the son of Texas cheated out of his birthright, is another kind of story — the loser, the "have-not," despite his accumulated millions. His continued marginalization in the story drives home the point that tolerance is fragile, always threatening to dissolve. While Juana is accepted into the Benedict family and into the film's social fabric (she is a female and *makes* family), Jett's poverty of birth and pedigree exclude him. Stevens appears to have less tolerance for Jett; he remains, as Ivan Moffat wrote of him, at the "lower depths of a great nation." Early on he tells Leslie not to confuse him with the Mexican workers at Reata. Stevens does not, eventually ennobling Juana for the sake of drama and leaving Jett behind.

While *Giant* ends with its conflicts intact, these conflicts have little potency while set up against the backdrop of Stevens's predominantly large, open, blissfully colorful landscape. The sheer size of it drums up enough giddy energy to flatten, diffuse conflict — enough so that whatever *is* threatening — even the political act of putting a baby's brown face on the huge screen — cannot seem so for long. This is a film about *making* and enduring. Even *Giant*'s props were large, and scattered far and wide after the production shut down. The Reata house was left standing and used to store grain for a period of time. On May 5, 1962, Rock Hudson wrote Stevens telling him he had been up in a SAC B-52 bomber and used the house, now moved to Roswell, New Mexico, as a target during a low-level bomb run; he wrote, "hit a bulls-eye on my first try."

8

The One Who Cannot Be Left Behind

The Diary of Anne Frank

History is precisely the way we are implicated in each other's traumas.

— Cathy Caruth

Forgive me, they haven't given me the name "little bundle of contradictions" for nothing!

— Anne Frank, Friday, July 21, 1944

After directing two successful films situated in the American west, Stevens turned his attention back to Europe to direct what appeared to be a more intimate story, Albert Hackett and Frances Goodrich's Pulitzer-winning Broadway play, *The Diary of Anne Frank*, the story of a thirteen-year-old Jewish girl who hid with her family from the Nazis for two years. Anne Frank then was sent to a concentration camp where she died just before her fifteenth birthday, two months before the war ended. In 1954, before he began shooting *Giant*, Stevens signed a two-picture contract (which then turned into a one-picture deal) with Twentieth Century Fox, and when he learned that the studio owned the Anne Frank property, he was convinced that he should be the one to direct it. It had been more than a decade since he returned from Europe and now he finally had material for what was truly his war film.

It is understandable that the writings of this young Jewish girl would touch Stevens given his experiences at the Dachau concentration camp. More than that, he believed that Anne's diary was an important cultural document, ironic testimony that Anne had outlived Hitler's plan to empty Europe of its Jewish population. Stevens's film on Anne Frank would be the first commercial picture to bring up the Holocaust, albeit indirectly, from within the walls of the Secret Annex where Anne and her family hid.

In approaching *The Diary of Anne Frank,* however, Stevens was forced to confront memories of his experiences at the concentration camps in 1945 that he may not have wanted to revisit so pointedly. A few years after the war he and his friend, attorney Vincent Hallinan, sat down to watch some of the color footage Stevens shot in Dachau; they could take only a few minutes of it before turning it off and Stevens relegated the footage to his Bekins storage in North Hollywood, California. Now, confronting the experience again, thirteen years later, he averted his eyes from the horror of the camps as much as he could — and as much as the 1950s would impel him to do. No one was ready yet to talk about the Holocaust. But when Stevens did look closely at Anne Frank and the diary she produced, he learned a large lesson: that not only was his life inextricably caught up with Anne's, but so were other lives in the audience implicated in the trauma of that one defining moment in history. In his film he would try to find an aesthetic to express the power of that inclusive moment in history.

At Dachau Stevens's reaction was not unlike that of other Americans who entered the camps at the end of the war. Deborah Lipstadt recorded interviews with American news correspondents who spoke about their first reactions upon seeing the concentration camps: "Even now that correspondents were witnessing the grim results of the Final Solution, they could not grasp what they were seeing. . . . They found it difficult to admit to themselves — and their readers — what they were witnessing. . . . They did not associate what they were now seeing in these camps, where most of the survivors were Jews." Not only could the correspondents not talk about what they saw, they could not even "grasp" it.[1] There was something terrible, evil even, found there. It was only years later that

Stevens was able to describe its pervasiveness: "Of all the outrages of human nature [that] bring these latent and deep-rooted emotions to the surface . . . [there is] *nothing* like a concentration camp. Everything evil will be exposed in a day . . . it's deplorable because it undercuts one terribly. . . . The [German] army, what they stood for was the worst, worst possible thing that's happened in centuries."[2] The country, the world, was caught up in a collective gasp that soon settled into a refusal to discuss publicly what occurred in the camps. The event that came to define the darkest moments of the century was still too immediate, too horrifying an event to absorb into collective consciousness — even as Stevens made his film.

When Stevens went to Amsterdam in 1957 to scout locations for *Anne Frank,* he took along a yellow loose-leaf notebook used as a diary, just as he had done so many times before. Standing on the street in front of Anne's house, walking up the stairs to the Secret Annex, Stevens produced his own kind of diary, no doubt feeling an intimate connection with Anne, enough so to write in his notebook, "Why, oh why did Anne have to die? Was it so that we would learn something?"[3] He stretched his imagination out to meet her. Anne Frank was a thirteen-year-old girl who viewed the world through the lens of romantic optimism. Her diary is a mix of real and direct discussion of the horror of what was happening around her as well as a wish to hold that horror in abeyance. "I have, as it were, a dual personality," she wrote in a 1944 entry. "One half embodies my exuberant cheerfulness. . . . This side is usually lying in wait and pushes away the other, which is much better, deeper and purer."[4]

The film Stevens produced resembles the "dual personality" Anne described in her diary. He entreated the Anne who also dreamed of hundreds and thousands of eyes someday reading her prose by drawing as many spectators as possible into Anne's experience. While Stevens's film cannot escape the horrors of the Holocaust that drove the Frank and van Daan families into their hiding place, it sometimes looks as if it would like to — as if the film wanted to get Anne out of that Secret Annex so that she could be a typical teenager. The more Anne was a typical teenager the less she was a Jew who died in Bergen-Belsen and the less Stevens would have to look back at the Holocaust and at Dachau. Stevens produced a film with its own duplicitous nature in this regard, a blend of fact colliding with fiction and realism often covered over by romanticism — also honoring the way Anne experienced herself in her diary. This suited his view of filmmaking only too well, since he had always believed that films were more invigorating, more attractive versions of the world outside. Refashioning Anne this way for *The Diary of Anne Frank* was Stevens's way of expressing his truest connection to her. Everyone wanted to look away: Anne, Stevens, the audience. Their connection was the extent to which they could — and could not.

Text without Borders

Anne Frank's diary is a text always in the process of being revised. Even today the diary is thought to be still incomplete, making it a document that is continuously pending. In light of the way Anne produced the diary — her constant revision of it even before she left it on the floor of the Secret Annex — it is a story that always changes shape. Anne's intention to write and then revise pages for an imagined public audience is the diary's most prominent feature. While some scholars have called the invented "Kitty" to whom Anne writes evidence of her secreting information, creating a secret place, it is more likely that "Kitty" is Anne's first "public" reader. Her wish for a reading public would demand that the diary be revised until it could please a broad audience.

The very first diary was a red and white checked photo book given to Anne by her father on her thirteenth birthday (she herself helped pick it out). The critical edition of the *Diary* charts the diary's revision: Anne's first diary begins on June 12, 1942, with the well-known line, "I hope I shall be able to confide in you completely, as I have never been able to do in anyone before; and I hope that you will be a great support and comfort to me." This diary covers the period from June 12 to December 5, 1942, including additions in 1943 and 1944 "when she also used up some of the pages she had previously left blank." "Daddy has tracked down another new diary for me" she wrote in a new exercise book begun on December 22, 1943, more than a year after the last diary entry in the first book, which indicates that that portion of the diary is lost. The second book continues until April 17, 1944. A third book was started on April 17, 1944 but has no end date; the last entry in this book is August 1, 1944.[5]

On March 28, 1944, four months before she made her last August entry, Anne heard the minister of education, Gerrit Bolkestein, announce on Radio Oranje that the Netherlands State Institute for War Documentation planned to collect diaries and letters from ordinary citizens to keep a history of the war. Anne was thrilled at the thought that her diary could actually be included in this historical record. "Of course, they all made a rush at my diary immediately," she wrote the day after hearing the broadcast: "Just imagine how interesting it would be if I were to publish a romance of the 'Secret Annex.' The title alone would be enough to make people think it was a detective story." Writing that she wanted to be a journalist she decided to make the tales from the annex interesting enough to be included in this national project. "You've known for a long time that my greatest wish is to become a journalist someday and later a famous writer. . . . I want to publish a book entitled *Het Achterhuis* after the war. Whether I shall succeed or not, I cannot say, but my diary will be a great help." So Anne rearranged her diary again. According to Gerrold van der Stroon, in the critical edition of the *Diary*, she rewrote her first diaries on loose sheets of copy paper. Thus a second version in her handwriting came about. She revised her diary again, expanding, abbreviating and changing names. She also made a list of name changes: "'Anne' became 'Anne Robin,' 'v. Pels' became 'v. Daan,' 'Pfeffer' became 'Dussel,' 'Kleiman' became 'Koophuis,' 'Kugler' became 'Kraler,' 'Bep' became 'Elly.'"[6] Anne was still rewriting when the *Sicherheitsdienst* (the German Security Service) raided the Annex on August 4, 1944. After the raid, Miep Geis, who helped hide the Frank family, collected all the pages of the diary that the Green Police (the Dutch Gestapo) had thrown on the floor of the Secret Annex.

A complete diary will never be reconstructed as it is known that Anne's second version has not been found in full. Also, after the war when Otto Frank returned from Auschwitz and Miep Geis gave him the diary, he copied the contents on a typewriter but omitted parts of the diary that he thought inessential or too personal. He did not want to offend people Anne mentioned who might still be alive, nor did he want to share Anne's comments about her mother. He translated the diary into German and sent it to his mother who lived in Switzerland.

In addition to its always tenuous shape, Anne's diary reads as a self-divided work, reflecting the often-conflicted way Anne experienced herself. In her lengthy final diary entry, just before the Gestapo arrested the group hiding in the Secret Annex, she writes about her duplicitous nature and likens part of herself to a "love film," something not to be taken too seriously, but ironically the kind of film Stevens would make of *her:*

> I've already told you before that I have, as it were, a dual personality. One half embodies my exuberant cheerfulness, making fun of everything, my high-spiritedness, and above all, the way I take everything lightly. . . . This side is usually lying in wait and pushes away the other which is much better, deeper and purer. You must realize that no one knows Anne's better side and that's why most people find me so insufferable.
>
> Certainly I'm a giddy clown for one afternoon, but then everyone's had enough of me for another month. Really, it's just the same as a love film is for deep-thinking people, simply a diversion, amusing just for once, something which is soon forgotten, not bad, but certainly not good. I loathe having to tell you this, but why shouldn't I, if I know it's true anyway? My lighter superficial side will always be too quick for the deeper side of me and that's why it will always win. You can't imagine how often I've already tried to push this Anne away, to cripple her, to hide her, because, after all, she's only half of what's called Anne; but it doesn't work.[7]

Anne cunningly declares the superiority of her "lighter, superficial" side, pretending not to have the strength to push it down and allow the "deeper, purer" side to emerge. But the "lighter," fictional side is the stronger of the two. Considering what lies outside her window, fiction, lightheartedness, and fantasy are a preferable world to inhabit, especially for a young girl who has barely left childhood behind her.

Anne's fictions carried her even to Hollywood — long before Stevens carried her there himself. Like many teenage girls Anne pasted photos of movie stars on the walls of her tiny bedroom in the Annex. Her desire for public attention inspired her also to visit Hollywood in her own writings. In short stories written concurrently with the diary entries, and later published as *Tales from the Secret Annex*, she penned a long fantasy, "Dreams of Movie Stardom": "I was seventeen, an attractive girl with flirtatious eyes and a wealth of dark curls — a teenager filled with ideals, illusions, and daydreams. In one way or another, the day would come when my name would be a household word and my picture would occupy a place of honor in the memory book of every damp-eyed bobby-soxer." In the story she visits Hollywood and stays with the three Lane sisters; she is discovered by a Hollywood producer and briefly flirts with stardom. At the end of the story, however, she realizes that Hollywood is not for her. She stays on for her visit with the Lane sisters nonetheless. "I was deeply grateful. Undisturbed, I hugely enjoyed the rest of my unforgettable vacation. As for dreams of movie stardom, I was cured. I had had a close look at the way celebrities live."[8]

The fantasy life Anne finds so comforting eases the pain of her isolation from the social world she knew and the physical world in which she might walk (late in the diary she tells Peter, the son of the van Daans, in hiding with the Franks, how she offsets the harshness of the war by imagining she is outdoors among fields of grass and flowers). It also offsets the sense of isolation she carries inside herself. "I don't seem to lack anything," she writes. "But it's the same with all my friends, just fun and joking, nothing more. I can never bring myself to talk of anything outside the common round. We don't seem to be able to get any closer, that is the root of the trouble. Perhaps I lack confidence, but anyway, there it is, a stubborn fact and I don't seem to be able to do anything about it. Hence this diary. In order to enhance in my mind's eye the picture of the friend for whom I have waited so long, I don't want to set down a series of bald facts in a diary like most people do, but I want this diary itself to be my friend, and I shall call my friend Kitty."[9]

Much of the time Anne found ways to ignore the horror outside her window. But sometimes she could not: "Everything has upset me again this morning, so I wasn't able to finish a single thing properly. It is terrible outside. Day and night more of those poor miserable people are being dragged off, with nothing but a rucksack and a little money. On the way they are deprived even of these possessions. Families are torn apart, the men, women and children all being separated. Children coming home from school find that their parents have disappeared. Women return from shopping to find their homes shut up and their families gone. The Dutch people are anxious too, their sons are being sent to Germany. Everyone is afraid. . . . No one is able to keep out of it, the whole globe is waging war and although it is going better for the Allies, the end is not yet in sight." On one hand, the fear can feel stratospheric. On the other hand, mixed in with fantasy it is simply her life. While others are mentioned by name and nationality, the Jews, whom she describes at the beginning of the entry, are not. They are too familiar to her, too close to bare naming. The chaos she sees outside reflects the conflict she feels within. "Then I fall asleep with a stupid feeling of wishing to be different from what I am or from what I want to be; perhaps to behave differently from the way I want to behave, or do behave. Oh, heavens above, now I'm getting you in a muddle too." Ironically, Anne's last words in the diary make reference again to fictionalizing herself: "If I'm quiet and serious, everyone thinks it's a new comedy and then I have to get out of it by turning it into a joke."[10]

Shaping the Production

Stevens intended to create a truthful but hopeful portrait of Anne's days in hiding; he wanted to present a view of Anne as a typical teenager rather than a young Jew slated to die in the death camps. On January 17, 1958, six weeks before principal photography began, Anne's original diary was flown from Holland to Los Angeles, paid for by Otto Frank, where it was kept in a bank vault when it was not being studied. Stevens would use the diary to create a facsimile of it for the camera and for press junkets.

The facsimile that Stevens and his staff produced is a remarkable document in itself—a blend of fact and fiction that is a microcosm of the way truth and fancy merge in the film. Combining historical truth with artifice, Stevens had an exact replica made of Anne's handwriting and interspersed it with childhood photographs of Anne and her family. They were then combined with childhood photographs of Millie Perkins, the actress chosen to play Anne Frank, and photographs of the actor Joseph Schildkraut, who would play Otto Frank. There lay Anne's handwriting reproduced on the page; there on the page lay Anne herself, reproduced in photographs.

The facsimile shows Stevens's seriousness in "reconstructing" Anne by reconstructing the document that represents her in the world. He wished to make the diary the visual centerpiece of the film, the "real" artifact that organizes the film's narrative and segues between events. Creating the facsimile also brings Stevens closer to Anne since he is now also the facsimile "author" of a diary. The document collapses their histories together, creating a closeness between two authors. Yet he cannot always manage to keep Anne and her family realistic; for example, in a script note where he jotted down some thoughts about the Franks before he began filming: "The whole thing is a matter of survival, a story of survival for your entertainment. Anne Frank wrote with the intention of entertaining her readers. She had no thought of being a sacrifice, a martyred heroine — no thought of not surviving 'her time of trial,' and as she wished, she did survive. Her little checkered covered diary, which was the personification of Anne's thinking, survived, and with it Anne." He also exalted the Frank family: "The Franks were a kind of royalty of the human race — regal in dignity and wisdom and spirit — and the wealthy ones of the human race; a great wealth of dignity and nobility and good humor." Finally in the note he gave some (disorganized) thought to his audience for the film. "The story of Anne Frank — popular/fiction," he wrote, "The truth of Anne Frank is as strange as any fiction. Her story indicates that this strange fiction could happen to us — the audience. . . . The New York audience that saw the play was an audience from the world that had shut the war out completely. The film is for the world that has experienced war's rough usage. *Audience.* What do we know about ourselves — that part of us where these mysteries lie? This is our audience curiosity here. . . . Films not made to please Hollywood. This a great local mistake." Stevens knows his film will get a wider audience, both those who shut the war out and those, in Europe, who experienced the war. Finally, Stevens wrote down those inevitable words to himself, "Remember from the start this is a love story," the same words he used in planning *Alice Adams,* the view he held of Dreiser's Clyde and Sondra in *A Place in the Sun.* He had no trouble adapting this feature of the Hacketts' play. Anne's story would be romantic.

Stevens also knew that late 1950s America was not yet ready to see the face of the Holocaust without some veil placed over it. Certainly it was evident in the population of Holocaust survivors who immigrated to the United States after the war. In his study of the impact of the Holocaust on American life, Peter Novick writes, "It is said that survivors' memories were so painful they repressed them, that only after the passage of many years could they bear to speak of what they had undergone." He also describes the broad repression of discussion about the Holocaust in postwar America in general. "By the late 1940s and throughout the 1950s, talk of the Holocaust was something of an embarrassment in American public life. This was not, as many have claimed, because of any shame or guilt on the part of Americans concerning their response to the Holocaust. Rather, it was a consequence of revolutionary changes in world alignments. These changes required far-reaching ideological retooling in the United States, after which talk of the Holocaust was not just unhelpful but actively obstructive."[11] Several factors added to this silence: three years after the end of the war, America bombed Hiroshima, an event that created guilt — spoken and unspoken — for many Americans. How could one discuss the Holocaust without also raising memories of the atrocity committed by the United States on Hiroshima?

Also, American Jews themselves wanted to blend in with other Americans and not be seen as victims or singled out as the targets of thousands of years of racism. This was a time when economic prosperity took hold in the United States. America was the most powerful nation in the world and American Jewry wanted to share in the national prosperity. American Jews did not want to be haunted by the horrors brought over, in one way or another, from Europe.

It is not surprising, then, that in annotations he jotted down in his paperback edition of *Anne Frank: The Diary of a Young Girl,* Stevens looked for an Anne Frank who was neither tragic nor particularly Jewish — a view that coincided with Otto Frank's preferred conception of his daughter and that depicted the "ordinariness" of her character in the stage play. Anne must be "universal." Stevens read through the book making notations to develop an Anne who would draw massive audiences. He wrote in its first pages, "Tremendous woman budding here — She will be interesting under any circumstance." Alongside her entry for July 8, 1942, when Anne describes how she and the family pack clothing and walk to the Secret Annex, he wrote of Anne, "Happy, packing for an adventure," evoking a line he later inserted into the screenplay, "I'm living a great adventure!" playing up a teenage hopefulness in Anne's view of her world. Tellingly, next to her entry dated January 13, 1943, as she describes the miserable condition of the children she sees walking in the street below her window, Stevens noted, "this can be a story of the whole war, not only of the Jews." Next to an entry dated a week later, when Anne writes that she would like to "shout at Margot," Stevens wrote, "Big scene for girl, every girl," investing in her a "typical" teenage angst mixed with optimism, even as she hid from the Germans. He underlined passages that he could label the "description of a teenager—Good." Stevens described his film to Herbert Luft of Chicago's *Centinel* in the fall of 1958: "It's a microcosm of family life telling us the valiant story of a group hiding out in a time of great stress and of the magnificent triumph over fear by a teenage girl." Calling the Holocaust "a great time of stress" partly denies its great horror; referring to Anne's "magnificent triumph over fear" sentimentally recasts her as heroic. He was preparing a film that will disavow a trauma where it can.

"Mr. Stevens, I Want to Go Home"

Before Stevens acquired *The Diary*, Samuel Goldwyn was slated to produce it but left the project after apparently feeling insulted and badgered by what he considered Otto Frank's constant dictating to him. For the rest of his life, legend has it, he looked upon *The Diary* as "the one that got away."

Otto Frank, Anne's surviving father, figured prominently in the play's evolution and in the film's early development. He had gotten an agreement from Fox that husband and wife screenwriting team Frances Goodrich and Albert Hackett would write the screenplay since they had already won a Tony and a New York Critics Drama Award for their play *The Diary of Anne Frank*. This was settled before Stevens came onto the project, which he did after his agent Charlie Feldman wrote to production chief Buddy Adler. "Today George told me what he has in mind for *The Diary of Anne Frank*," Feldman wrote. "It was so thrilling to hear him tell what he would like to do with this story that I felt I would be remiss if I did not bring this to your attention. His views so overwhelmed me that I came from the lunch feeling that he not only could have one of the greatest properties of all time but probably one of the most important 'hit pictures' ever made. There is no doubt that he is the only person in the world who can make a really tremendous box office picture out of this subject. A couple of months ago I told you Stevens wanted to do this yarn. I am repeating it to you today, but today I urge you to assign Stevens to this production immediately or in the near future." The next day Feldman wrote to Stevens, "Frankly, George, as I told you yesterday, I never liked this property, but after hearing your ideas concerning same,

I was overwhelmed, *and I think now as you do that you should do the yarn.*"
Though Fox production notes do not substantiate it, Stevens later said
that he had to persuade Fox to make the film because the front office
worried about its dark subject.

Still, Stevens's entrance onto the project was preceded by an intense
drama already in its second act. Goodrich and Hackett, who were themselves not Jewish (a fact that made them feel self-conscious when they
began writing what would eventually be eight drafts of the stage play),
were embroiled in a lawsuit with the writer Meyer Levin, a correspon-
dent for the Overseas News Agency at the end of the war and allegedly
another of the first Americans to enter Dachau and Buchenwald. Right
after the war, Levin wrote a piece in the *New York Times* about Anne
Frank's diary after reading it in its French edition. His article was in-
strumental in the diary finding a British publisher. He and Otto Frank
agreed that Levin would write a play based on the diary. After some time,
Frank rejected Levin's effort, dubbing it not "stage worthy" enough.
Frank then entered into negotiations with new producers for the New
York stage with the Hacketts set to write the play. After seeing the
Hacketts' work, however, Levin sued, claiming that they plagiarized
from his version. He eventually won his suit but considered it less than
the victory he wanted.

Levin claimed that the real reason Otto Frank rejected his version of
the play was because it was too "Jewish" and for the rest of his life, which
he spent in Israel, he was obsessed with his loss. His book on the subject,
The Obsession, itself generated more discussion and other books on the
subject. As Ilan Avisar has written, "Levin maintained that he was victimized by a cultural 'doctrinaire censorship of the Stalinist variety,' for
offering something too Jewish. Although in the commercial version the
Jewish identity of the Franks is never concealed, and they are even shown
celebrating Jewish holidays, what is completely missing is any attempt to
present the Franks' predicament as essentially Jewish, within the context
of the history of Jewish experience." According to Levin, Avisar says,
"the Jewish producers [of the play], writers like Lillian Hellman, and
even Otto Frank, pressed for a universalized presentation out of anxieties
about a work that may seem too Jewish. The worst blatant example had
to do with the character of Anne. The 'American' Anne states: 'We are
not the only people that've had to suffer. There've always been people

that've had to . . . sometimes one race . . . sometimes another.' But the real victim of the Nazi genocide felt the Jews had to suffer because it is 'our religion from which the world and all peoples learn good.'"[12] As an antidote to the kind of argument Levin leveled at Otto Frank and the play's New York producers, World War II historian David Barnouw has commented that the Franks were "a happy German family who happened to be Jewish. It was Hitler who made them Jews."[13]

Stevens entered into the suit by proxy, with an understandable show of support for his writers, the Hacketts. In correspondence between the three when the Hacketts went to New York for the trial, a set-up emerged: the Hacketts were the victims, Stevens their sympathizer, and Levin the clear villain. On December 19, 1957, the Hacketts wrote to Stevens that Levin "was caught in lie after lie. . . . He was forced to admit that when he said he was the agent for the play that it was not true." Stevens wrote back seeming amused and supportive but not deeply concerned about the suit. "For satisfaction to be had by your reader," Stevens wrote, "the jury must march back in after deliberating and find Meyer Levin guilty. What a miserable, unfortunate man — suing for $1,500,000 — hanging a threat like that over anyone's head. He must undo himself if he is on the stand long enough. . . . How terribly unfortunate that dear Mr. and Mrs. Frank should be so imposed upon."

Stevens set about reworking and developing the Hacketts' script. The relationship between director and writers was cordial at times, strained at others, though the Hacketts did send a note to Stevens at the end of the production congratulating him on the authenticity of the finished script. Again Stevens developed the script with Fred Guiol and Ivan Moffat. Though not on the payroll as writer or associate producer Moffat nonetheless in the fall of 1957 handed Stevens one of his characteristic treatises on dramatic structure. "If the prologue was reduced to a suggestion of doom, instead of an explicit statement that Anne was dead," he said, "the story might benefit in two ways: one, the audience would not be looking at dead characters; two, it would impose the necessity for real suspense and excitement within the terms of the story while it was actually being told. The shock at the end might then be infinitely more memorable." Evoking the young lovers Moffat had imagined for *A Place in the Sun,* he wrote, "The participation of the audience with the hopes and fears of the young lovers would be intense. The feeling of 'peep show into dead past' would be lessened." Stevens did not let Anne and Peter's relationship dominate to that degree, however.

Early in the production Moffat's suggested sense of drama was intense, fanning the fire of Stevens's own occasional attraction to melodrama: "If, at the beginning, or even under titles, we see [Otto] Frank, coming to the warehouse, looking at it with sober and somber regard, perhaps starting to climb the stairs — himself thin and threadbare — the story could then begin with the strange and yet-to-be-explained suspenseful spectacle of a thirteen-year-old girl slipping out of her house after saying a quick temporary goodbye to her mother, a profound goodbye to her cat. Her movements show that she is on the run but afraid to show it. She fears the cars of the Green Police. Passers-by on bicycles and in cars look at her sympathetically. She several times can't help breaking into a run. Rain comes to make her haste. Finally she enters a warehouse door and her father is waiting for her to conduct her up to the world of hide-away, of half-terror, half make-believe." Though Stevens did not use the idea, he did build on Moffat's suggestion of an ending where "the Germans win simultaneously" with Anne and Peter's love. He saw a parallel between the Germans' arrival and Anne and Peter's kiss just before the group is arrested, but he framed it from within the two lovers' desperate passion at the same moment the Green Police break down the doors — thereby giving it drama but saving it from extreme melodrama and suspense.

Stevens went to Amsterdam in September 1957 to scout locations, first stopping at Bergen-Belsen, where Anne died. He told William Kirschner in 1963, "I was curious about the area where Anne Frank had been. . . . I walked all over the place trying to get it all straight in my mind, the actuality of what had gone [on] in there, because it's something that the mind tends to throw off, this business of living."[14] But memories returned as Stevens made a connection with Anne Frank. He met with Otto Frank and Miep Gies and visited the Secret Annex, recalling later the moment he walked up the step in the hiding place:

> I went up there with Otto, who had never been back in that house since the day that they were all taken away by the Green Police . . . and we went through the factory, which then was locked up, because it was going to become a shrine . . . we went to the floor where they had little paneled living quarters, as it was described in her book, and then there

was a garret above that. . . . And as I was walking up the ladder behind Otto Frank, there was this window that was open. It was a gabled window, and it had blown open, and as we walked up the ladder there was a pigeon, or some other large bird, we didn't see it, but it made a great rustling of its wings and it flew and went out the window. And this man was a strong man, but he weakened on that ladder; you know, the sense of life being there and not to be seen, and being winged — it goes back in the senses to mystical thoughts, and he was terribly shaken by that . . . as if it had been her spirit . . . because she used to use this [ladder]. And we sat up there in the garret for a long time. He was up there to tell me things, and finally when he got his breath, he said, "Let's go for a canal boat ride and escape this, and then we'll come back another day."[15]

Stevens was moved by his meeting with Otto, who later became a frequent visitor to the set when he went to Hollywood to consult with Stevens. He commented on the likeness in spirit between the actress chosen to play Anne, Millie Perkins, and his daughter, but refrained from commenting on the production itself. By his own choice, he never saw either the play or the film.

In his notebook Stevens jotted down facts Otto told him about Anne and her sister, Margot — along with facts told to him by a Bergen-Belsen survivor who knew Anne. On one page he wrote:

> In Auschwitz, you can live until you are killed. In Belsen, you could not live that long. Auschwitz was fascinatingly clean — Lysol-clean — the sick were gassed — the cremations didn't smoke. People could talk, occasionally shower.
>
> In Bergen, there was nothing — no food — no water — no hope. We all had typhoid.
>
> In November Anne was in Belsen. She had Christmas in Belsen. Some happiness that day. They lived in tents until the tents were blown down. Then Anne moved into a block. . . . Margot died around the end of February or early March. Anne died a few days later, calmly.

On another page, Stevens wrote about the film's production. "We can have wild doves or pigeons at the window in the attic and hear their sounds." He also noted facts about Anne's childhood: "One winter, the canal froze. Anne loved the big ice skating rink but later she was kept away because she was Jewish." Then he jotted down the information about Bergen-Belsen: "Anne worked putting stones from one point to another. . . . A girl dancer in Eastern part of Germany, a Communist, was with the girls in Belsen. . . . Anne saw the Hungarian children in the rain going to the gas chamber. She said — 'Oh, look at their eyes.' She saw naked gypsy girls marching to the gas chamber. . . . The two girls [Anne and Margot] died early in March. Belsen was liberated April 10th. . . . Anne was in Strafflayer which is a punishment camp." Stevens came away from Amsterdam again sobered and feeling close to Anne Frank. On September 17 he wrote in his notebook, "Don't pull any punches on grimness in contrast to the lightness of this love story."

Stevens kept his story limited to the families' points of view and focused inside the Secret Annex walls. "There is so much to know and to show about the strange horror and excitement of Wartime Amsterdam," he wrote, "I think that we will do best if we show it only from the hiding place windows." Otto Frank had given him a detailed description of the Secret Annex that he kept in his notebook: "Curtains on the window of the main room. Blackouts down during the day. . . . Blue paint on downstairs window. . . . Blackouts very carefully baffled. . . . Three ply blackouts." He also learned details about the families: "Van Daan was a great reader . . . dictionary on wall . . . very heavy curtains in front office lined black curtains — over regular white muslin curtains underneath three big windows." He made a sketch of the families' sleeping quarters and noted that Dussel (Pfeffer) was a very religious man who conducted the Hanukkah services. In the film, however, he is a nonreligious Jew whose ignorance of the Hanukkah celebration gives the families, and the story, the opportunity to instruct him and the audience about the meaning of the holiday.

Stevens achieved an unusual realism by using actual footage from Auschwitz, gotten from the Germans, for the scene of Anne's nightmare of her friend, Sanne. "That's the only way they could stand up. . . . They were moving together, shoulder to shoulder, and so they would go through hours of the night getting stimulation, one from the other . . . so I just put that in for truth's sake . . . it wasn't something I schemed up on the back lot. . . . I think I take the girl . . . and work a kind of identification of her into it."[16] Production files show that at one time Stevens considered closing the film with scenes of Anne in a concentration camp. In his cutting

notes, he wrote: "if we do a c.u. [close-up] of Anna [*sic*] in the concentration camp for the finish, to be used like the one we did on Sanne [the scene
of Anne's nightmare] . . . this shot should say we have all those dreary,
weary people around Anna [*sic*] and she is the only one with resolution,
courage and strength and the tiny expression on her face indicates a note
of optimism among all the dreary faces around her. And the note of optimism should be provocative to optimistic response, due to the fact she is
the only one with a spark of courage." The scene is a clash between the sentimental "spark of courage" in Anne's eye and the brutality camp life, or so
he instructed the film's composer Alfred Newman.

Stevens's decision to keep the action limited to the Secret Annex enabled him to gaze fully at the one "reality" he wanted more than any
other: Anne's diary. From the beginning he planned to open the story
with a close-up of the diary, perhaps Anne writing in her diary. This shot
of course would align him with her — he as the author of the shot that
recreates Anne Frank in the act of writing. On the front of the first page
of his paperback he wrote: "use insert and actual handwriting." Below
that he wrote, "move a pen under it as if the writer is reviewing it . . .
open up on the diary; make the diary the first important thing we have
to look at."

But the plan to keep the action limited to the hiding place inadvertently created some friction with the studio. Fox President Spyros
Skouras was committed to using the CinemaScope process. Never a fan
of the process, Stevens was convinced that its huge proportions would
destroy the sense of intimacy he wanted. But after a letter from his agent,
Charles Feldman, in October 1957 he was forced to change his mind.
Feldman had met with Skouras in New York and wrote Stevens that
"Spyros would resign from the company if [CinemaScope were not
used]. . . . It just can't be done. There was nothing I could do about
it. . . . Fox is dedicated to the Cinemascope process." Ironically, however, the large CinemaScope cameras were conducive to creating the
"small" feeling Stevens saw as the film's design. The huge cameras were
difficult to move freely within the cramped spaces of the replicated Secret Annex Stevens had built as the set — no matter what arrangements
Stevens made to accommodate them — thereby giving the story just the
sense of claustrophobia, imprisonment, and intimacy it needed. George
Stevens Jr. noted that "the horizontal inclusiveness of the lens was the

problem; so much more is in the frame. So Stevens designed beams and uprights into the set that could be used in framing." Also, the Cinema-Scope lens "ballooned the actors' faces in close-ups, so Dad pho-tographed Millie Perkins' close-ups with nonanamorphic lens and had the picture presized in the lab to the CinemaScope aspect ratios."[17]

Throughout the production, Fox's publicity department moved full throttle to exploit its upcoming drama about Anne Frank. But little seemed as urgent a subject for exploitation as the hunt to find the actress who would play Anne. Stevens sent out a press release stating that he sought an actress who would be "a living counterpart of Anne." But Stevens was ambivalent. Early on he wanted Audrey Hepburn to play Anne. But Hepburn was in her late twenties at the time, a handicap de-spite her proven box office clout. In an undated letter he wrote to her, "I am so happy today for all of the people to whom this story means so much and for all of the others that will learn about poor little Anna [*sic*] through the art of poor little Audrey." The partnership was short-lived and both Stevens and Hepburn later claimed responsibility for Hepburn dropping out of the running.

The studio launched a worldwide search to find an actress to play Anne Frank. The search took on a life of its own and became a cause of its own. In a long memo dated August 8, 1957, Fox publicist John Del Valle detailed an aggressive campaign designed to find an actress for the part. Essentially, the plan was to *rediscover* Anne — or perhaps to invent her anew: "We are not looking for an actress, but for the girl who will BE Anne Frank in the sensitive performance of this greatest role that could come the way of a young girl anywhere. . . . It would be made clear that this is a role that a girl may play only once, either in real-life or in make-believe" and that "the intention is not the usual one of building a star, but rather the extraordinary one of filling a single great role." He emphasized that the search should be launched worldwide and that "we should stage a press conference at the studio . . . at which Mr. Stevens should make the announcement" to the worldwide press. He continued: "In keeping with the unusual nature of the announcement, Mr. Stevens might be flanked at the press conference by some highly prestigious pe-diatrician, a recognized authority upon the physio-emotional aspects of young girls at the age of transition, a man perhaps from UCLA or USC.

The medical authority would be present to lend scientific credence to the announcement and to answer questions on the subject." Also, "an Anne Frank household might be synthesized of Amsterdam non-professionals who resemble the originals, to occupy scenes from the Diary which are to be embodied in the motion picture." Lastly, he suggested that when Anne's diary was brought to Hollywood by her father, "for the start of the picture . . . the father would give interviews in New York City and again on arrival in Los Angeles, displaying his daughter's graphic record which now becomes the subject matter of an extraordinary motion picture." The publicity machine took Anne Frank and produced an elaborate plan to invest her into every facet of contemporary life. There would be little way to escape her or her facsimile.

Among an ever growing list of potentials, Stevens considered the German actress Romy Schneider for the part, prompting a disgruntled fan in Holland to send an angry letter: "The stupid news about the possible candidacy of the German girl, Romy Schneider, as the Jewish girl, Anne, has had one good result in that they have shown up in all their impossible, bad publicity and gruesomeness, how uneducated their publicity people of the film business are. Twice in a row, for publicity sake, they turned the head of several hundred girls with supposed chances for a film career, whereas it was probably all set who was going to play the lead in this expensive business of Fox films. . . . With all this fooling around with the memories of Anne Frank it is gruesomely clear how little feeling the makers of the picture really have for the significance of the Anne Franks in Europe — and in Holland especially." Still, negative publicity was publicity nonetheless, even if Stevens was not always willing to participate in the huge campaign. Del Valle sent him another memo several days after the launch was proposed, urging him to pose at a press conference before a large picture of the real Anne Frank. "You have indicated a reluctance to pose with the portrait of Anne Frank for the news photos," he wrote, "lest it be construed as not in good taste. . . . I know and completely respect your thinking in this, but feel strongly that your dignified visual association with the prototype of the role you must fill will be both well regarded and constructive." Del Valle stressed that Stevens's appearing with the photo "would be lending your own great prestige to the project so that readers everywhere would associate it in their minds that this is not just another run-of-the-mill picture" but "one of which great things may be expected because your name is attached to it." Stevens did appear before the huge photos.

If Stevens saw this film as an important event of international proportions, he was well on his way to convincing others of this. The Fox casting call was heard around the world and young girls from the United States and Europe wrote to him asking to be considered. At one point the search again pitted him against Meyer Levin, initiating a round of correspondence between them. In October of 1957 Levin sent Stevens a photograph of his stepdaughter, suggesting that he test her for the part because at age twelve she already had "fantastic sex appeal." He wrote Stevens a second letter on November 10, reminding him of his lawsuit against the Hacketts: "It is a pity that there cannot be a decision on her very shortly," he said, "as the Anne Frank case comes up in court at almost any time now. . . . It would perhaps have been a way out of the impasse, were she the one for the role." Stevens wrote back, "I have found it incompatible with my nature to at any time put someone in an important part in a film for any reason other than that person seems best suited for the part. . . . The choice from among them must be made on merit, and a proposal to favor any one of them for any special interest, as you propose, cannot be considered."

To this Levin fired back a response: "I am startled and shocked to find that you considered my letter a 'proposal.' If you will read it again I am sure you will find that there is no suggestion in it that you give any extra consideration to anyone that I proposed for your film. . . . What I did want to bring out was this: that *should* my daughter prove the right person for the role, it would be a great pity if the matter of timing in regard to my court case on the Diary would harmfully intervene." Levin suggested that he and Stevens meet during Levin's upcoming trip to Los Angeles: "If you would care to spend a few moments with me, I would regard it as a favor, for I should like to erase the impression you seem to have of me, if possible." Levin also suggested that during that meeting Stevens could take a look at a 16mm print of his film *The Illegals,* which he was bringing with him.

The Diary needed its Anne and the search had by now become its own best publicity stunt. But Ivan Moffat always insisted that Stevens was simply looking for a teenage Elizabeth Taylor — a beauty, that is — not necessarily a thirteen-year-old girl who resembled Anne. Moffat's comment holds some merit, since the unknown actress Stevens eventually chose, Millie Perkins, a nineteen-year-old model from New Jersey, strongly resembled Audrey Hepburn. Perkins exuded the kind of spiritedness Stevens envisioned for his Anne, though her older age and physical beauty proved to be a block for some audiences and critics. Stevens nurtured Perkins and at one point took care to send out press notices indicating that Perkins "developed beautifully" and had an "opportunity to make full expression of her potential, which is high." After the film opened it was difficult for Stevens to think of Perkins as anyone other than Anne Frank; partly out of a wish to protect Perkins and partly out of a wish that she always be Anne Frank, he advised her to say no to some acting offers that soon came her way.

Another controversy threatened to erupt during casting. Rumors spread from Europe that German actress Gusti Huber, chosen to play Anne's mother in the film and on the Broadway stage, was said to have pro-Nazi sympathies. Several years earlier while still in Germany Huber was said to have refused to appear in a production that included Jewish actors. Stevens looked into the matter and conferred with Jewish leaders in Los Angeles. Eventually the rumor proved to have little merit. The Jewish actress Shelley Winters wrote Stevens a long letter telling him of her interest in playing any part in the film and was subsequently cast as Mrs. van Daan.

At times Stevens seemed ambivalent about participating in publicity events, but found time to write to an assistant during the shooting that, "Anne Frank . . . is a symbol of humaneness and compassion. To teenagers she represents their own precocious awareness of things seemingly beyond their years. . . . Mr. Frank's approval of our choice, is, of course, of great interest to us. . . . Yes—it is one of great dramas of our time, and I agree with *Datebook* [teen magazine]; it is the most tender and poignant teenage romance since *Romeo and Juliet*." He did say no, though, to another public relations plot to have Millie Perkins record a 45 rpm record, a song that would be played on teen radio shows across the country as a way to ensure the film's popularity with a younger audience.

Perkins recalled that on the set, Stevens was distant, serious, and focused on getting the job done more than in getting close to his cast. "He wore dark sunglasses so that no one could see what he was thinking or feeling."[18] He played actual recordings of Hitler's speeches at Nuremberg and the bells of the same Westertoren church that Anne heard during her time in the Annex without telling the actors beforehand. During the scene of the crucial air raid attack he also had the entire set shaken violently without forewarning the actors. According to Perkins, he was meticulous and absorbed. But when she went to his office one day, not knowing any better, and told him she wanted to go home to New Jersey, he listened attentively and found a way to convince her to return to the set. He could be distant one moment and affectionate the next.

Stevens shot *The Diary of Anne Frank* from March through August 1958 and began editing immediately after that. As was his customary practice, he spent days and nights in the cutting room, telling his editors what he wanted cut and checking their work thoroughly after they had finished. He spent as long editing as he did filming, recalled Del Valle: "He had two projection machines working simultaneously: reversible projection machines, and by pressing buttons or handles or whatever, he had some sort of a console there, he could play one scene and another against each other in the cutting room, which is remarkable, I think, in editing. . . . And he had a book prepared for him, probably by the Script Supervisor, with every printed scene, and often he printed the same scene . . . in numerous camera angles, and there was a master frame from each scene which was cut and put into a cutout . . . and a page of this book with a description of the scene and all the facts pertaining thereto. . . . [So there would be] just the frame and all the text around it . . . and this frame would be a key part of that particular take."[19]

After four California previews, *The Diary of Anne Frank* opened in New York and Los Angeles in March 1959. Reviews were largely positive, though Hollis Alpert, writing in the *Saturday Review,* while calling the film a magnificent movie thought less of the "aura of bigness with which the movie is surrounded," saying, "Anne Frank does not need this much glorification. . . . Anne's growing into the first stirrings of womanhood is told as thought it is a major drama."[20] Despite its good critical reception the film faired poorly at the box office. One problem persisted: Fox took the film so seriously it slated it to run in road show schedules, thereby allotting only two performances daily. Box office revenue never recovered fully from that decision and *The Diary of Anne Frank* marked the beginning of Stevens's fall at the box office.

The Poetry of Inclusion

Stevens's film seeks a universal audience of spectators who find their lives inextricably bound up — like Stevens's — with the words and experiences of a fourteen-year-old girl who died at a death camp just weeks before the Allies arrived. The tragedy and trauma of the Holocaust, the film implies, was an event that continues to live and implicate us in Anne's experience through Anne's diary. As the critic Cathy Caruth has written about collective trauma, "History, like trauma, is never simply one's own . . . history is precisely the way we are implicated in each other's traumas."[21] She quotes Freud: "History is not only the passing on of a crisis but also the passing on of a survival that can only be possessed within a history larger than any single individual of any single generation."

In creating the Holocaust's most famous young victim, Stevens shaped her into a generally optimistic, typical teenage girl just budding into womanhood. The story — part fact, part fiction, part love story — turned away from Anne Frank's particularly "Jewish" ending to make it more tolerable for audiences in a decade where people were reluctant to talk about the Holocaust and preferred to dwell in the optimism of economic recovery. Even though Stevens may not have returned from Europe with an unguarded optimism, he knew the mood of his audience, and knew that an optimistic, hopeful Anne Frank would be accepted better and offer him the largest audience he could get. Anne Frank is the teenager who sees a garden of flowers where the fictional Peter fears his own death.

Reading Anne's diary, Stevens knew how to present Anne Frank as a symbol, a voice that offered movie audiences not a blithe sense of optimism but rather a new way to experience and view their own histories and to understand the fundamental link between their histories and those of others. Stevens may have found it difficult to confront fully and consciously the repetition of the Holocaust's worst images, but the breadth and the largeness of the war compelled him now to commit to celluloid an aesthetic to express the simultaneity of many lives, many voices, most of all his own, that he found in Anne Frank's text. Visiting Anne's house, knowing Otto Frank, and recalling his experiences at the death camp compelled Stevens to shape a film that would implicate many lives in a single, shared historical moment of cinema.

Stevens creates a poetics of inclusion in *The Diary of Anne Frank*—a purely visual, cinematic means of articulating the simultaneity of tragedy that makes it possible for the spectator to hear the various voices that cry out from the wound of war's trauma. Stevens reaches for film's visual grammar to convey this simultaneity, and he finds it in two particular poetic techniques he had always been fond of: the dissolve, used more urgently here than previously, collapsing one image onto another and therefore one experience into another, and the tracking shot, the means by which his camera moves over a distance collecting images together that now share a history simply because they occur in the same sweeping gesture of the camera. As he had done with *Shane*, collapsing two meanings, or two actions, within one shot, *simultaneity* becomes the film's fundamental aesthetic. The extent to which this film would succeed as a commodity and as an emotional necessity for Stevens lay with the extent to which he could communicate to his audience the implication of so many lives inextricably bound up in one trauma.

Midway through *The Diary of Anne Frank*, Stevens employs the film's most expressive use of the dissolve and the tracking shot; their simultaneity makes the poetry of inclusion appear even more urgent. Together they denote the crushing weight of history as it collects images and sweeps them up into one particular moment. Miep and Kraler bring the old dentist, Mr. Dussel, to the Secret Annex and he first sits on the sofa updating the two families on what has been taking place outside their windows. He lists names of neighbors who have recently been picked up by the Green Police and shipped to concentration camps. This is shocking news to the Franks and the van Pels; Anne is hit hard by the news that her best friend, Sanne, was one of the children taken away. After the group breaks up and Margot and Anne show Mr. Dussel to the room he is to share with Anne, he carefully walks over to the window and stops just short of opening the curtain to look out, instinctively knowing the danger of doing so. He leaves the room, followed by the others, and the camera rests at a medium shot of Otto Frank sitting on a chair trying hard to absorb the terrible news he has just heard. While the shot focuses on Frank's troubled face, Stevens slowly dissolves to an exterior scene of a band marching down the street (we assume it is a street in Amsterdam, but its implication of course is larger). The band marches and Stevens layers the shot with the soundtrack of stirring German patriotic music.

But before the band marches out of the frame, the screen dissolves onto another image of a map of the world, with the music still playing. The map turns out to be tacked to a wall above the bookcase that hides the passageway to the Secret Annex. The camera moves down slowly to this bookcase and rests there, having come full circle from inside the hiding place, going outside to the street, to the world of danger, and then to an even larger world signified by the map. Then the camera moves back to the Secret Annex. It is urgent that the spectator experience the multiplicity of lives and realities included here. The Franks hide in the Annex but they are not safe from the world outside. What may seem like two realities may be more closely related than the families and the spectators believe.

Stevens first uses the dissolve to express the diary's dominance as the place from which the entire story evolves. It in fact owns the story and provides it with its narrative frame. When Otto Frank returns to the Secret Annex in the film's first scenes, Miep and Kraler find him in the garret and Miep hands him the diary. Otto sits down, opens the diary and begins reading. An overhead shot of the diary, with its handwritten entries and photographs of the young girl fill the frame as he reads and the page takes possession of the story. Fact and fiction merge briefly when the photograph turns out to be one of the real Anne, not Millie Perkins. Out of this page springs Anne's voice (Millie Perkins's narration), taking the audience to a flashback of Anne explaining that the family is about to go into hiding. Stevens uses another kind of dissolve here as well, the simultaneous experience of visuals (the shot of the diary page) and sound (Anne's voiceover). With this dissolve the film stays in the past tense, leaving behind a brief prologue.

Throughout the film the diary page returns to claim the story. When Otto first gives Anne the diary, she sits down to write. With her father still watching, the camera focuses on a medium shot of Otto's face as the frame dissolves to a page in the diary. Otto and the diary are caught together within the frame, each an extension of Anne's sense of security. Later, just before Anne discovers her feelings for Peter (Richard Beymer), she stands in Peter's room alone, writing in the diary. Her voice narrates, as it does frequently in the film, giving voice to words written in the diary. Anne says there is a miracle taking place in her body; she is changing into a woman. As she speaks, the frame is another overhead shot of the page Anne writes on while she speaks.

The dissolves also link the world of the Secret Annex to the seemingly more dangerous exterior world, the city of Amsterdam, and by extension, the whole of occupied Europe. In a dramatic scene, when Amsterdam is under attack by the Allies, bombs explode all around the hiding place and the Annex shakes violently. The families gather before the open skylight in Peter's room and look out at the destruction all around the city. They see magnificent lights explode after a bomb has been dropped. In the last explosion, with shooting lights emanating from it, Stevens dissolves to the flickering lights of the Hanukkah menorah as the families sit at the dinner table to celebrate the holiday. The simultaneity of these two kinds of lights brings together the largeness and the powerful force of the war with the more delicate lights of the menorah, fleeting and tenuous. The symbolism is plain enough: the possibility exists that either of these lights could be extinguished at any given moment, the destruction of war or the lives of the families in the Secret Annex.

Recalling that all of these scenes emanate from the pages of Anne's diary—now cinematically as well as literally—the diary contains a voice that draws in others. The dissolve serves Stevens well. For example, when Anne has a nightmare in which she sees the face of her friend Sanne as she stands in line in a concentration camp, the shot links two nightmares—Anne's life and her friend's—as Stevens closes in on full, intimate shots of their faces. Cutting between them three or four times sutures together their fates. Anne appears safe in bed in the Annex, but matching her close-up with that of Sanne is also a premonition of Anne's similar fate. The poetry of Sanne swaying back and forth in a line of other women at once calls up the documentary feel of the shot while the lyrical sway of the women and the haziness that creeps around its edges signifies its dreamlike quality.

Within the same scene of Anne's nightmare, another kind of dissolve occurs. Anne screams after she hears gunshots, which she believes emanate from her dream of the concentration camp. In truth the gunshots are fired from the street below her window when soldiers shoot at a man running down the street. At the same time, however, two couples are walking down the street, slightly drunk, when one of the women screams with laughter after they pause in a doorway. Stevens collapses several events together within seconds that purposefully confuses the spectator:

the gun shots, which might be coming from Anne's dream *or* from the street below her, and then her reaction, the scream, which the camera then shows us, is simultaneous with the woman's scream. Another man walking down the street might have heard Anne's scream; then again he might have confused it, as the spectator did, with the woman's scream. Is Anne safe or is she in danger? Does someone now know the families are upstairs? The audience knows this one moment of simultaneity is almost a trick, perhaps a holdover from Stevens's early days in silents, but it nevertheless offers the audience the same sense of danger — of unknowing — the families experience. It is another moment of simultaneity between fictitious characters (but we know better) and those in the audience that watches with some sense of distance but also with a strong identification.

Stevens also achieves a sense of simultaneity with the tracking shot, moving his camera from one image to another thereby relating them along the way. The two most frequent tracks occur between the different floors of the four-floor replica of the factory and attic he had built on the set. At various times, especially during the first half of the film, he moves the camera from the factory at the bottom of the building and up to the offices where Miep and Kraler work, then up to the bookcase and (using a dissolve to get through the door) on up the stairs to the attic where the families live. He takes the camera up the stairs themselves, or at different times he moves up in front of all the floors, giving the audience the sense of moving up and down different floors of a house feeling as though one were actually inside each room.

In moments of danger the camera tracks the inside of the stairs that lead to and from the bookcase and the floor below — and sometimes even down to the front door at street level. In the several scenes where either burglars or German soldiers come into the building, the camera is positioned to follow them up and down the stairs. When one of the Franks or van Daans steals silently down the stairs, the camera moves intimately along side of them, linking the attic with the office floors and collecting a shot of the street door as well. In the burglary scenes, especially, Stevens moves the camera from the office floor where the burglar attempts to open the office safe, at times in close-up, to the faces of the family members above as they lie on the floor listening for signs either of what the intruder is doing or that he has left the building.

Although Anne's voice dominates the story, either in a voiceover, on a diary page, or as a character in the drama, her link to her father is personally and historically significant. Otto Frank often takes up a central psychological space in the story. As her father he bears the crushing weight of history as it bears down on his family. For this reason, the camera seeks him out as the dominant member of the group. Stevens often shows Frank in close-ups, as his knowledge of what will happen to his family often mirrors the spectator's knowledge. Much like Anne, he has secrets inside himself. He knows or at least suspects that his family is in grave danger despite the show of hopefulness he gives them, and shows a different face to his family than he does to the camera. When Otto Frank gives his daughter the diary and tells her that she will have "a fine life" in the hiding place, she hugs him, believing him. But the camera moves to a medium shot that captures Anne's hopefulness and her father's deep sadness and worry. His face carries the weight of a generation's fear — no less than does George Eastman's sad face as he holds onto Angela before heading off into the forest, taking with him the sadness of a generation just returned from war.

Otto Frank is never simply a character but instead is a face and soul belonging to history, and the camera has a special relationship with him to indicate this. As with Stevens's tracking shots and dissolves, Otto Frank is a link to the past and present, a character of simultaneity who puts into motion the important work of his daughter's diary. He survives the death camps and his return to Amsterdam is the focus of the film's prologue and epilogue (both of which were cut after the film's release, then restored). When he returns to the factory at the beginning of the film he is a link to the past and the present. He is also linked to the building that first was his office, then his designated hiding place for his family, and now a force that takes up the most physical space in the film. When Otto arrives at the hiding place, beaten down but having survived the camps, the camera looks down at him on the street. But the camera is *inside* the building looking out through a window and down. The spectator takes up the position of the camera so that it may even appear that the building is a character waiting for Otto to enter into it. Stevens and his cameraman shot the scene as if out of the third-story front window of the building. Stevens wanted a flowing single shot as Frank comes from the street and up the stairs to the Annex. The scene was shot in process: the shot begins with Schildkraut's double (he was not in Amsterdam for the scene), then pans off into a piece of black cardboard and dissolving with Otto Frank right through the set, and then centers down the stairs as he comes through the front door of the building. Art director George Davis recalled how Stevens agreed with his idea for the scene. "We'll make the first thing a process plate," he told Stevens, "and we'll stick it out the window of one . . . of the little bedrooms, and we'll open up the shot on that process plate, and the process plate will have Mr. Frank on it, in the pan over, and so on and so forth, and we'll move — we'll pan off that process plate, over across the set and down, and pan down to the front door, in the stair hall, and up to where our real actor will come." To this, Stevens said, "You're a bloody genius!"[22]

With Otto Frank's link to his daughter, to the camps, and to the building now awaiting him, the camera privileges his place in the film. His face is the subject of many close-ups and medium shots, more than of the other characters. Anne feels closest to him; he has (in the film's diegesis, at least) given her the diary once inside the hiding place. Yet the camera sets up the simultaneity of Otto and Anne Frank most firmly when Otto begins reading her diary. His voiceover reads the page and then her voiceover literally *takes* over to narrate the bulk of the story. At the close of the story, Otto again reads her diary, and it is his voice we hear. He not only frames his daughter's story and words, but Stevens positions him as the link between Anne's diary and the history it both serves and creates.

The simultaneity of image, character, and event in *The Diary of Anne Frank* ultimately rests with Stevens, however, whose disturbance at "living" among the death camps once again does not compromise the film's great historical sense of itself. In fact, it may increase that kind of sensibility.

While Stevens was aware of the uncomfortable emotional material he and audiences had to confront during the production of *The Diary of Anne Frank*, he nonetheless kept sight of the "image" he had in mind to "provoke thought." He held close the larger historical importance of the diary and of the film he could make of it. Knowing cinema's powerful hold on the American people, he knew also that his film had to reenact the diary's power to translate trauma and to reveal the multitude of voices within that site of trauma. In a large sense, then, the film takes up the position of the diary. It repeats the trauma each time it is viewed by a spectator, an audience. It is a constant repetition of trauma as it collects a mass audience and a massive embrace of other voices, other lives. Ultimately, history owns Anne Frank's diary and this film simultaneously, just as Stevens hoped it would when he said, "the voices that were heard in Europe for years were those of Hitler and Goebbels, yet the voice that persists is Anne's."

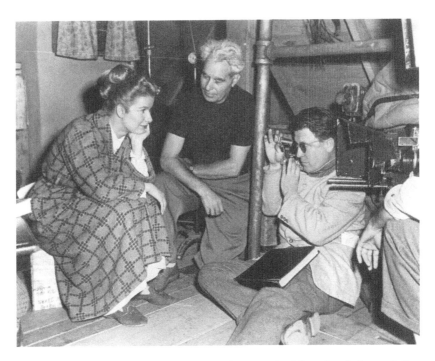

Stevens and Barbara Bel Geddes on the set of *I Remember Mama* (1948), Stevens's first film after returning to Hollywood from the war. Reproduced courtesy of the Academy of Motion Pictures Arts and Sciences.

"The two most beautiful actors in the world": teenage Elizabeth Taylor with Montgomery Clift in a scene from *A Place in the Sun* (1951).

Alan Ladd as Stevens's lonely, chivalric gunfighter in *Shane* (1953).

Stevens with *Giant* cast members Mercedes McCambridge, Elizabeth Taylor, Rock Hudson, and James Dean (l. to r.) during the long, hot shoot in Marfa, Texas, in 1955. Reproduced courtesy of the Academy of Motion Pictures Arts and Sciences.

Stevens and Otto Frank, Anne's father, look out the window while on the stairs of the Secret Annex in Amsterdam during preparation on *The Diary of Anne Frank* (1959). Reproduced courtesy of the Academy of Motion Pictures Arts and Sciences.

Stevens (second from right) and cast members Gusti Huber, Diane Baker, Ed Wynn, Lou Jacobi, and Millie Perkins wait for the Green Police during shooting on *The Diary of Anne Frank*. Reproduced courtesy of the Academy of Motion Pictures Arts and Sciences.

Good friends: Stevens and Carl Sandburg at Sandburg's home in South Carolina before production on *The Greatest Story Ever Told*. Reproduced courtesy of the Academy of Motion Pictures Arts and Sciences.

Learning from the master: Stevens directs Warren Beatty on the set of Stevens's last film, *The Only Game in Town*. Reproduced courtesy of the Academy of Motion Pictures Arts and Sciences.

PART III

Life and Times

9

Democratic Vista
The Greatest Story Ever Told

Do I contradict myself?
Very well then I contradict myself,
(I am large, I contain multitudes.)
                    —Walt Whitman, "Song of Myself"

In December 1958, while still shooting *The Diary of Anne Frank*, and after a long series of negotiations, George Stevens Productions contracted with Twentieth Century Fox again, this time to produce and direct *The Greatest Story Ever Told*, an adaptation of Fulton Oursler's 1949 book of the same name. The relationship between the two films is based on more than simply their simultaneity in Stevens's career. *The Greatest Story Ever Told* was a logical next step after *The Diary of Anne Frank* in the evolution of his postwar aesthetic; it was another way that Stevens continued to create art from his experiences in the war. His view of Dachau left an indelible imprint that seemed to drive his aesthetic forward to the ever-larger expression, as if he were trying to gain on the enormity of life-changing images he saw in the war. He filmed the story of Anne Frank as one of the most significant episodes of the twentieth century. As his friend Frank Capra later put it, Stevens thought of his experiences at Dachau when he imagined filming a story of Jesus' message: that human beings should embrace one another instead of putting each other to death for their differences. The story of Jesus was the logical culmination of Stevens's postwar vision — as if something *he* could call the "greatest story" could be his only destination. *The Greatest Story Ever Told,* after all, was not his only "religious" postwar film; for Stevens, God's grandeur is evident in *Shane*'s large vistas — revered by the film's characters *and* spectators.

Stevens and Ivan Moffat had just begun writing a script for *The Greatest Story Ever Told* when they met for lunch at the Brown Derby in early December 1960 and Stevens told Moffat that the film would never become a comic book version of Jesus' life. That is, it would not follow suit with the recent spate of Biblical epics produced in Hollywood during the 1950s. Instead, his would be reverent, and universal, a word he often employed when he thought about the masses he would attract to his film. *The Greatest Story Ever Told* would be the ultimate movie on Jesus. Though it would refrain from making a spectacle of itself, after his film on Jesus there would be no need to make another.

Two years later, with a completed script in hand — the only time in his career that Stevens received actual screenwriter credit — he took cast and crew and embarked on location shooting in Page, Arizona. Then the unthinkable — but in hindsight the logical — occurred: over the next three years, slowly but with unwavering momentum, Stevens's great epic on Jesus began to unravel until it met an unfortunate end in movie houses. Glaringly shy of the audience Stevens imagined, *The Greatest Story Ever Told* took a beating from movie critics along the way. During its production, *The Greatest Story Ever Told* threatened to get out of hand time and again, though Stevens tried his best to curb the small disasters as they came: weather was unreasonable and unforgiving; Stevens took longer and longer to contemplate and shoot scenes; other directors were summoned to come in and shoot sequences just to bring the film in and get it finished. By February 1965, Stevens had on his hands the most stunning work of art he had ever directed and the most beautiful failure of his career. What would have been the magnum opus of his career was now his beautiful half-failure of a film. His painfully wrought rendering of the life of Jesus was an experience from which he, truthfully, never recovered. He was not at a loss for offers after that: Warren Beatty courted him for a year to direct *Bonnie and Clyde;* Fox offered him *Butch Cassidy and the Sundance Kid* in 1968; he planned and then walked away from producer Sam Spiegel's *Nicholas and Alexandra* in 1967, as well from directing *This Property Is Condemned.* Then in 1969 he directed one more film, the high profile *The Only Game in Town,* believing he could direct it just as he had directed comedies at RKO in the 1930s: he would direct an intimate film and do it quickly.

But it was too late for such economy. Stevens had seen the negative side of grandiosity with *The Greatest Story Ever Told*—the physical and emotional place to which he, ironically, and who knows how consciously, had aspired since the war. When he turned around to direct the smaller *The Only Game in Town,* it turned into an elaborate web of delays. It, too, failed to make money at the box office; Stevens jokingly told interviewers that, yes, he would like to direct another film, "but I don't know if I could find a studio with enough money to bank roll me."

When Stevens first conceived of what *he* probably thought of as his crowning achievement, biblical epics still loomed large in Hollywood. But it took him six years to make *The Greatest Story Ever Told,* a period during which he became emotionally and physically drained. The life of Jesus Christ was such a large topic, he told himself, that he remained constantly uncertain of how to approach it. So he approached it from every conceivable angle (just as he shot film), so much so that he lived and thought only through the camera, almost myopically through his story of Jesus Christ. The more absorbed he became in planning his long epic and the more absorbed he *had* to be in simply getting it done, the more he lost touch with his sharp storytelling capabilities. He planned *The Greatest Story Ever Told* to be a story of ideas and to the extent he wanted it to be the last word, the last and largest *idea* about Christ, he simultaneously found its largeness almost too much to manage. When he embarked on the film he wanted his audience to be *everyone.* But when he emerged from shooting and editing his five-year project he no longer had a clear idea of who that audience might be. He emerged with a beautiful but not entirely lived-in epic: idea-driven, meditative, and slow. Every beautiful vista and every exquisite frame looked as if it were a painting instead of a living landscape. In attempting to achieve such visual perfection such commitment to an *idea,* such as it was, Stevens strained his filmmaking capabilities. He never lost his stunning relationship with his camera, but his relationship with his audience was now another matter entirely. The moral universe he entered into with *A Place in the Sun* and *Shane* dissolved into one of only art, stultified, and no longer a living thing.

To the Mount: The Production

While still at Twentieth Century Fox, Darryl Zanuck acquired the screen rights to Fulton Oursler's 1949 book, *The Greatest Story Ever Told*, in 1954, at about the same time that Stevens, still in preproduction on *Giant*, became interested in it. When Zanuck left Fox in 1956 to start up his independent production company, trade papers announced his plans to produce *The Greatest Story Ever Told*, a film that never materialized. Then, in 1958, while in production on *The Diary of Anne Frank* at Fox, George Stevens Productions contracted with the studio to form "The Greatest Story Productions" "for the purpose of producing a film of the same name."[1]

But Stevens's contract with Fox was the end result of two long years of negotiations that tried Charlie Feldman's patience. Two months earlier, Feldman implored Stevens to give it up. "I can truthfully tell you, George," he wrote to Stevens on April 21, 1958, "that in all the years that I have been in business I have never devoted as much time (let alone the time of my associates) in trying to clean up a one-picture commitment. I have reached the point, George, where it is just physically impossible for me to go on and attempt to negotiate anymore. It really has gotten me down, and with your blessing I beg of you to allow me to call off negotiations." Feldman was serious enough to test the waters at other studios. "It goes without saying, George," he wrote on May 5, "*every studio in town wants to make a deal with you* and every one of them is willing to give you the best deal or a better deal than that particular studio gives to anyone else." Columbia and United Artists both offered Stevens 50 percent of the gross-receipts after break-even, and autonomy in production; Metro had never made a deal on 50 percent of the gross to the director but was "mulling over" Feldman's proposal. To top it off, Jack Warner told Feldman "I must have George. . . . I've got to make a deal with him." During this time, Fox also offered Stevens *Cleopatra*, to which he said, no, thanks. Darryl Zanuck also turned it down when they offered it to him.

But after six more months of negotiations, Stevens signed with Fox on November 25, 1958. Stevens would shoot the film in CinemaScope 55 with a total budget "not to succeed six-and-a-half million." He would deliver *The Greatest Story* to the studio "ready for public exhibition" on December 20, 1960, and for this he would receive a salary of $1 million — $100,000 to be paid yearly from 1958 to 1967. Two years later, on April 18, 1960, Fox extended the film's release date to September 20, 1961, and subsequently to 1963.

Stevens's million dollar salary, plus profit participation, set an industry precedent that had far-reaching implications — not only for the business but for Stevens. It was an early indicator of the fantastical boundaries within which *The Greatest Story Ever Told* was conceived. The film's executive producer, Frank I. Davis, said in a 1982 interview, "Sitting on this side of the table now, it [was] a bad precedent. There was a logic that Charlie employed — and I remember discussing it at the time — that George was going to spend three years of his life on this. A director — even a good director — may direct even more than one picture a year, and here's the top director who'll be spending this much time, and so it's totally justifiable in terms of the talent of the man and the mammoth nature of the project and the time that it's going to take to bring it off."[2] The film was an especially ambitious project for a director who was not a particularly religious man. As Ivan Moffat said later, "He was out of his element when it came to making a film about Jesus Christ."[3] He was embarking on a subject of enormous proportions.

A director who had always been in touch with his audience — who had a firm understanding of what that audience wanted — Stevens now seemed *unsure* of who his audience was. He began to question his connection with his audience, a questioning he ironically reiterated February 1965, just before the film's release: "When you come to this story, unless you have spent years in study in this area, you are unequipped to know enough, to understand enough, and to know how it relates to all of its audience, or what is in the varied minds of the audience."[4] Stevens is tentative, cautiously approaching a subject that is too big, too disperse, too monumental to know or to pin down. What would an audience require? "When the image comes on the screen, what do they think? How does the figure look?" he said. Why is the audience moved? Why do some believe and others not? For the very first time in his career, Stevens was not certain if he knew how to excite the audience.

As Stevens asked himself these questions when he embarked on production, he also worked to find out everything possible there was to know about Jesus' story, to research a myriad of writers and artists who passed down and interpreted his story through the centuries. Stevens said, "A film has to interest audiences everywhere to be a film at its best. It is now the film's function to ask that the viewer accept the belief in its fullest."[5] Yet Stevens reached for many belief systems in his film. His democratic vista contains a multitude of beliefs made homogenous to satisfy what he perceived to be a multitude of beliefs.

Stevens particularly liked Oursler's novel because its universal quality would offend no one. "Oursler does not deal in terms of doctrine as taught by any individual religion," he noted, "yet seeks to present certain basic truths found in all faiths. It does not oppose any religion or sect, or plead the cause of any individual denomination. There are those who believe unquestionably, unequivocally — not only Christians and Jews, but also Muslims, Buddhists, Taoists and Hindus. The faithful are found in every religion. None have the right to question the sacred implications of another's faith."

In a note dated March 24, 1960, a skeptical but realistically-minded Stevens said,

> Oursler has written the emotional approach throughout the story, rather than the intellectual approach. The real fascination of the Christ story is that a man died and then a man lived again. . . . The interesting part of the story is the way and how of Christ going to the Cross. It isn't so much that we find out Pilate's, Herod's or Caiaphas' responsibility in this Trial. The people are seeking their King — they are trying to escape the responsibility — they must have a King and they must have a God, represented by the High Priest, who promises them hope. They must have someone who represents the law. So they set up the machinery to make that work and bring about a Trial. The machinery of the Trial is set up to maintain the order that the group is imposing upon itself. The desire for this examination of the individual caught in his own trap of the Court and the law is always very popular in fiction. What intrigues me is to see a group of people who must

have a King, a Messiah, a Christ, or must have a definition of God that they can see and touch. They bring it about, but the nature of their social structure is such that they destroy that which they have created.

Stevens sees a definite dramatic tension taking shape; he sees the emotional drama in the story of an individual in conflict with the social world around him.

Stevens's point of view of the individual caught in and punished by the trappings of social structures were by now his emotional and intellectual staples — as he had already demonstrated in *Alice Adams* and *A Place in the Sun*. Added to this, *The Greatest Story Ever Told* even elaborates the story of social inequities and tragedies Stevens saw at Dachau. Of Herod, Pilate, and Caiaphas, he said, "the great group and their self-interest in being anonymous because they cannot speak out, are all one. This is a great moral disaster. Then we find the groups dividing up and becoming very strong for two reasons — one . . . is to carry their own point of view forward in the world, and the other . . . is to escape the responsibility of this moral disaster."

Stevens took the idea and gave it context: "One thing that bothers me is how we can turn the effect of the story away from what we like to accomplish. It is widely done, but it is possible. There is a way to say that the Jews killed Christ. We see this [implied] in treatments, because that is the way to take the responsibility away from where it belongs . . . on the backs of the people who stood at the foot of the hill. We must take all of the people — it is unfair to take any one part of the people, such as only the Jews. Other people found a scapegoat and absolved themselves. One of the most important reasons to tell the story of Christ is to tell it in such a manner that it does not impose false responsibility on the ancient Jews. They were the whole of the people — the good and the bad of the whole world. How we love to localize when it is a case of capital punishment — such as the [Carol] Chessman case. As soon as it hits home, the whole subject of capital punishment is hushed up."

Stevens wrote in his copy of Oursler's book that the film's dialogue should be written in the "easiest possible conversational tone." Then he turned his attention to color conception of particular scenes. For the stable scene he envisioned "heavy brown color — dark — with a ring around back light." For Jesus' birth he said, "control color — soft —

focus." Annotating an early Fox playscript, when Christ says, "the spirit of the Lord is upon me," Stevens writes "make the audience cry with this word (the simple strings will do it . . . eight violins, two violas, two cellos)." Later he notes "the work to be done is to point out the skeptics and in the film convince the skeptics . . . the film must convince the skeptics after making its skeptics." In addition, he included plans to display a calendar on the screen, using large tablets and tracing up to 1 B.C. Plans were large and far reaching, however scattered, however vague.

In his effort to produce an informed and all-encompassing film, Stevens doled out reading and research assignments to close staff members. At an early point associate producer George Stevens Jr. read *Harmony of the Gospels;* head researcher Tony Van Renterghem looked at the Standard Version of the Bible; associate producer Tony Vellani read the Douay Confraternity; assistant director Bill Hale looked at the New Testament; and Stevens read the King James version of the Bible. The group established a list of films to see, including *Solomon and Sheba, King of Kings, The Robe, Intolerance, The Ten Commandments, Ben Hur,* and *Fourteen Stations of the Cross.* He also added travelogues of Israel and a Spanish Passion Play.

Stevens also called in religious advisors, including rabbis and Christian leaders. He brought in a large group of Inbal Dancers from Jerusalem for the shooting. He kept a file called "Racial Prejudice" in which he collected pieces of what he called "hate propaganda," including a newspaper article on "Martin Luther King at . . . Communist Training School," W. C. George's article "The Biology of the Race Problem," as well as an invitation to a lecture at the University of Judaism in Los Angeles called "Vigilantism: The Southerner as Extremist." He sent a memo to his staff that "we should keep a file of any interesting articles we find on religious subjects. We could make photo static copies for each individual's file — then keep all of the clippings in a folder marked Current Topical Reading in the Conference Room, so that it will be available to everyone. . . . Also, we should delegate different books to each individual to read. The reader could then suggest to the rest of us any aspect of the book that might be interesting for the film. It would be a good idea for the reader to give us some knowledge of the author and his thinking — that would give us some familiarity of each individual's thinking on each book." Plans became broader still. When he was planning a trip to Rome, Turkey, and the Holy Land, he wrote, "We should keep in mind the different ways a tape recorder could be used during the trip. One thing we might record would be the different sounds, music, dialects, and languages. These are for our guidance. We might also want to use the tape recorder to make tapes of conversations." The approach was all-inclusive, maybe even diffuse.

According to the film's publicist, Ann Del Valle, in a January 1964 progress report, "George Stevens' concept for the film was 'basic'—the greatest story was to be 'the straight narrative with no embellishment.' Stevens is quoted as saying, 'An important part of our design is that we want to get at the heart of the matter . . . the simplicity of the people of the time and simplicity of the thinking as well as the profundity. But many of these thoughts are humble and simple and related to the most ordinary kind of existence as well as aspects of it that relate to a sublime kind of existence. . . . A film of this kind should approximate the telling of the whole story. I think that is the responsibility of the film and we want this film to be inclusive and comprehensive. From the beginning to the end. From the early prophecies in the Old Testament that become so important throughout the development of the New Testament on through to the conclusions. . . . In our film the costumes will not be the first thing to look at, nor the sets. The thing we want to interest our audience in is the ideas expressed in the film.'" Associate producer Tony Vellani later added, "the way it was conceived from the beginning was a film of ideas. George wanted to stay away as much as possible from the pageantry, from the things we are accustomed to, and he wanted to express thoughts. Indeed we did an extraordinary amount of preparation for the picture. We knew the Gospel as well as anybody could, really, backwards and forwards. We had done research for two years . . . when we made changes from the reality of the time, the way it can be conceived today, we did it with purpose." As an example, Vellani said, "like The Last Supper—George always wanted to do it in the manner of Da Vinci; he always did . . . to make a reference on the picture to famous artists of the past, the famous minds in the history of Western man who had dealt with this particular theme."[6]

Stevens and Fox producer David Brown considered possible screenwriters, among them Ray Bradbury, Reginald Rose (who wrote *Twelve Angry Men* and *The Days of Wine and Roses)*, along with William

Saroyan, Joel Sayre, and Ivan Moffat. Brown wrote to Stevens on April 22, 1960, about approaching poet Carl Sandburg:

> We have the unprecedented problem of preparing dialogue which can stand alongside the words of Christ. . . . I can think of no writer of films who would not feel honored to work under Mr. Sandburg's guidance. . . . We will go after three or four or possibly more writers of the caliber of Ray Bradbury to work in concert but each to concentrate on a specific area of the New Testament in the preparation of the first draft screenplay. . . . They will then each write their own particular portion of the story in first draft screenplay form. Somewhere along the line, probably after a rough assemblage of a first draft screenplay has been received from the writing team, you and a skilled craftsman with whom you have worked — such as Ivan Moffat — can begin the task of blending and bridging the various elements in one harmonious whole. Following this or perhaps during the entire operation Mr. Sandburg could function as Editor-in-Chief, going over each element of the screenplay, particularly with respect to dialogue. It is to be hoped that . . . he will feel impelled to add some touches of his own.

The plan already seemed scattered, nevertheless Moffat began work on a script in spring 1960, just about the time that Stevens and Brown approached Sandburg at his home Flat Rock, North Carolina, about editing. Sandburg signed on as a creative consultant on June 27 and arrived in Los Angeles on July 18, 1960, to collaborate on the script; he was paid $125,000 for six months of work. Long an admirer of Sandburg, Stevens was said (on the production company's progress report) to admire his "soaring lyricism" and "his humane and Olympian point of view." Stevens said, "I want to get his poetry on the screen — his sense of ordinary conversation. He is a profound man, yet he thinks with humility." At a June 1960 press conference announcing Sandburg's coming on board Stevens quipped that when Sandburg called him "Boss," Stevens got even by calling Sandburg "god."

After that, however, no one could ever determine what Sandburg actually contributed to the script, but at least some amusing stories of his behavior surfaced — including talk of Sandburg's habit of falling asleep during story meetings; or of his walking into story meetings with no jacket, complaining that he was cold, being offered a jacket to put around his knees, and then walking out of the room at the end of the meeting without returning the jacket; he eventually collected quite a number of them. However, Sandburg did write an imagined conversation between Mary Magdalene and Judas Iscariot for the film:

JUDAS: Mary of Magdala, or as they call you, Mary of Magdalene. It is told that you went on your knees before Jesus, and the tears came, and you washed his feet with your tears, and then wiped them with your hair. So it is told. It is true?

MARY: Yes, it is true.

JUDAS: This is a form of worship? You mean it as worship? It can only be worship.

MARY: Yes, you say truly. It is worship. I love him, adore him, and I worship him. All his words and acts are sacred to me.

JUDAS: Do you never doubt he is the Messiah, the Christ?

MARY: I never doubt. What do you mean by questioning me? Are you not one of his twelve disciples? Why do you question me?

JUDAS: Are you not one of the best known sinners in Jerusalem?

This exchange unfortunately adds little insight into Sandburg's contribution to the script, although the press made much of his presence at story conferences. Stevens and Brown came up with his official screen credit: "In Creative Collaboration with Carl Sandburg" since it was reported that indeed Sandburg wrote some dialogue and talked over scenes at length with Stevens. He gave Stevens a book of religious painting reproductions, including works by Michelangelo, Rembrandt, Giotto, Botticelli, Sassetta, El Greco, and Fra Filippo Lippi. They probably helped Stevens more than any other of Sandburg's contributions.

Fox head Spyros Skouras was especially determined to get a biblical epic for the studio and was anxious to see a script from Stevens as soon as possible. It appears from script notes that writing the script took the better part of the year. As early as November 2, 1960, a progress report from George Stevens Jr. noted various delays in the production, one owing to a writers' strike, another stemming from the studio's failure to work out a percentages deal for Sandburg. The report also mentioned that "Mr. Skouras had plans to buy out Samuel Bronston's *King of Kings.* . . . When it was found that this was impractical, Skouras said on the phone 'George, you've got to give me the picture sooner.'" Skouras transferred all his elaborate planning to produce a biblical epic onto *The Greatest Story Ever Told,* suggesting a broader, more elaborate concept for the film than even Stevens planned. He asked Stevens to get "an all-star cast and also outdo MGM's *King of Kings* active publicity campaign." Stevens Jr. noted that Skouras's idea was to "cast *The Greatest Story* with the biggest stars in films; he mentioned specifically Greg Peck and Liz Taylor." Stevens Jr. wrote "this was agreed to by George Stevens and George Stevens, Jr. as 'a fine idea,' and we, of course, proceeded in that fashion." He also said, "This sort of casting is a wide departure from the original concept, which was to do the film with a modest cast and perhaps one or two stars."

As Stevens's writing team — now Ivan Moffat, Stevens, Sandburg, and James Lee Barrett (who had written for television and would later write *The Undefeated, The Green Berets,* and *Bandolero!*) — wrote the script, Skouras told a stockholders' meeting in October 1960 that *The Greatest Story Ever Told* would go into production sometime between March and May 1961. Then he let Stevens know he planned to go ahead with the picture *The Day Christ Died,* worrying Stevens that all his story ideas would be used in that film. On October 12 Skouras phoned Stevens asking him when he thought he might start shooting *The Greatest Story.* Stevens said probably in May 1961, and Skouras answered "George, it would help me if you would say March," adding, "George, I am going ahead and make *The Day Christ Died.*" When Stevens asked what kind of a picture it was, Skouras said, "Oh, you know, it is the story of the last hours of Jesus," adding, "And George, I am going ahead and make this picture even if I have a lawsuit." When Stevens asked Skouras whom he expected to sue him, Skouras answered, "I'll have to tell you that . . . when I see you." He changed the subject and asked Stevens how the script was going and Stevens answered, "It is developing magnificently." Skouras responded, "George, it would help me if you would send me some pages."

On August 31, 1961, however, despite a firm commitment to the project, and despite one cast member, Max von Sydow, already signed, Twentieth Century Fox notified George Stevens Productions that it was pulling out of the deal to produce *The Greatest Story Ever Told.* Stevens was given two years to find another producer, after which, if he did not, Fox would reclaim rights to do so. In September the Stevens company sent notice of the situation to the trades that it held sole ownership of the property. Fox cited internal management problems and other financial commitments as the reason for the pull-out: studio head Buddy Adler had just died of cancer and in the interim a series of production heads, including Peter Levathes, took over. The studio also had *Cleopatra* to worry about; in Europe the Elizabeth Taylor-Richard Burton picture outran every attempt to put controls on the production: *Cleopatra* became Stevens's problem also. Charles Feldman met right away with Arthur Krim at United Artists and the studio committed to financing and distributing *The Greatest Story Ever Told.* Fox paid Stevens the minimal guaranteed compensation, without United Artists assuming any of it, and Stevens moved off the Fox lot and set up offices as an independent producer in the Culver City offices that once housed both David O. Selznick's and Desilu Studios. Stevens signed with United Artists on November 6, 1961, and the studio, as distributor, agreed to a budget "not to exceed seven-and-a-half million," giving Stevens complete creative control. Stevens would own 75 percent of the film, United Artists 25 percent.

Stevens kept working. Finishing the script took up most of 1961. Its sources, Stevens said, were the gospels of Matthew, Mark, Luke, and John, and other references in the New Testament based on Old Testament prophecies. The whole Bible was well represented, he added. Stevens wrote in his date book in the week of November 1961 that intense work was being done on the script and that sometimes they worked all through the day. Finally, on Saturday, November 14, he wrote, "Finished script handed to me by Bill Hale at 2 p.m. — at last! Magnificent script . . . very tired . . . we leave studio at 9 p.m."

Stevens traveled to the Holy Land as part of his search for locations but found that the landscape had eroded. At one point he even considered shooting in Spain. Believing that the story needed an artistic retouching, he especially wanted the landscapes to look physically magnificent. Eventually he chose two areas closer to home: one in Page, Arizona, which would serve as the site of the Jordan River; the second was Pyramid Lake, Nevada, the site for the Sea of Galilee. Max von Sydow, the first actor Stevens cast, arrived in Los Angeles in June 1962 expecting to begin work. But more delays followed. Arnold Picker at United Artists decided it would be a good idea to present *The Greatest Story Ever Told* in Cinerama, the three-camera process that at that time used three separate panels and created two vertical lines on the screen. Stevens was reluctant to use it, but the Cinerama Company advised him that they had developed a new device to solve the problem of the vertical lines. After experimenting with it he agreed to go ahead with it.

All considered, casting ran smoothly given Stevens's plan (via Skouras) to cast a parade of well-known actors. Dorothy McGuire was Mary, Robert Loggia was Joseph, Charlton Heston was John the Baptist, and Telly Savalas was Pontius Pilate. In addition his cast included Pat Boone, Carroll Baker, David McCallum, Sidney Poitier, Angela Lansbury, Jose Ferrer, Martin Landau, Shelley Winters, and Ed Wynn. He cast John Wayne in a brief appearance as the Centurion. He now said that he wanted to cast the world's greatest actors for the world greatest story. Fans sent Stevens plenty of advice on casting matters, much of which ended up in his newly created "Crank" file — including advice from one woman that Elizabeth Taylor should have a starring role in the film since "this could be a way for her to make a humble Thanksgiving to God for her life being restored not too long ago." (A tracheotomy saved Taylor's life in 1961.) Another fan told Stevens to cast Fidel Castro as Jesus Christ because "with his beard he looks like a holy man." Still another letter objected to Carl Sandburg having anything to do with the script because he was a Communist.

On Location

The start date was postponed to September 1962. Then an additional delay allowed time for the company to build the two hundred units of portable housing necessary for the cast and crew. But the builder was no more adept at coming in on schedule than the production would be — the aluminum units took longer than expected. Executive Frank Davis later said, "Stevens was pretty calm through all of this. He saw one blessing in the situation that later was to cause us great problems. . . . He felt that shooting in the daytime, which it would be, with the summer sun overhead, we would get a flat picture, and shooting when the sun was at a lower angle you would get a much better image and one that he found satisfying artistically. So we went through the problems of getting the houses built, set and some trees, and then getting all of these people fed. . . . We were really running a city." The true start date in Arizona turned out to be October 28, and the entire cast and crew gathered, "sprinkled a little water and said a prayer," and took one whole day to do it.[7] In a 1982 interview, actor Michael Anderson, who played James the Younger, recalled that the second day of shooting was no more productive than the first. "We all thought . . . right, okay, we're going to work . . . and we sat there for three weeks and Stevens took a chair and he sat where we could all see him on a hill overlooking the entire valley, and he did not move. . . . He came down for an hour to rehearse and then he would go back up, and we were ready to shoot this thing. And it went on for days and days and days. Finally we rehearsed the scene a little bit and . . . a little bit more and then he went back up for five, six hours. . . . Nobody really knew what that meant. We all realized at that point that we were not going to knock this movie off."[8] Anderson's account, true or not, points to the time-consuming nature of this beast. As writer James Lee Barrett said, "He knew the story he wanted to tell. . . . I haven't seen anybody do it since . . . you'd have an enormous wall where eight-by-five index cards were. Scene numbers and all of that, telling who's in a scene and what's going to happen in a scene and how it progresses . . . and he'd stand there for an hour looking at it, and then he'd take one scene from here and move it over to here . . . this was all in his own head."[9] The shoot required endless, and enormous, logistics. Dorothy McGuire remembered going into filming "as one would go into battle. . . . As a cast we went up in sections when we were needed for shooting. He brought us up early so we'd absorb the atmosphere . . . with its mesas and buttes . . . and not be psyched out by this experience but that it would become part of us."[10]

The sets were larger than life in size and concept; for Stevens they were also heavily weighted down by his desire to make each frame a study in religious iconography. To add to it, he insisted on getting master shots, medium shots, and close-ups from every angle possible, causing the actors to sit for longer periods of time. As an extra source of anxiety, the Arizona weather was unforgiving. "Shooting was slow," Davis said, recalling one of Stevens's more serious set backs at the Page location. "It was cold out there . . . the water was cold for the baptism and all of that, and we were dropping behind and dropping behind, and then . . . I think it was about December 7 or 8 it snowed. Now our problem was that we had to finish that location in order to get to the studio. . . . We were hoping to get here by Christmas because that's the way we had scheduled [Charlton] Heston's time . . . if we ran over it would be expensive. So they melted the snow and then brushed the snow. . . . Ed Wynn and Van Heflin and Max von Sydow . . . all out there sweeping . . . and shoveling snow. The next day, it snowed again and the company had to leave the area for six months."[11] Troubles mounted for Stevens. The caterer was also losing money and not getting paid. Then, the housing had to be moved to Pyramid Lake, but there was no time to do it and new construction was set up there.

The size of it all was almost hypnotic, not only the length of the shoot but the physical landscape Stevens had to manage in order to choreograph the hundreds and thousands of extras for the larger scenes. He could almost get physically and psychologically lost in it: "We did so much of it in the Glen Canyon area of Arizona and north up there into other parts of Utah. I was using a helicopter a lot, because the trails were bad and the roads are no good, and I had to bring people in, and I got in the habit of picking locations and putting down on them, and generally understanding what they were. . . . I had a helicopter there to save time, to move from one place to another myself. And I had to ground myself from the helicopter because I was losing my sense of earthliness. How grand things can be in the mind's eye, from the ground, when there's height leading up into these areas beyond our understanding. . . . Everything from the helicopter was so much more fascinating than standing on the earth . . . just looking at it from another point of view . . . and it is kind of a drug, the helicopter and the grand landscape."[12]

The locations were a constant problem, Davis said. They company transferred back and forth and back again from Page "and over to Pyramid and then back [to Los Angeles] shooting on the back lot at Desilu Studios where they built the streets of Jerusalem." The temple itself was a huge set with a mat painting behind it. Eventually United Artists became concerned. Stevens would come up with a prospective finish date yet was not able to pick up speed to meet that date. "He seemed to be losing time," Davis said, because "it was a monumental undertaking, more than he certainly ever conceived at the onset." The shoot turned into one large logistics problem. "I believe for George," he said, "it was a most, most, most difficult experience. Because George was not unmindful of his responsibility to United Artists. I'm not sure that they fully comprehended that . . . so obviously he had to be in conflict with himself. You know, 'Do I tear these pages out of the script, do I forget this scene, do I accept this first take or these first five takes when I don't think that they are good, or do I press on for that sixth, seventh or eighth. . . . Do I stop before I'm ready?'"[13]

When Stevens could no longer speed up he met with Arthur Krim and agreed to let other directors step in to pick up some of the scenes just to get the picture finished. According to Davis, however, "he was not prepared to compromise the film . . . and it must have been difficult for George Stevens to allow Jean Negulesco [and] David Lean to come in and participate in photographing scenes of his film while he's off on location doing other work. He was very grateful . . . and he respected what they did. He was not unhappy with what they did." While Negulesco shot the Jerusalem street scenes, Lean shot the Herod sequences, and since the part of Herod had not yet been cast, Lean asked that Claude Rains play him. Stevens was pleased with the work, even though Lean was uncomfortable at first. Davis recalled his saying, "'This is a real tough thing to do. . . . You can't fool 'em, George. You can't fool 'em.' And George kind of paused and said, 'No, David, you can't.' They were talking about the audience."[14]

Shooting ended August 1, 1963. Stevens shot over six million feet of film in nine months on the set. Exhausted, he took a little time off, then edited for seventeen months, until February 1965, with editors Harold Kress and Argyle Nelson Jr. and assistant Don Guideus. Stevens came in during the afternoon, took time to plan, had dinner, then worked from about seven in the evening until late in the night. The final cost of *The Greatest Story Ever Told* hit $20 million, making it then the most expensive film ever shot in the United States. The picture had no previews; its first public screening was the New York press screening. Its Ultra Panavision 70 aspect ratio, 2.75 to 1, made it massive and commanding. In its initial road show engagement *The Greatest Story Ever Told* was projected in single-lens Cinerama. Later Stevens shaved the running time from 225 minutes down to 193 minutes. For its later wide release Stevens cut it again to 141 minutes.

"Is God Dead?"

By the time United Artists released *The Greatest Story Ever Told* in 1965, Fox's bloated, $40 million, four-year disaster, *Cleopatra*, had already cured moviegoers of spectacles, even biblical epics. The times were not receptive to a film as long, as labored, and as reverent as Stevens's story of Jesus. The timing of the film's release and the now well-known *Time* magazine cover asking boldly in February 1965, "Is God Dead?" could not have helped much. Stevens himself voiced his disappointment in the coincidence in later interviews. In his public statements he looked calm, tired even.

The film brought its own set of internal story problems. Stevens's look at Jesus was meant to be a "film of ideas," a quality that slows the film down and even burdens it with a deliberate pace, dialogue that many took to be labored and studied, and an almost sterile and "painted" — albeit exquisitely — emotional and physical landscape. Stevens set out to tell the story of Jesus not only through dramatic events, but through scenes set as if from within the religious paintings that depict them. Scene after scene in this ecumenical film makes reference to the paintings that inspired each of them. These scenes are rendered as beautiful artifacts without looking lived-in by flesh-and-blood characters. They are further stultified by the long line of actors, in cameo, who march to the screen and unwittingly distract the spectator from connecting with them. Spectators find themselves looking for the next famous face to appear. Dialogue and expression often seem melodramatic, as if trying to stir up the emotion flattened out by the carefully designed sets — a good example being Van Heflin's overzealous look of wonder at seeing Jesus' miracle. To complicate matters, despite beautiful shots such as the large silhouette of Jesus just before he brings Lazarus back to life (reminiscent of an earlier more intimate, character-driven Stevens), Stevens's sweeping camera (sadly his good friend and cameraman Bill Mellor died during the production) pulls back to reveal vistas so expansive they are almost distant and emotionally numbing. His production comments ring true: the view was more breathtaking when he viewed it from the mammoth perspective and the great height of a helicopter. But where, in all that space, was there a character that stayed long enough or came close enough to the spectator to share a moment? Where in all the space and the grandeur, could Stan and Ollie have given each other a look, felt a flash of empathy? In studying his subject with such reverence Stevens seemed at last to have lost his connection with his audience.

Stevens said in a February 1965 *New York Times* interview, "I have tremendous satisfaction that the job has been done — to its completion — the way I wanted it done; the way I know it should have been done. It belongs to the audiences now . . . and I prefer to let them judge."[15] But the film failed to connect with a broad audience in any meaningful way. The film was a long time coming. It was greatly anticipated and widely reviewed, earning great praise as well as harsh criticism. Shana Alexander, who could well have represented the East Coast critics who generally blasted *The Greatest Story Ever Told*, wrote in *Life* magazine, "The pace was so stupefying, that I felt not uplifted — but sandbagged!" Bosley Crowther wrote in the *New York Times*, "The most distractive nonsense is the pop-up of familiar faces in so-called cameo roles, jarring the illusion." Judith Crist, who wrote for the *New York Herald Tribune*, was heard to be laughing during the screening and called certain scenes in the film "lost between a Christmas-card approach and an arty aftermath," particularly the Last Supper scene "the stalest of lithographs." She also said, "*The Greatest Story Ever Told* succeeds in a number of areas where other Hollywood spectaculars have failed. . . . But it is unfortunate that it does not succeed ultimately in elevating its theme visually or intellectually beyond the dime-store-picture-Sunday-school-holy-primer level to which its predecessors have accustomed us. . . . The result, however, is what might be called a Hollywood Reverential, a film so in awe of its subject that it dares approach it only in the most traditional terms as a slow and solemn pace." Whether or not the New York critics were leveling a diatribe against Hollywood and its tradition of "big" and "extravagant" movies in a time when they were seduced by foreign imports, the East Coast response was particularly negative. *The Greatest Story Ever Told* fared better with critics across the country. *Variety* called it "a big, powerful moving picture demonstrating vast cinematic resource. . . . The film looks like the money it cost, or at least most of it and though it may need some selling, there is a lot to sell. . . . What Stevens puts on view, over-all, is panoramic cinema." The *Hollywood Reporter* said, "With Stevens's concentration on Jesus . . . most of the other characters are lost," but also said, "George Stevens has created a novel, reverent and important film with his view of this crucial event in the history of mankind." The *New York Daily News*, leading a faction of East Coast reviewers who praised *Greatest Story,* called it "a magnificent film . . . handled with reverence, artistic appreciation and admirable restraint."[16]

The production took its toll on Stevens in more ways than one. Publicists Ann and John Del Valle said about the last part of the shoot: "That was about the time when there were the big sets at the back of the studio. And he began to look like he could just hardly keep going. And I began to notice then that with people he enjoyed — for instance if Lucille Ball came on the set, that was a refresher to him — that he wasn't as genial. And he didn't visit with his own crew the way he had before. And . . . by the time that it ended, if it had been another week to go. . . . I don't think he would have made it. Nobody can keep going like that. . . . [Still] he knew what he had done. There was no question. And there's no question that he was happy with that picture. . . . But . . . if you take from each sequence one frame of film, I promise you have an absolutely beautiful painting."[17]

Stevens had been moving toward grandiosity since the war. But with this film's size his focus turned inward — not to the audience but by necessity to the huge subject at hand. *The Greatest Story Ever Told* is a study of Jesus, a contemplation that of course became very personal for Stevens. His gaze was so intense, so all-encompassing, that perhaps it unintentionally excluded others' eyes. Had he been younger, Stevens could have recovered easily from a box office disappointment and returned. But *The Greatest Story Ever Told* was his life's work, produced at a time in his life when stories had become large ideas and ideas were deeply ingrained into his sense of self. Studios would now look at him with skepticism but still make offers; after all he was still considered to be America's great filmmaker. But after the sheer size of the experience of this film, energy and enthusiasm were harder to muster. It was easier now to look past the rewards and disappointments of the film — of *film.* In the aftermath, when he visited Carl Sandburg just before Sandburg's death in 1967, Steven could not have helped but take satisfaction in the friendship he and Sandburg shared — and to note that it especially grew from their work together on *The Greatest Story Ever Told.* There was much to give him pleasure. He may have lost the book Stan Laurel gave him years ago but he kept a "piece of the rock" Sandburg gave him during their last visit. Walking down the hill from Sandburg's front porch, Stevens turned around to wave goodbye. Then he looked at the rock Sandburg had given him that he now held in his hand. Sandburg had inscribed in it, "To George from Carl."

10

Postscript
The Only Game in Town

> He had the kind of character in his face that
> looked like you could pour seven months of rain
> water out of it if he got wet.
> — Warren Beatty

Stevens went to Paris in July 1968 to shoot what would be his last film, *The Only Game in Town*, and rented William Wyler's former townhouse at 19, rue Weber. *The Only Game in Town* was a romantic comedy starring Elizabeth Taylor as a chorus girl named Fran and Warren Beatty as a piano player but more often gambler named Joe. Fran and Joe are emotionally down and out Las Vegas characters that play a game of romantic hide-and-seek before finally admitting that they might love each other. On September 30, 1968, the day he began shooting *The Only Game in Town*, Stevens wrote to Fred Zinnemann and described the film as "a very nice little story, mostly in two rooms of a small apartment. Through the windows we see the backing which shows a very pleasant view of the Las Vegas Strip." He added, "I present the possibilities in this dull fashion so, if the film proves interesting, you will think generously, as you do, how remarkable are the fellows of my craft."[1] Two months earlier he had married his longtime companion, Joan McTavish, and was awaiting her arrival in Paris. In the meantime he was again keeping a date book and writing to longtime friends.

Stevens had not directed since *The Greatest Story Ever Told.* When he read Frank Gilroy's script for *The Only Game in Town*, which was based on Gilroy's own play, he said, "Well, it's a nice little story. I'm going to make it the way I used to make comedies at RKO; I'm going to get in and shoot it and get it done."[2] But it took longer than that. After Twentieth Century Fox producer Fred Kohlmar brought the story to his attention, Stevens had to convince studio head Richard Zanuck that he could make the film without turning it into a long, expensive project. David Brown remembered that, "Zanuck . . . questioned him very severely on whether this was going to be expensive, whether George could contain his desire to make an enormous production of something, taking years and years, and George said to please remember that 'I was one of the originators of the quick production — two-reelers'; . . . [he] wanted to go back to work. . . . He had to work, and when he worked, that took care of everything."[3] Fox contracted with Stevens for the film on April 15, 1968.

Frank Sinatra was originally set to play opposite Elizabeth Taylor, but Stevens's notebook entry for July 30 indicates the tides to come: "Bad news all around re: start of picture — Taylor's health; Sinatra's disposition."[4] Taylor had gained a lot of weight and was again frequently ill, all complicated by her $1.5 million asking price, which Fox thought too high. But then Sinatra pulled out and Warren Beatty entered the picture. Stevens wanted to cast Beatty, who was only too happy to work with him and said he did not even need to see the script before committing. But Beatty's younger age created yet another problem, altering the script's older man-younger woman dynamic. Mia Farrow's name came up, along with Julie Christie's. Stevens wanted Zanuck to hire Farrow, but Taylor wanted to stay and Zanuck did not want to offend her, on top of which Fox agreed to shoot *The Only Game in Town* in Paris where Taylor's husband, Richard Burton, was working on *The Staircase* with Rex Harrison. The Las Vegas setting for *The Only Game in Town* was created on a Paris sound stage, giving the scenes a surreal look. The cast and crew shot in Paris from September 30, 1968, to February 13, 1969, when they relocated to Las Vegas and shot for a week before heading back to the Fox lot in Los Angeles where principal photography finally finished on March 3.

The film opened almost a year later, on January 23, 1970, to respectable reviews and box office numbers. But audiences probably saw what Stevens saw: that Taylor's character was too cynical, perhaps too old, for Beatty's character, who was a young, optimistic-against-all-odds piano player who finally strikes it lucky in love and money at the end. Joe gambles and wins the money to get the two of them out of Las Vegas while Fran grudgingly makes a commitment to him. But it is a hard-fought battle, and by the time Fran admits that perhaps she loves Joe, it is difficult for audiences to believe her. The film is overcome by its slow pace and its cynicism.

To some, *The Only Game in Town* might have seemed an odd choice for Stevens, who spent the last twenty years filming outdoors where he loved it best. But since *The Greatest Story Ever Told* he considered directing a wide range of projects before eventually walking away from them, or them from him. He thought about *The Stalking Moon* but ultimately did not like the story; he thought the script for *Butch Cassidy and the Sundance Kid* was showy. At one point Lew Wasserman also asked him to keep an office at Universal Studios, but he turned the offer down because there was no particular project attached to it. While in Paris in 1968 he kept an enthusiastic eye on the stage production of *The Great White Hope* but the playwright, Howard Sackler, and his agent, thinking Stevens might make the film too costly, sold it instead to Fox. *The Confessions of Nat Turner* also held interest and Stevens researched it thoroughly, but David Wolper outbid him on it. Three year passed before Stevens directed *The Only Game in Town*.

Even though *The Greatest Story Ever Told* failed to connect with audiences Stevens remained a powerful figure, an industry icon. He was, after all, still George Stevens. He thought about the future of filmmaking, about young directors, and spoke at university retrospectives of his work, saying at one point that he thought highly of the French New Wave directors and the implications of the auteur theory for filmmaking. A Johnsonian Democrat, he was involved with the National Endowment for the Arts, working with Gregory Peck and Elizabeth Ashley to help get the American Film Institute off the ground, and he never stopped attending or being active in the Directors Guild of America through the early 1970s.

"George would call up and we'd meet for lunch," his friend Jim Silke said. Silke first met Stevens when he interviewed Stevens for his *Cinema* magazine. They would talk movies, sometimes attend screenings. They met for lunch almost monthly during the late 1960s; sometimes they would eat at the Cave des Roys, a men's club on La Cienega Boulevard in Beverly Hills, or at Ships, a coffee shop just down the street. One particular time Silke met Stevens for lunch at the MGM commissary in Culver City—not the Green Room, which Stevens considered too public and would jokingly call the "enemy." But they were seen, Silke recalled. "I went to New York that night for about a week, and when I returned, there were twenty-two phone messages from friends who wanted me to get a script to Stevens. One was from my own lawyer!"[5]

There were also lunches with Warren Beatty long before Stevens cast him in *The Only Game in Town*. Beatty was after Stevens for a time to direct *Bonnie and Clyde*. Beatty remembered that, "I asked George to direct it. And we would have long silent meetings in Chinese restaurants. And he would think, silently. And I would learn from these long pauses. He would make suggestions that were symbolic, I thought, like 'Are you sure about the haircuts?' Then we'd eat Chinese food for twenty minutes. And I could never get him to do the movie but I sure had a lot of meetings with him. I'll never know whether he came close to doing the picture. . . . I began to think of him as a slow-moving freight train."[6]

In March 1975, a reunion was planned for Stevens and his war buddies, the men who filmed the battles of the war and who walked into Dachau. Members of the U.S. Army Signal Corps Special Motion Picture Unit were en route from around the country to meet again with Colonel George Stevens. But the reunion ended differently than anyone planned. On March 7, Stevens and his wife, Joan, were vacationing in Lancaster, California, when Stevens became ill and was taken to the hospital. He died of a heart attack during the night. Stevens's secretary, Edna Shively, wrote in Stevens's office date book:

GEORGE STEVENS DIED MARCH 8, 1975
Friday, March 7, 1975, Mr. & Mrs. Stevens spent a very pleasant evening with friends at the Bermuda Inn. Conversation during the evening included a discussion of the men's similar World War II experiences. George Stevens became ill during the night. The following morning they reached Dr. Howard Baer in Los Angeles. Late in the afternoon . . . GS [was] admitted to Antelope Valley Hospital and Medical Cen-

ter and placed under Intensive Care. . . . Later in the evening GS insisted on being moved into a private room, as he hoped to be released the next morning. Following medication for rest and sleep, Mr. Stevens died in his sleep about nine o'clock and efforts for the next hour to restore the heart were unavailing.[7]

Stevens's funeral was held at Forest Lawn in the Hollywood Hills. Charlton Heston gave the eulogy for the group of family and friends assembled at the Old North Church. Later, Stevens was buried up on the cemetery hill, overlooking Warner Bros. studios and the city of Toluca Lake where he had lived before and after the war.

Capra, now an old man, might not have known about the jeep Stevens called Toluca, but he remembered his friend well. Years after Stevens's death, he said, "I just loved the man and I'm sure he loved me. And when I die . . . I'm certainly going to look George up. . . . I think we'll start another Liberty Films up there . . . and maybe we can get out of heaven once in a while and go to some of these other places, just like George went to hell in the army when he went to Europe . . . and wouldn't it be wonderful if we could make pictures in heaven that we could send down here. . . . When it comes down to doing it, I want to do it with George."[8]

Back in 1968, while staying at 19, rue Weber, Stevens wrote to his friend Irwin Shaw in Switzerland about the death of their war buddy, Gene Solow:

> I was in London the weekend before Gene Solow died. It would have been so simple for me to locate him if I had known he was there. I had heard from him last, some months earlier, from Spain. The news of his death was received here in a clipping about a week later from Los Angeles. At the time I was within an hour or closer to Solow during the few days before his fatal illness and at the time of his passing, only a shout away, and it seemed stupid and ridiculous that I didn't even know.
>
> Getting the note from you was the good thing. So much time has passed. I have always rather felt that I would be seeing you tomorrow or somewhere soon. I guess it takes the death of a friend to squash the pipe dream that life is forever and that the good things are coming tomorrow.
> —George

Notes

Filmography

Bibliography

Index

Notes

Chapter 1. George and Rex, Stan and Ollie

1. Yvonne Stevens, interview by Irene Atkins, August 1980, transcript, *George Stevens: A Filmmaker's Journey* Collection, Margaret Herrick Library, Academy of Motion Picture Arts and Sciences, Beverly Hills, Calif. Material from this collection reproduced with the permission of George Stevens Jr.

2. Ibid.

3. Newspaper article, private collection of George Stevens Jr.

4. Henrietta Drake to George Stevens Jr., May 11, 1984, private collection of George Stevens Jr.

5. George Stevens, date book entry, 1922, George Stevens Collection, Margaret Herrick Library, Academy of Motion Picture Arts and Sciences, Beverly Hills, Calif. Material from this collection reproduced with the permission of George Stevens Jr.

6. Ibid.

7. Ibid.

8. Leonard Maltin, "George Stevens: Shorts to Features," *Action*, November-December, 1970, 12-14.

9. George Stevens, date book, 1922.

10. Sumiko Higashi, *Cecil B. DeMille and American Culture: The Silent Era* (Berkeley: University of California Press, 1994), 10-11.

11. Ibid.

12. George Stevens, date book, 1922.

13. Ibid.

14. George Stevens, interview by Kevin Brownlow, October 12, 1970, transcript, George Stevens Collection.

15. Jim Silke, "George Stevens Talks about Movies," *Cinema Magazine*, December-January, 1964-65, 18-19.

16. Quoted in Kevin Brownlow, *The War, the West and the Widescreen* (New York: Random House, 1979), 351.

17. Ibid.

18. Ibid.

19. Silke, "George Stevens Talks about Movies," 18.

20. Ibid., 19.

21. George Stevens, interview by Eduardo Escorel, Associacao De Cineaseas, Rio, Brazil, June 25–27, 1969, transcript, George Stevens Collection.

22. Patrick McGilligan, *Film Crazy: Interviews with Hollywood Legends* (New York: St. Martin's Press, 2000), 80.

23. Randy Skretvedt, *Laurel and Hardy: The Magic Behind the Movies* (Beverly Hills: Moonstone Press, 1987), 49.

24. George Stevens, interview by Eduardo Escorel.

25. Maltin, "George Stevens: Shorts to Features," 13.

26. Ibid.

27. Silke, "George Stevens Talks about Movies," 18.

28. Yvonne Stevens, interview by Irene Atkins.

29. Yvonne Stevens, interview, Ontario Educational Communications Authority, June 1978, transcript, George Stevens Collection.

30. Production notes, *The Devil Horse*, George Stevens Collection.

Chapter 2. The RKO Years

1. Yvonne Stevens, interview by Irene Atkins, August 1980, transcript, Filmmaker's Journey Collection.

2. Jerry Hoffman, review of *The Cohens and Kelleys*, *Los Angeles Herald Examiner*, March 8, 1933.

3. Review of *Laddie*, *Variety*, February 25, 1935.

4. Review of *Laddie*, *Hollywood Reporter*, February 25, 1935.

5. Muriel Babcock, review of *Nitwits*, *Los Angeles Herald Examiner*, June 14, 1935.

6. George Stevens, interview by Robert Hughes, February 1967, transcript, George Stevens Collection.

7. George Stevens, USA Film Festival, Dallas, Texas, April 1971, transcript, Filmmaker's Journey Collection.

8. Production notes, *Alice Adams*, George Stevens Collection. Unless otherwise noted, all quotations and notes pertaining to this film are from these files.

9. Elizabeth Kendall, *The Runaway Bride: Hollywood Romantic Comedy of the 1930s* (New York: Cooper Square Press, 1990), 69–89.

10. George Stevens, interview by Robert Hughes.

11. Yvonne Stevens, interview by Irene Atkins.

12. George Stevens, USA Film Festival.

13. Review of *Annie Oakley*, *Variety*, October 26, 1935.

14. Review of *Annie Oakley*, *Hollywood Reporter*, October 26, 1935.

15. Yvonne Stevens, interview by Irene Atkins.

16. Recounted by Jim Silke, interview by the author, August 7, 2003.

17. Review of *Swing Time, Hollywood Reporter,* August 24, 1936.

18. Review of *Swing Time, Variety,* August 24, 1936.

19. Review of *Quality Street, Los Angeles Times,* March 6, 1937.

20. Review of *Quality Street, Hollywood Reporter,* March 6, 1937.

21. Yvonne Stevens, interview by Irene Atkins.

22. George Stevens, interview by Joseph McBride and Patrick McGilligan, the Brown Derby restaurant, Hollywood, Calif., September 1974, transcript, Filmmaker's Journey Collection.

23. Review of *A Damsel in Distress, Time,* December 6, 1937.

24. Peter Bogdanovich, "Interview with George Stevens," *Esquire,* July 1966, 106.

25. George Stevens, interview by Robert Hughes.

26. See Rudy Behlmer's excellent history of the production of *Gunga Din* in *America's Favorite Movies: Behind the Scenes* (New York: Frederick Unger, 1982), 87–103.

27. George Stevens, USA Film Festival.

28. Commentary by George Stevens, *Gunga Din* (Image Laserdisc, Collector's Edition, 1995).

29. Khwaja Ahmd Abbas, review of *Gunga Din, Filmindia,* February 1939.

30. George Stevens, seminar, American Film Institute, 1970.

31. Review of *Gunga Din, Variety,* January 25, 1939; *New York Times,* January 27, 1939; *Newsweek,* February 6, 1939.

32. Pandro Berman cable to George Stevens, February 8, 1939. General files, George Stevens Collection.

33. General files, George Stevens Collection.

34. Review of *Vigil in the Night, Los Angeles Times,* February 16, 1940; *Daily News,* March 9, 1940.

Chapter 3. The Women

1. George Stevens, USA Film Festival, Dallas, Texas, April 1971, transcript, Filmmaker's Journey Collection.

2. George Stevens, "Q & A with George Stevens," *Screen and Radio Weekly,* 1939, George Stevens Collection.

3. George Stevens, USA Film Festival.

4. Ibid.

5. Joanne Dobson, "Reclaiming Sentimental Literature," *American Literature* 69, no. 2 (June 1997): 263–65.

6. Production notes, *Penny Serenade,* George Stevens Collection. Unless otherwise noted, all quotations in this chapter pertaining to *Penny Serenade, The Talk of the Town, Woman of the Year,* and *The More the Merrier* are from these files.

7. Review of *Penny Serenade, Variety,* April 16, 1941; *Hollywood Reporter,* April 16, 1941.

8. Roland Barthes, *The Pleasure of the Text,* trans. Richard Miller (New York: Hill & Wang, 1975), 10.

9. Teresa de Lauretis, *Alice Doesn't: Feminism, Semiotics, Cinema* (Bloomington: Indiana University Press, 1984), III, 121.

10. George Stevens, interview by Joseph McBride and Patrick McGilligan, the Brown Derby restaurant, Hollywood, Calif., September 1974, transcript, Filmmaker's Journey Collection.

11. George Stevens, USA Film Festival.

12. George Stevens, interview by Kevin Brownlow, October 12, 1970, transcript, George Stevens Collection.

13. Yvonne Stevens, interview by Irene Atkins, August 1980, transcript, Filmmaker's Journey Collection.

14. Review of *Woman of the Year, Variety,* April 1, 1942; *Motion Picture Herald,* January 17, 1942.

15. MGM Press Book Collection, University of Southern California Cinema-TV Library, Los Angeles, Calif.

16. Mary Anne Doane, "The Economy of Desire: The Commodity Form In/Of the Cinema," in *Movies and Mass Culture,* ed. John Belton (Brunswick, N.J.: Rutgers University Press, 2000), 125.

17. MGM Press Book Collection.

18. George Stevens, interview by Robert Hughes, February 1967, transcript, George Stevens Collection.

19. John Oller, *Jean Arthur: The Actress Nobody Knew* (New York: Limelight Editions, 1997), 140.

Chapter 4. Toluca Ville

1. George Stevens, interview by Robert Hughes, February 1967, transcript, George Stevens Collection.

2. World War II photos file, George Stevens Collection.

3. George Stevens Jr., interview by the author, August 2003.

4. George Stevens, interview by Robert Hughes.

5. George Stevens, interview by Bruce Petri, March 1973, transcript, George Stevens Collection.

6. George Stevens, World War II Journals, Notebooks, and Correspon-

dence, George Stevens Collection. Unless otherwise noted, all quotations from notebooks are from these files.

7. Frank Capra, interview by George Stevens Jr., April 1982, transcript, Filmmaker's Journey Collection.

8. George Stevens, letter to Joel Sayre, December 6, 1944, World War II Journals, Notebooks, and Correspondence.

9. George Stevens, interview by Bruce Petri.

10. Ivan Moffat, interview by Susan Winslow, April 1982, transcript, Filmmaker's Journey Collection.

11. George Stevens, interview by Robert Hughes.

12. Ibid.

13. Ibid.

14. Frank Capra, interview by George Stevens Jr.

15. George Stevens, date book entry, 1946, George Stevens Collection.

16. Ibid.

17. Joseph McBride, *Frank Capra: The Catastrophe of Success* (New York: St. Martin's Griffin, 2000), 506.

18. Yvonne Stevens, interview by Irene Atkins, August 1980, transcript, Filmmaker's Journey Collection.

19. Frank Capra, *Name Above the Title: An Autobiography* (New York: Macmillan, 1971), 373–74.

20. Ibid., 386.

21. Jim Silke, "George Stevens Talks about Movies," *Cinema Magazine,* December-January, 1964–65, 18–19.

22. McBride, *Frank Capra,* 508; Yvonne Stevens, interview by Irene Atkins.

23. DeWitt Bodeen, interview, Ontario Educational Communications Authority, June 1978, transcript, George Stevens Collection.

24. Ibid.

25. Ibid.

26. Ivan Moffat, interview by Susan Winslow.

27. DeWitt Bodeen, interview by Susan Winslow.

28. Review of *I Remember Mama, Variety,* March 9, 1948; *Hollywood Reporter,* March 9, 1948.

Chapter 5. I See America Kissing

1. George Stevens, interview by Robert Hughes, February 1967, transcript, George Stevens Collection.

2. F. O. Matthiessen, *Dreiser* (New York: William Sloane Associates, 1951), 191.

3. W. A. Swanbeg, *Dreiser* (New York: Charles Scribner's Sons, 1965), 254.

4. Matthiessen, *Dreiser*, 194.

5. David Thomson, *Showman: The Life of David O. Selznick* (New York: Alfred A. Knopf, 1992), 117.

6. Ibid.

7. *New York Times,* July 8, 1931.

8. *Variety,* August 11, 1931.

9. *Nation,* September 2, 1931.

10. George Stevens, interview by Eduardo Escorel, Associacao De Cineaseas, Rio, Brazil, June 25–27, 1969, transcript, George Stevens Collection.

11. George Stevens, interview by Robert Hughes.

12. George Stevens, Forum, Ohio State University Retrospective of Stevens's films, April, 1973.

13. George Stevens, annotations in his Signet paperback of Dreiser's *An American Tragedy,* George Stevens Collection.

14. Jim Silke, interview by the author, December 12, 2001.

15. Production notes, *A Place in the Sun,* George Stevens Collection. Unless otherwise noted, all quotations and notes pertaining to this film are from these files.

16. George Stevens, Ohio State University Retrospective.

17. George Stevens, interview by Robert Hughes.

18. Ivan Moffat, interview by the author, August 2000.

19. Ibid.

20. Ibid.

21. Ibid.

22. Scott Eyman, *Print the Legend: The Life and Times of John Ford* (New York: Simon and Schuster, 1999), 449.

23. Ivan Moffat, interview by the author.

24. Ibid.

25. Theodore Dreiser, *An American Tragedy* (New York: Signet Classics, 1964), 219.

26. George Stevens, Ohio State University Retrospective.

27. George Stevens, interview by Robert Hughes.

28. Ibid.

29. Patricia Bosworth, *Montgomery Clift* (New York: Harcourt Brace Jovanovich, 1978), 185.

30. Ibid., 184–85

31. Ibid., 185.

32. Ivan Moffat, interview by the author.

33. Bosworth, *Montgomery Clift,* 187.

34. Shelley Winters, *Shelley: Also Known as Shirley* (New York: William Morrow and Company, 1980), 283.

35. Ivan Moffat, interview by the author.

36. Review of *A Place in the Sun, Hollywood Reporter*, July 18, 1951; *Newsweek*, September 10, 1951.

37. Jim Silke, interview by the author.

38. George Stevens, USA Film Festival, Dallas, Texas, April, 1971, transcript, Filmmaker's Journey Collection.

39. George Stevens, interview by Robert Hughes.

40. *Los Angeles Times*, July 29, 1951.

41. R. W. B. Lewis, *The American Adam: Innocence, Tragedy, and Tradition in the Nineteenth Century* (Chicago: University of Chicago Press, 1955), 5.

42. Barney Hoskyns, *Montgomery Clift: Beautiful Loser* (New York: Grove Weidenfeld, 1991), 85.

43. Jim Silke, interview by Susan Winslow, August 1982, transcript, Filmmaker's Journey Collection.

44. George Stevens, interview by Kevin Brownlow, October 1970, transcript, Filmmaker's Journey Collection.

Chapter 6. The Art of Gun Slinging

1. Production notes, *A Place in the Sun*, George Stevens Collection.

2. Production notes, *Shane*, George Stevens Collection. Unless otherwise noted, all quotations and notes pertaining to this film are from these files.

3. Chuck Rankin, "Clash of Frontiers: A Historical Parallel to Jack Schaefer's Shane," in Jack Schaefer, *Shane: The Critical Edition* (Lincoln: University of Nebraska Press, 1984), 8.

4. George Stevens, USA Film Festival, Dallas, Texas, April 1971, transcript, Filmmaker's Journey Collection.

5. Patrick McGilligan, *Film Crazy: Interviews with Hollywood Legends* (New York: St. Martins Press, 2000), 91.

6. George Stevens, interview by Joe Hyams, *New York Herald Tribune*, April 19, 1953.

7. Ibid.

8. Schaefer, *Shane: The Critical Edition*, 273; Richard Slotkin, *Regeneration Through Violence: The Mythology of the American Frontier 1600–1860* (Middletown, Conn.: Wesleyan University Press, 1973), 8.

9. George Stevens, Forum, Ohio State University Retrospective of Stevens's films, April 1973.

10. Rick Lyman, "Coming Back to Shane: Watching Movies with Woody Allen," *New York Times*, August 3, 2001.

11. *Saturday Review of Literature,* December 3, 1949.

12. McGilligan, *Film Crazy,* 91–92.

13. Ibid., 92.

14. Schaefer, *Shane: The Critical Edition,* 66.

15. Recounted by Alan DeLynn, interview by Susan Winslow, July 1981, transcript, Filmmaker's Journey Collection.

16. Schaefer, *Shane: The Critical Edition,* 272.

17. George Stevens, interview by Joe Hyams.

18. Commentary by George Stevens Jr., *Shane* DVD (Hollywood, Calif: Paramount Home Video, 2000).

19. Jean Arthur, interview by Susan Winslow, July 1981, transcript, Filmmaker's Journey Collection.

20. George Stevens Jr., correspondence with the author, April 18, 2003.

21. Elisha Cook Jr., interview, Ontario Educational Communications Authority, June 1978, transcript, George Stevens Collection.

22. George Stevens Jr., interview, Ontario Educational Communications Authority, June 1978, transcript, George Stevens Collection.

23. Frank McConnell, *The Spoken Seen: Film and the Romantic Imagination* (Baltimore: Johns Hopkins University Press, 1975), 160.

24. George Stevens, interview by Eduardo Escorel, Associacao De Cineaseas, Rio, Brazil, June 25–27, 1969, transcript, George Stevens Collection.

25. Schaefer, *Shane: The Critical Edition,* 65, 258.

26. Darry F. Zanuck, letter to Sol Siegel, in *Memo from Darryl F. Zanuck: The Golden Years at 20th Century Fox,* ed. Rudy Behlmer (New York: Grove Press, 1993), 245.

27. Commentary by George Stevens Jr., *Shane* DVD.

Chapter 7. Our Town

1. See Roy Harvey Pearce, introduction to *The Continuity of American Poetry* (Princeton, N.J.: Princeton University Press, 1961).

2. George Stevens, *Hollywood Reporter,* November 19, 1956.

3. World War II veteran Sol Feldman, interview by the author.

4. Alan Nadel, *Containment Culture: American Narratives, Postmodernism and the Atomic Age* (Durham, N. C.: Duke University Press, 1995), 91.

5. David Halberstam, *The Fifties* (New York: Balantine, 1993), 585.

6. Shelley Nickles, "More Is Better: Mass Consumption in Postwar America," *American Quarterly* 54, no. 4 (December 2002): 588.

7. Trevor Willsmer, "Giant: The Making of an Epic Motion Picture," *Giant Collector's Special Edition* VHS booklet (Burbank, Calif: Warner Home Video, 1996), 10.

8. Ibid.

9. David Brown, interview by Susan Winslow, October 1981, transcript, Filmmaker's Journey Collection.

10. "The High Road," *Hollywood Reporter,* October 23, 1953.

11. Production and script notes, *Giant,* George Stevens Collection. Unless otherwise noted, all quotations and notes pertaining to this film are from these files.

12. Jim Silke, interview by the author, August 7, 2003.

13. Louella Parsons, *Herald Examiner,* November 6, 1954.

14. George Stevens, USA Film Festival, Dallas, Texas, April 1971, transcript, Filmmaker's Journey Collection.

15. Jack L. Warner Collection, University of Southern California Cinema-TV Library, Los Angeles, Calif. All references pertaining to Jack Warner are from this collection.

16. Mercedes McCambridge, *The Quality of Mercy* (New York: Times Books, 1981), 206.

17. Jane Withers, interview by the author, May 2003.

18. Bob Hinkle, interview by the author, March 2003.

19. Earl Holliman, interview by the author, May 2003.

20. Richard Dyer McCann, "George Stevens' Director's Techniques," *Christian Science Monitor,* September 25, 1956,

21. Philip K. Scheur, "Lone Rider: Galahad Roving Plains of the West," *Los Angeles Times,* June 7, 1953.

22. George Stevens, USA Film Festival.

23. Stephen Crane, "The Bride Comes to Yellow Sky," *The Portable Stephen Crane,* ed, Joseph Katz (New York: Viking Press, 1969), 392.

24. Willsmer, "Giant: The Making of an Epic Motion Picture," 10.

Chapter 8. The One Who Cannot Be Left Behind

1. Deborah E. Lipstadt, *Beyond Belief: The American Press and the Coming of the Holocaust, 1933–1943* (New York: 1986), quoted in Peter Novick, *The Holocaust in American Life* (Boston and New York: Houghton Mifflin, 2000), 65.

2. George Stevens, forum, Ohio State University, April 1973, transcript, Filmmaker's Journey Collection.

3. Production notes, *The Diary of Anne Frank,* George Stevens Collection. Unless otherwise noted, all quotations and notes pertaining to this film are from these files.

4. Anne Frank, *The Diary of a Young Girl* (New York: Pocket Books, 1952), 239.

5. David Barnouw and Gerrold Van Der Stroon, eds., *The Diary of Anne Frank: The Critical Edition* (New York: Doubleday, 1989), 59.

6. Ibid., 60–62.

7. Frank, *Diary of a Young Girl*, 239–40.

8. *Anne Frank's Tales from the Secret Annex* (New York: Bantam Books, 1994), 107, 113.

9. Frank, *Diary of a Young Girl*, 3.

10. Ibid., 57, 51, 241.

11. Novick, *The Holocaust in American Life*, 83, 85.

12. Ilan Avisar, *Screening the Holocaust: Cinema's Image of the Unimaginable* (Bloomington: Indiana University Press, 1988), 122.

13. David Barnouw interviewed in *History vs. Hollywood*, Van Ness Films, 2001.

14. George Stevens, interview by William Kirschner, August 27, 1963, transcript, George Stevens Collection.

15. George Stevens, Ohio State University Retrospective.

16. George Stevens, interview by Bruce Petri, March 1973, transcript, George Stevens Collection.

17. George Stevens Jr., interview by the author, October 2002.

18. Millie Perkins, interview by the author, October 2002.

19. John and Ann Del Valle, interview by Susan Winslow, May 1982, transcript, Filmmaker's Journey Collection.

20. Review of *The Diary of Anne Frank*, Hollis Alpert, *Saturday Review*, April 4, 1959.

21. Cathy Caruth, *Unclaimed Experience: Trauma, Narrative, History* (Baltimore: Johns Hopkins University Press, 1996), 24.

22. George Davis, interview, Ontario Educational Communications Authority, June 1978, transcript, George Stevens Collection.

Chapter 9. Democratic Vista

1. George Stevens, contract with Twentieth Century Fox, November 25, 1958, production notes, *The Greatest Story Ever Told*, George Stevens Collection. Unless otherwise noted, all quotations and notes pertaining to this film are from these files.

2. Frank I. Davis, interview by Susan Winslow, April 1982, transcript, Filmmaker's Journey Collection.

3. Ivan Moffat, interview by the author, June 2000.

4. Jim Silke, "George Stevens Talks about Movies," *Cinema Magazine*, December–January, 1964–65, 18–19.

5. Ibid.

6. Tony Vellani, interview, Ontario Educational Communications Authority, June 1978, transcript, George Stevens Collection.

7. Frank I. Davis, interview by Susan Winslow.

8. Michael Anderson, interview by Susan Winslow, October 1982, transcript, Filmmaker's Journey Collection.

9. James Lee Barrett, interview by Susan Winslow, May 1982, transcript, Filmmaker's Journey Collection.

10. Dorothy McGuire, interview by Susan Winslow, September 1981, transcript, Filmmaker's Journey Collection.

11. Frank I. Davis, interview by Susan Winslow.

12. George Stevens, Forum, Ohio State University Retrospective of Stevens' films, April, 1973.

13. Frank I. Davis, interview by Susan Winslow.

14. Ibid.

15. George Stevens, interview, *New York Times,* February 1965.

16. Review of *The Greatest Story Ever Told,* Shana Alexander, *Life,* February 25, 1965; Bosley Crowther, *New York Times,* February 16, 1965; Judith Crist, *New York Herald Tribune,* February 26, 1965; *Variety,* February 15, 1965; *Hollywood Reporter,* February 15, 1965; *New York Daily News,* February 15, 1965.

17. Ann and John Del Valle, interview by Susan Winslow, September 1981, transcript, Filmmaker's Journey Collection.

Chapter 10. Postscript

1. Production notes, *The Only Game in Town,* George Stevens Collection. Unless otherwise noted, all quotations and notes pertaining to this film are from these files.

2. Recounted by George Stevens Jr., interview by the author, August 2, 2003.

3. David Brown, interview by Susan Winslow, October 1981, transcript, Filmmaker's Journey Collection.

4. George Stevens, date book, 1968, George Stevens Collection.

5. Jim Silke, interview by the author, August 7, 2003.

6. Warren Beatty, interview by Susan Winslow, October 28, 1982, transcript, Filmmaker's Journey Collection.

7. Date book, 1975 (entry by Stevens's secretary, Edna Shively), George Stevens Collection.

8. Frank Capra, interview by George Stevens Jr., April 1982, transcript, Filmmaker's Journey Collection.

Filmography

As Apprentice and Assistant Cameraman

Heroes of the Street, 1922
The Flaming Arrow, 1922
Devil's Ghost, 1922
Destroying Angel, 1922
Michael O'Halloran, 1923
The Virginian (Preferred Pictures), 1923

Hal Roach Studios, 1924–32

Stevens worked at the Hal Roach Studios from 1924 to 1931 as assistant camera-man, cameraman, gag writer, and then director. Payroll ledgers for the year 1928 are missing. Prior ledgers show that Stevens received $150 per week from April 16 through May 7, 1927, as part of Roach Studios "Western Company." He received the same weekly salary for the rest of 1927 for work on other shorts. Studio pro-duction numbers are given where available and uncredited films are indicated.

As Assistant Cameraman and Cameraman

Battling Orioles (Pathé Films), 1924
The White Sheep, 1924
Black Cyclone (Pathé Films), 1925
Are Husbands Human? (Pathé Films), 1925
The Desert's Toll (MGM), 1926
The Devil Horse (Pathé Films), 1926
Be Your Age (Pathé Films), 1926
Are Brunette's Safe? (Pathé Films) (B-16), 1927
Bigger and Better Blondes (Pathé Films) (B-19), 1927
The Valley of Hell (MGM), 1927
No Man's Law, 1927

Lightning (Tiffany), 1927
The Girl from Gay Paree (Tiffany), 1927

L Series: Laurel and Hardy Silents

Slipping Wives, 1926
Putting Pants on Phillip, 1927
The Second Hundred Years, 1927
The Battle of the Century, 1927
Sugar Daddies, 1927
Leave em Laughing, 1928
The Finishing Touch, 1928
Early to Bed (L-12), 1928
Two Tars (L-13), 1928
We Faw Down (L-15) (not credited), 1928
Their Purple Moment (S-10), 1928
Liberty (L-16), 1929
Wrong Again (L-17), 1929
That's My Wife (L-18) (not credited), 1929
Big Business (L-19), 1929
Double Whoopee (L-20), 1929
Bacon Grabbers (L-21), 1929
Angora Love (L-22), 1929

L Series: Laurel and Hardy Talkies

Unaccustomed As We Are (L-23) (not credited), 1929
Berth Marks (L-24) (not credited), 1929
Men O'War (L-25), 1929
Perfect Day (L-26) (not credited), 1929
They Go Boom (L-27) (not credited), 1929
The Hoose Gow (L-28), 1929
Night Owls (L-29), 1930
Blotto (L-30), 1930
Brats (L-31), 1930
Below Zero (L-32), 1930
Hog Wild (L-33), 1930
The Laurel-Hardy Murder Case (L-34), 1930
Another Fine Mess, 1930
The Night Life, 1930
Our Wife (L-40) (not credited), 1931
Pardon Us, 1931

C Series: Charley Chase

Assistant Wives (C-1), 1927
All for Nothing (C-6), 1928
Aching Youths (C-9), 1928
Is Everybody Happy? (C-13) (not credited), 1928
The Booster (C-14) (not credited), 1928
All Parts (C-15), 1928
Chasing Husbands (C-16) (not credited), 1928
Off to Buffalo (C-18), 1929
Loud Soup (C-19), 1929
The Big Squawk (C-21) (not credited), 1929
Leaping Love (C-22), 1929
Snappy Sneezer (C-23), 1929
Crazy Feet (C-24), 1929
The Real McCoy (C-27), 1930
Whispering Whoopee (C-29) (not credited), 1930
Dollar Dizzy (C-33), 1930
One of the Smiths (C-39) (not credited), 1931
The Panic Is On (C-1), 1931

G Series: Our Gang (not credited)

Bear Shooters (G-32), 1930
A Tough Winter (G-33), 1930
Pups Is Pups (G-34), 1930
Fly My Kite (G-41), 1931

D Series: Max Davidson

Tell It to the Judge (D-5), 1928
Came the Dawn (D-8), 1928
Blow by Blow (D-9), 1928
Should Women Drive? (D-10), 1928
That Night (D-11), 1928
Do Gentlemen Snore? (D-12), 1928

S Series: All Star

Should Married Men Go Home? (S-11), 1928
The Boy Friend (S-13) (not credited), 1928
Feed em and Weep (S-14), 1928
Going Ga-ga (S-15) (not credited), 1929
A Pair of Tights (S-16) (not credited), 1929

Hurdy Gurdy (S-21), 1929
Madame Q (S-22), 1929
Dad's Day (S-23), 1929

S Series: Harry Langdon

Hotter Than Hot (S-24), 1929
Sky Boy (S-25), 1929
Skirt Shy (S-26), 1929
The Head Guy (S-27), 1930
The Fighting Parson (S-28), 1930
The Big Kick (S-29), 1930
The Shrimp (S-30), 1930
The King (S-31) (not credited), 1930

S Series: The Boy Friends

Bigger and Better (S-33), 1930
Ladies Last (S-34) (director), 1930
Blood and Thunder (S-35) (director), 1930
Love Fever (S-36) (not credited), 1931
High Gear (S-37) (director), 1931
Air-Tight (S-38) (director), 1931
Let's Do Things (S-39), 1931
Call a Cop! (S-1) (director), 1931
Mama Loves Papa (S-2) (director), 1931
The Kickoff (S-3) (director), 1931
Love Pains (S-4) (not credited), 1932
The Knockout (S-5) (not credited), 1932
You're Telling Me (S-6) (not credited), 1932

Universal Studios, 1932–33

The Warren Doane Comedy Series

Yoo-Hoo, 1932
Director: James W. Horne; Story: George Stevens, J. A. Howe
The Finishing Touch, 1932
Director: George Stevens; Story: Fred Guiol, George Stevens
Boys Will Be Boys, 1932
Director: George Stevens; Story: Fred Guiol
Family Troubles, 1933
Director: George Stevens; Story: James W. Horne, George Stevens

Hesitating Love, 1932
Director: James W. Horne; Story: George Stevens, James W. Horne
Who, Me? 1932
Director: George Stevens; Story: James W. Horne, Fred Guiol
Hunting Troubles, 1933
Director: James W. Horne; Story: George Stevens, James W. Horne
Pick Me Up, 1933
Director: James W. Horne; Story: George Stevens, James W. Horne
Alias the Professor, 1933
Director: James W. Horne; Story: James W. Horne, George Stevens
Rock-a-Bye Cowboy, 1933
Director: George Stevens; Story: James W. Horne, George Stevens
Should Crooners Marry? 1933
Director: George Stevens; Story: James W. Horne, Fred Guiol
Room Mates, 1933
Director: George Stevens; Story: Fred Guiol, James W. Horne
The Cohens and Kellys in Trouble, 1933
Director: George Stevens; Screenplay: Glenn Tryon; Original story: Victor
  and Edward Halperin

RKO Studios, 1933–40

As Director, Shorts

A Divorce Courtship, 1933
Flirting in the Park, 1933
Quiet Please!, 1933
Grin and Bear It, 1933
What Fur, 1933
Walking Back Home, 1933
The Big Mouthpiece, 1934
Rough Necking, 1934
The Undie-World, 1934
Cracked Shots, 1934
Strictly Fresh Eggs, 1934
Bridal Bait, 1934
Autobiography, 1934
Ocean Swells, 1934
Pickled Peppers, 1935
Hunger Pains, 1935

As Director, Feature Films

Bachelor Bait, 1934
Kentucky Kernels, 1934
The Nitwits, 1935
Laddie, 1935
Alice Adams, 1935
Annie Oakley, 1935
Swing Time, 1936
Quality Street, 1937
A Damsel in Distress, 1937
Having Wonderful Time (uncredited reshoots), 1938

Loaned Out to MGM

Hollywood Party (segment director), 1934

As Producer-Director

Vivacious Lady, 1938
Gunga Din, 1939
Vigil in the Night, 1940

Columbia Studios, 1941–43

Penny Serenade (producer-director), 1941
The Talk of the Town (producer-director), 1942
The More the Merrier (producer-director), 1943

MGM, 1942

Woman of the Year (director), 1942

Postwar Films

I Remember Mama (RKO, director), 1948
On Our Merry Way (United Artists, segment director), 1948
A Place in the Sun (Paramount, producer-director), 1951
Something to Live For (Paramount, producer-director), 1952
Shane (Paramount, producer-director), 1953
Giant (Warner Bros., producer-director), 1956
The Diary of Anne Frank (Twentieth Century-Fox, producer-director), 1959
The Greatest Story Ever Told (United Artists, producer-director, co-writer),
    1965
The Only Game in Town (Twentieth Century-Fox, director), 1970

Awards

Normandy Invasion Arrowhead, Legion of Merit, Unit Citation by General
 Dwight D. Eisenhower, five battle stars during World War II
Directors Guild Award, Best Director for *A Place in the Sun,* 1951
Academy Award, Best Director for *A Place in the Sun,* 1951
Director's Guild Award, Best Director for *Shane,* 1953
Irving Thalberg Award, Academy of Motion Picture Arts and Sciences, 1953
Directors Guild Award, Best Director for *Giant,* 1956
Academy Award, Best Director for *Giant,* 1956
D. W. Griffith Award, The Directors Guild, 1960

Bibliography

Avisar, Ilan. *Screening the Holocaust: Cinema's Image of the Unimaginable.* Bloomington: Indiana University Press, 1988.

Barthes, Roland. *The Pleasure of the Text.* Translated by Richard Miller. New York: Hill and Wang, 1975.

Behlmer, Rudy. *America's Favorite Movies: Behind the Scenes.* New York: Frederick Unger, 1982.

———, ed. *Memo from Darryl F. Zanuck: The Golden Years at 20th Century-Fox.* New York: Grove Press, 1993.

Bogdanovich, Peter. "Interview with George Stevens." *Esquire,* July 1966.

Bosworth, Patricia. *Montgomery Clift.* New York: Harcourt, Brace, Jovanovich, 1978.

Brownlow, Kevin. *The War, the West and the Wilderness.* New York: Random House, 1979.

Capra, Frank. *Name Above the Title: An Autobiography.* New York: Macmillan Co., 1971.

Caruth, Cathy. *Unclaimed Experience: Trauma, Narrative, History.* Baltimore: Johns Hopkins University Press, 1996.

de Lauretis, Teresa. *Alice Doesn't: Feminism, Semiotics, Cinema.* Bloomington: Indiana University Press, 1984.

Doane, Mary Anne. "The Economy of Desire: The Commodity of Form In/Of the Cinema." In *Movies and Mass Culture.* Edited by John Belton. Brunswick, N.J.: Rutgers University Press, 2000.

Dobson, Joanne. "Reclaiming Sentimental Literature." *American Literature* 69, no. 2 (June 1997).

Dreiser, Theodore. *An American Tragedy.* New York: Signet Classics, 1964.

Eyman, Scott. *Print the Legend: The Life and Times of John Ford.* New York: Simon and Schuster, 1999.

Ferber, Edna. *Giant.* New York: Doubleday and Company, 1952.

Frank, Anne. *The Diary of a Young Girl.* New York: Pocket Books, 1952.

———. *The Diary of Anne Frank: The Critical Edition.* Edited by David Barnouw and Gerrold Van Der Stroom. New York: Doubleday, 1989.

————. *Anne Frank's Tales from the Secret Annex.* New York: Bantam Books, 1994.

Halberstam, David. *The Fifties.* New York: Balantine Press, 1993.

Higashi, Sumiko. *Cecil B. DeMille and American Culture: The Silent Era.* Berkeley: University of California Press, 1994.

Hoskyns, Barney. *Montgomery Clift: Beautiful Loser.* New York: Grove Weidenfeld, 1991.

Kendall, Elizabeth. *The Runaway Bride: Hollywood Romantic Comedy of the 1930s.* New York: Cooper Square Press, 1990.

Lewis, R. W. B. *The American Adam: Innocence, Tragedy, and Tradition in the Nineteenth Century.* Chicago: University of Chicago Press, 1955.

Lyman, Rick. "Coming Back to Shane: Watching Movies with Woody Allen." *New York Times,* August 3, 2001.

Maltin, Leonard. "George Stevens: Shorts to Features." *Action,* November-December 1970.

Matthiessen, F. O. *Dreiser.* New York: William Sloane Associates, 1951

McBride, Joseph. *Frank Capra: The Catastrophe of Success.* New York: St. Martin's Griffin, 1992.

McCambridge, Mercedes. *The Quality of Mercy.* New York: Times Books, 1981.

McCann, Richard Dyer. "George Stevens' Director's Techniques." *Christian Science Monitor,* September 25, 1956.

McConnell, Frank. *The Spoken Seen: Film and the Romantic Imagination.* Baltimore: Johns Hopkins Press, 1975.

McGilligan, Patrick. *Film Crazy: Interviews with Hollywood Legends.* New York: St. Martin's Press, 2000.

Nadel, Alan. *Containment Culture: American Narratives, Postmodernism and the Atomic Age.* Durham, N. C.: Duke University Press, 1995.

Nickles, Shelley. "More Is Better: Mass Consumption in Postwar America." *American Quarterly* 54, no. 4 (December 2002).

Novick, Peter. *The Holocaust in American Life.* Boston and New York: Houghton Mifflin, 2000.

Oller, John, *Jean Arthur: The Actress Nobody Knew.* New York: Limelight Editions, 1997.

Pearce, Roy Harvey. *The Continuity of American Poetry.* Princeton, N.J.: Princeton University Press, 1961.

Rankin, Chuck. "Clash of Frontiers: A Historical Parallel to Jack Schaefer's *Shane.*" In Jack Schaefer, *Shane: The Critical Edition.* Lincoln: University of Nebraska Press, 1984.

Scheuer, Phillip, K. "Lone Rider: Galahad Roving Plains of the West." *Los Angeles Times,* June 7, 1953.

Skretvedt, Randy. *Laurel and Hardy: The Magic Behind the Movies.* Beverly Hills: Moonstone Press, 1987.

Slotkin, Richard. *Regeneration Through Violence: The Mythology of the American Frontier 1600–1860.* Middletown, Conn.: Wesleyan University Press, 1973.

Stevens, George. The George Stevens Collection. Margaret Herrick Library. The Academy of Motion Picture Arts and Sciences, Beverly Hills, California.

———. A Filmmaker's Journey Collection. Margaret Herrick Library. The Academy of Motion Picture Arts and Sciences. Beverly Hills, California.

———. "Q & A with George Stevens." *Screen & Radio Weekly*, 1939.

Stevens, George Jr. Commentary. *Shane* DVD. Paramount Pictures.

Swanberg, W. A. *Dreiser.* New York: Charles Scribner's Sons, 1965.

Thomson, David. *Showman: The Life of David O. Selnzick.* New York: Alfred A. Knopf, 1992.

Warner, Jack L. Collection. University of Southern California Cinema-Television Library, Los Angeles, California.

Willsmer, Trevor. *Giant: The Making of an Epic Motion Picture. Giant* Collector's Special VHS Edition. Warner Home Video, 1996.

Winters, Shelley. *Shelley: Also Known as Shirley.* New York: William Morrow and Company, 1980.

Index

Lightning Source UK Ltd.
Milton Keynes UK
UKOW06f1600240816

281369UK00002B/69/P